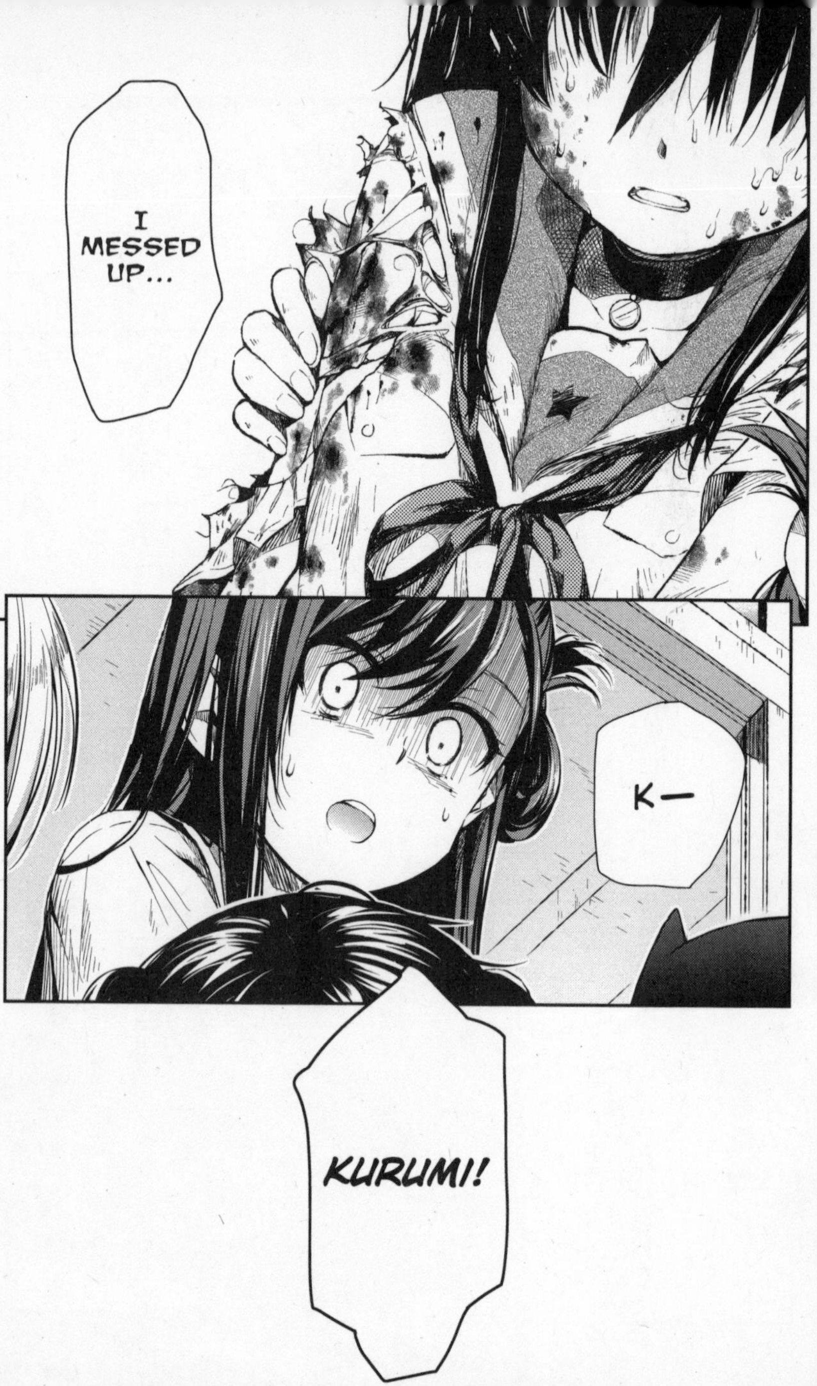
I MESSED UP...
K—
KURUMI!

Chapter 19 Scars

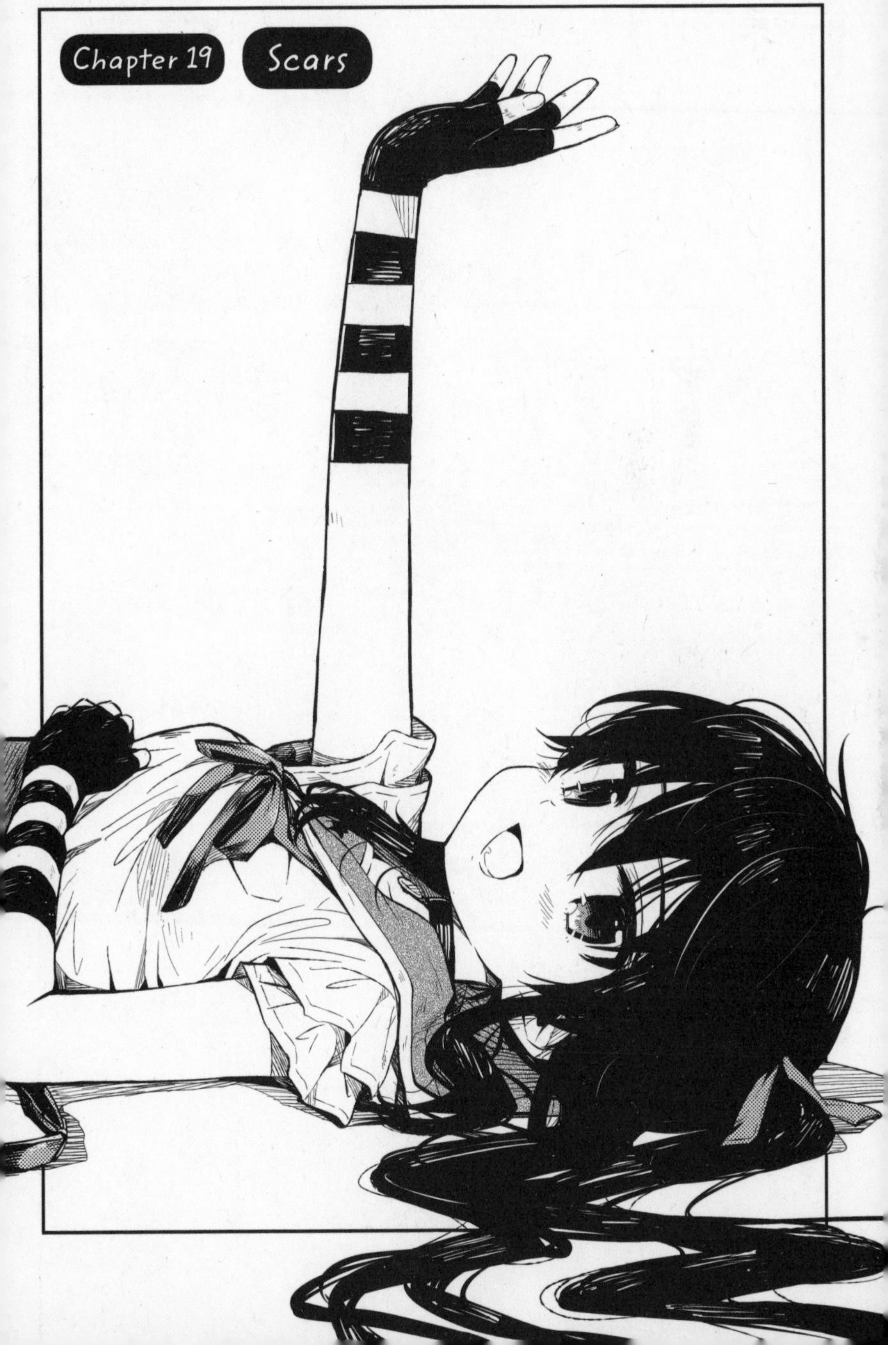

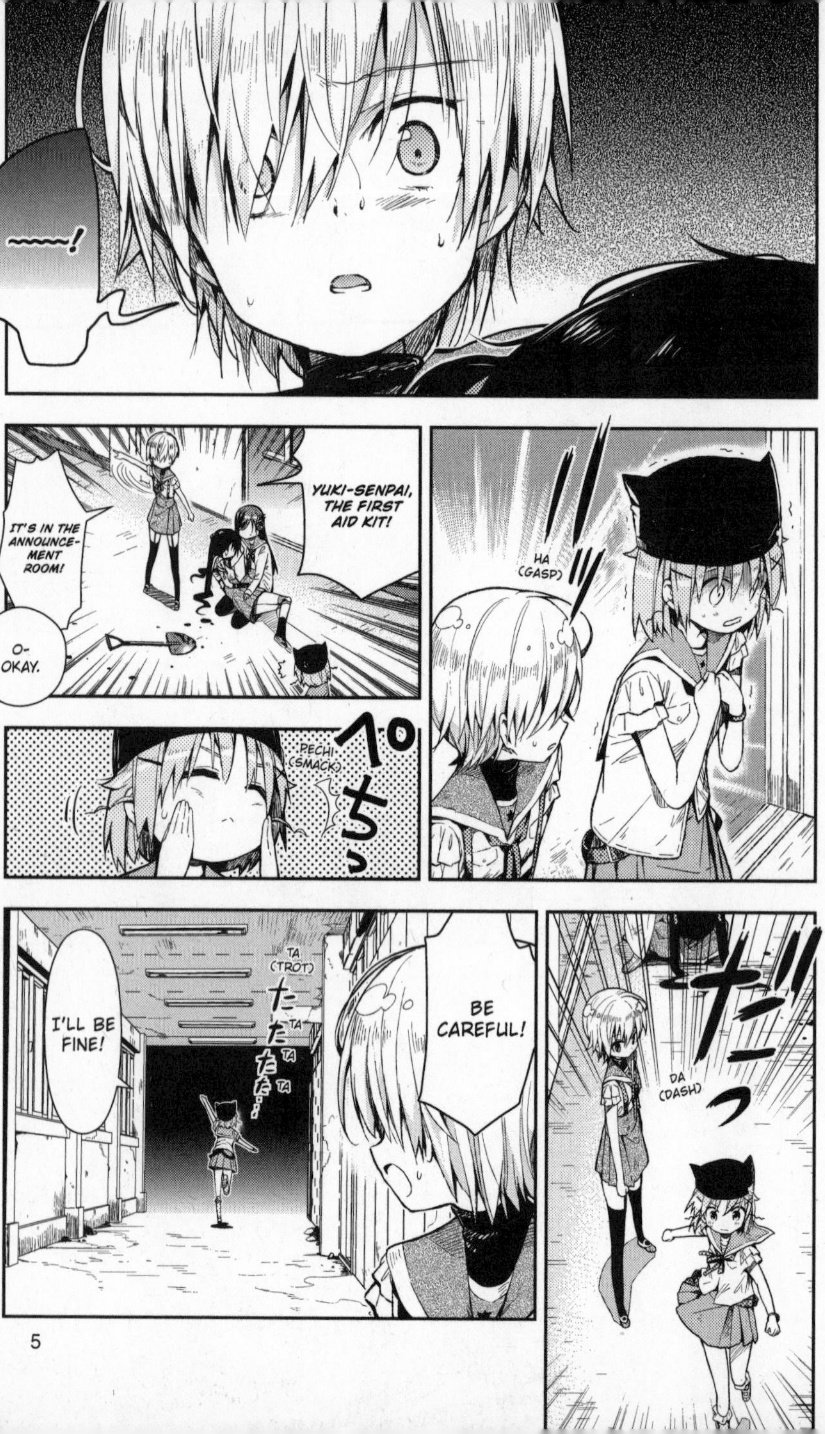

HA
(GASP)
YUKI-SENPAI, THE FIRST AID KIT!
IT'S IN THE ANNOUNCEMENT ROOM!
O-OKAY.
ぺちっ
PECHI
(SMACK)
ダーっ
DA
(DASH)
BE CAREFUL!
たたたた…
TA
(TROT)
TA
TA
TA
I'LL BE FINE!

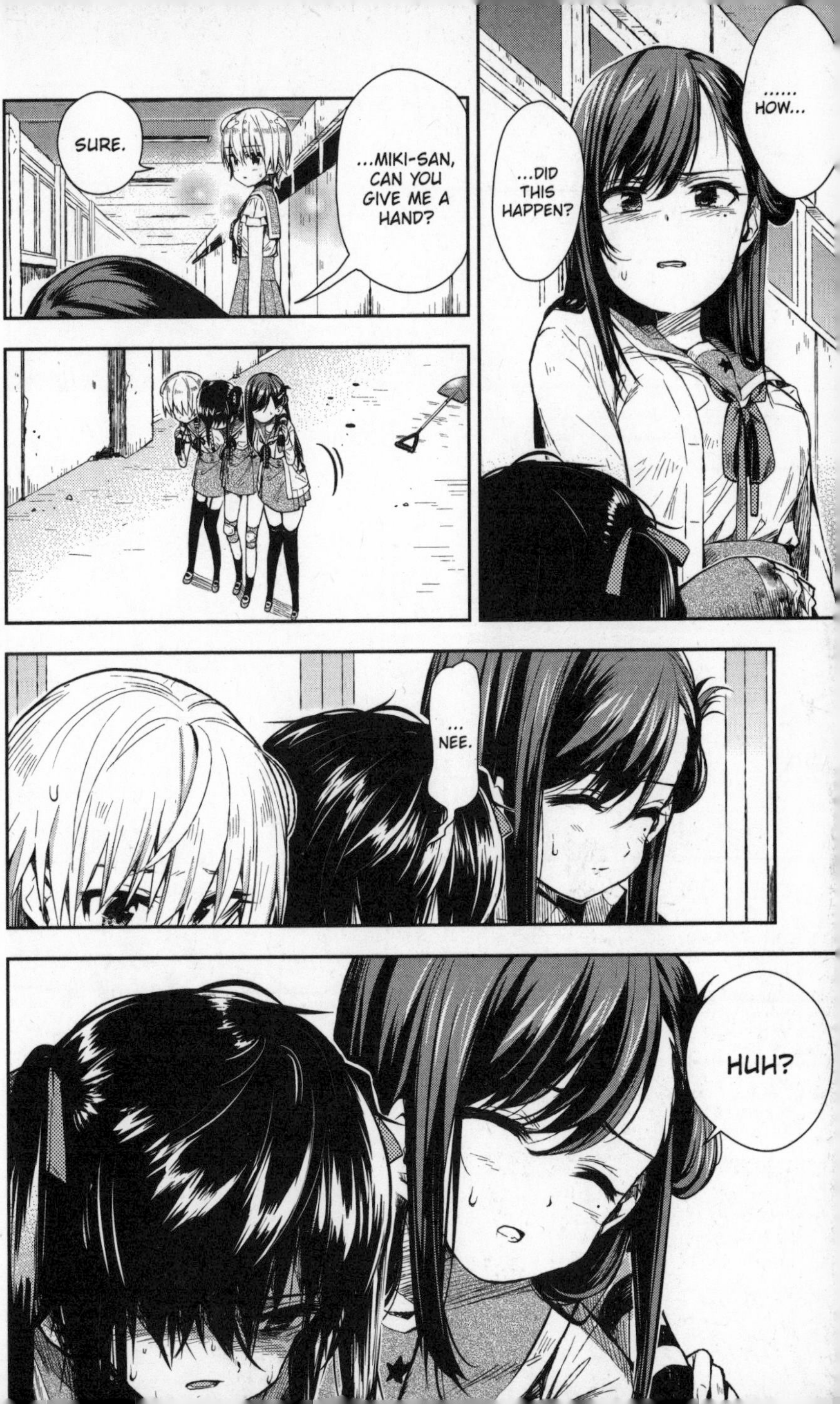
......HOW...
...DID THIS HAPPEN?
...MIKI-SAN, CAN YOU GIVE ME A HAND?
SURE.
...NEE.
HUH?

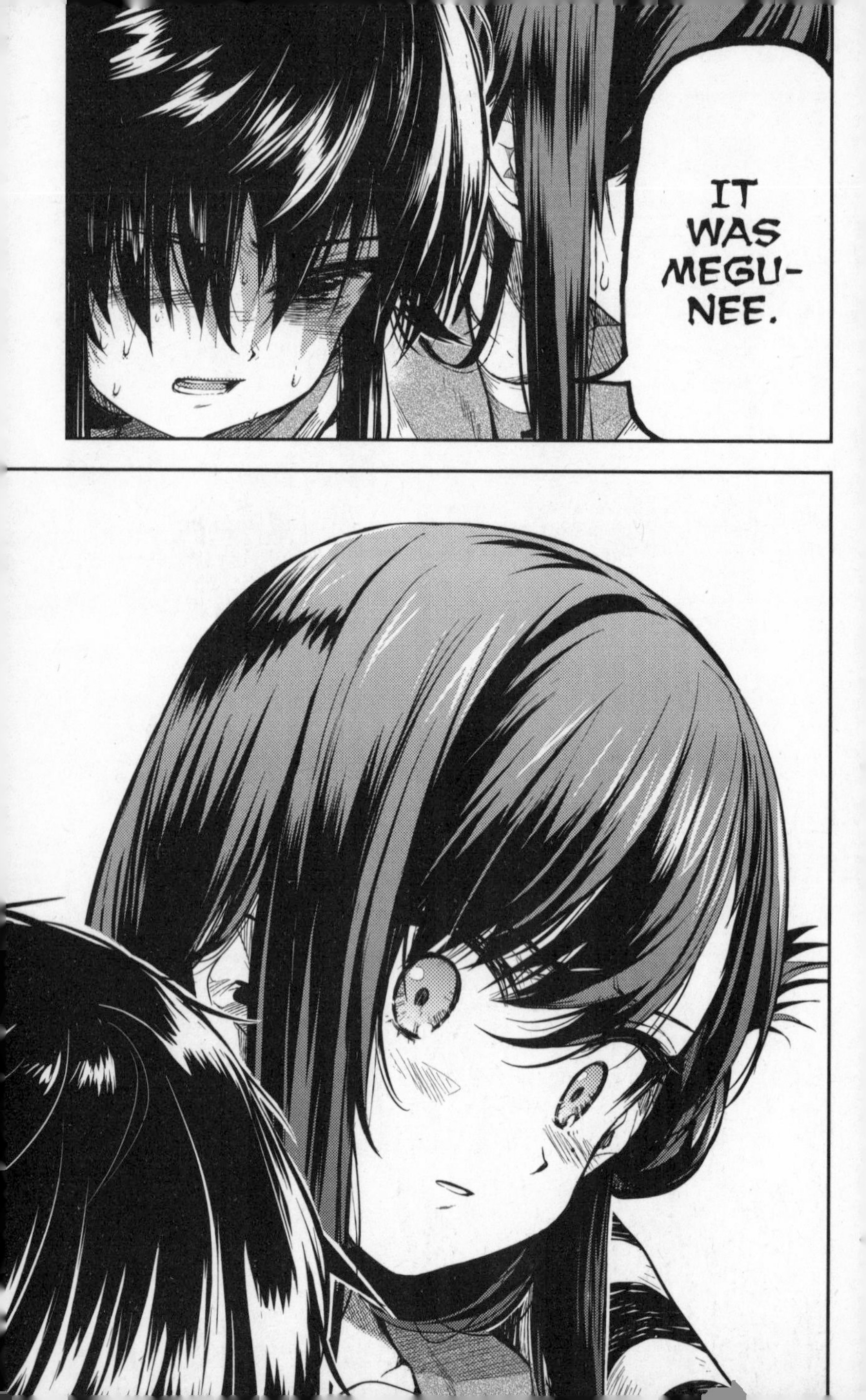
IT WAS MEGU-NEE.

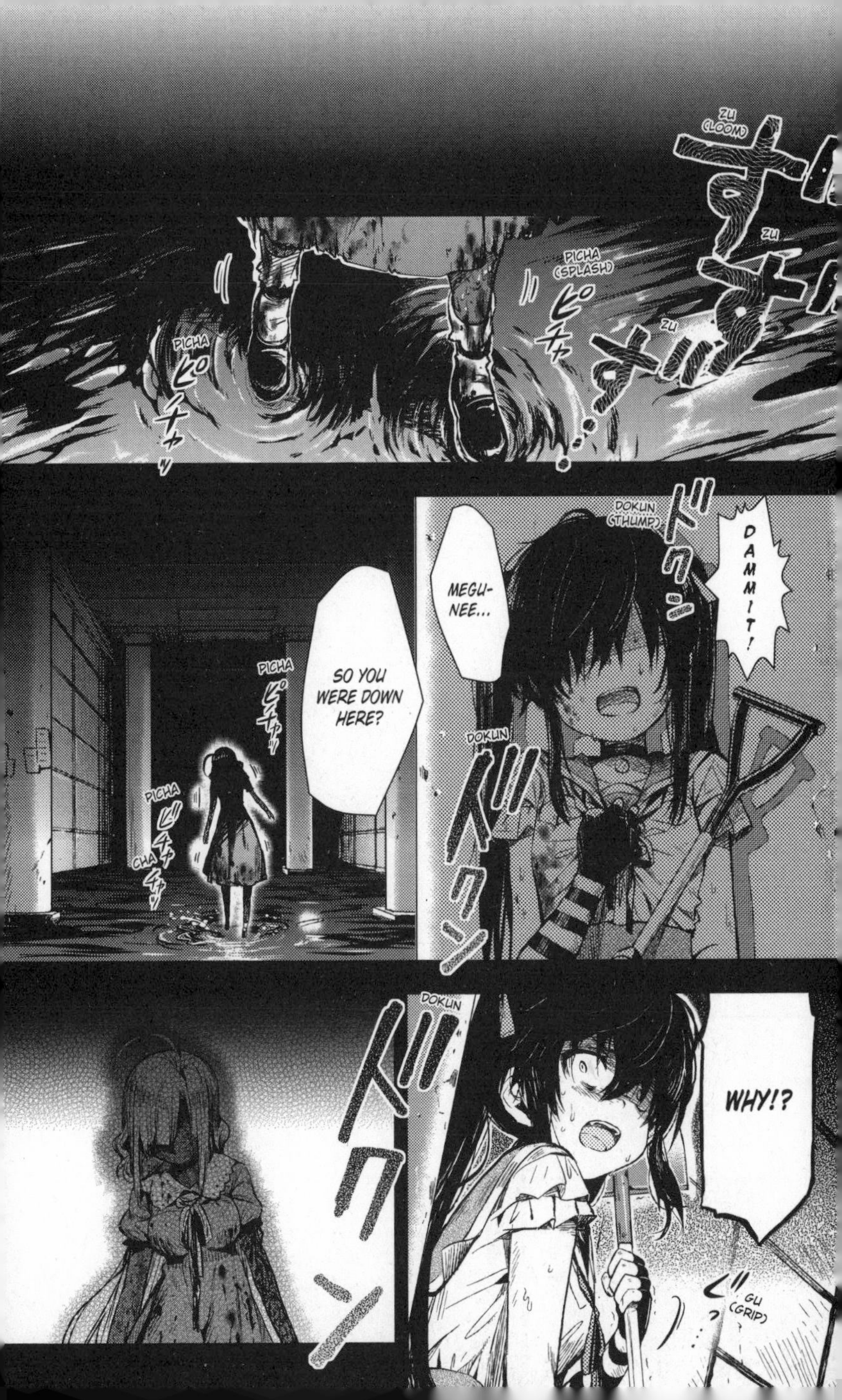
ZU (LOOM)
ZU
ZU
PICHA (SPLASH)
PICHA
DAMMIT!
DOKUN (THUMP)
MEGU-NEE...
DOKUN
SO YOU WERE DOWN HERE?
PICHA
PICHA
CHA
WHY!?
GU (GRIP)
DOKUN

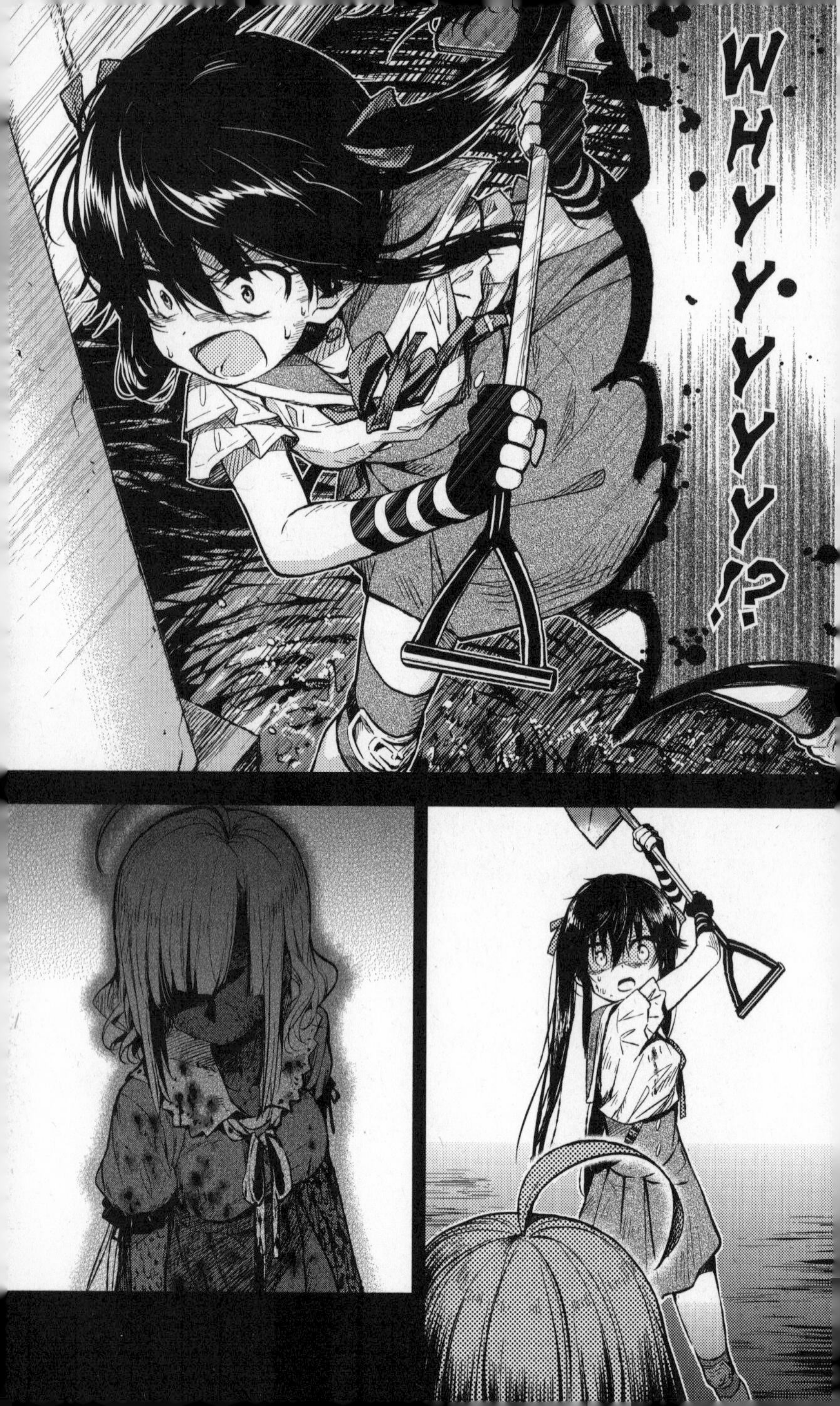
WHYYYYYY!?

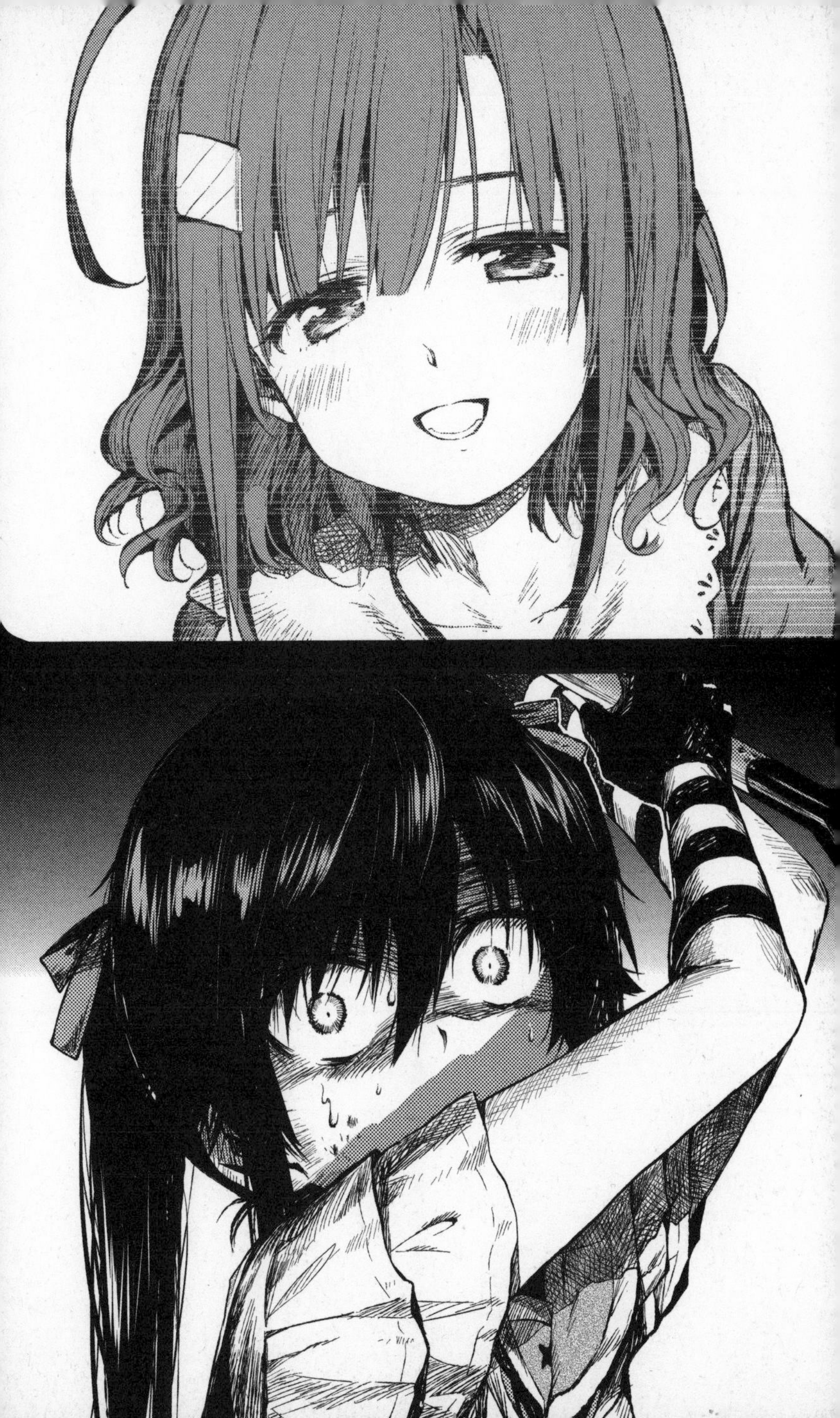

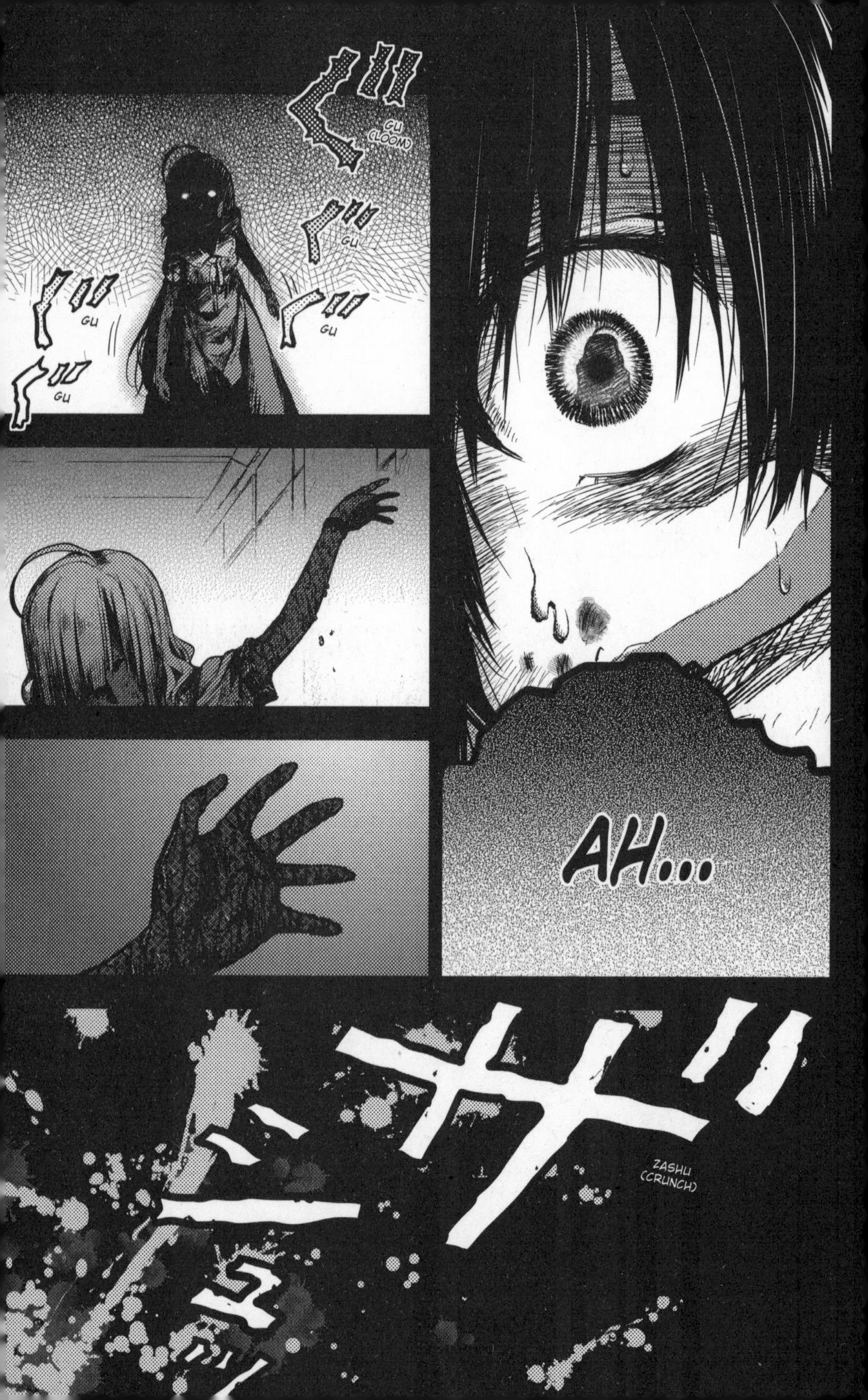
AH...
GU (LOOM)
GU
GU
GU
GU
ZASHU (CRUNCH)

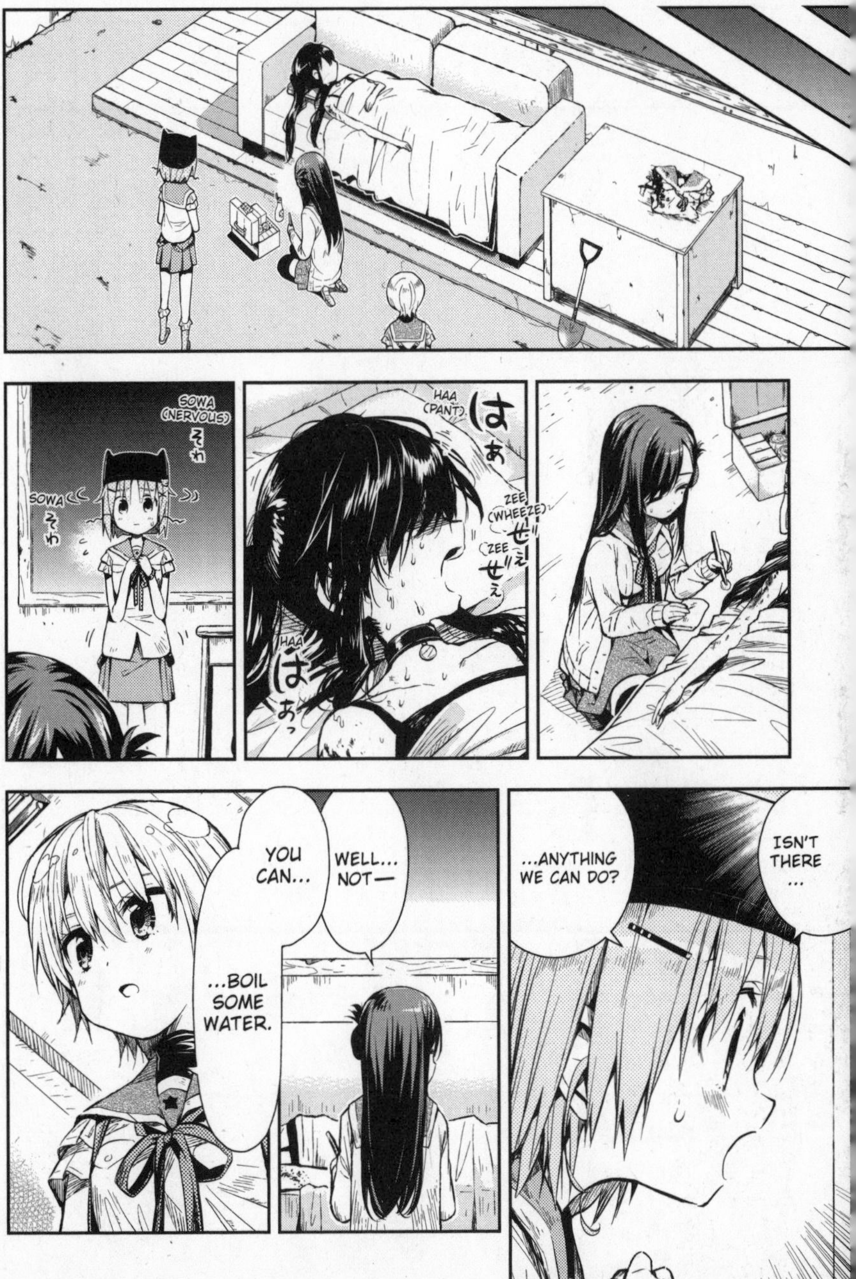
HAA (PANT)
はぁ
ZEE (WHEEZE)
ぜぇ
ZEE
ぜぇ
HAA
はあっ
SOWA (NERVOUS)
そわ
SOWA
そわ
ISN'T THERE ...
...ANYTHING WE CAN DO?
WELL... NOT—
YOU CAN...
...BOIL SOME WATER.

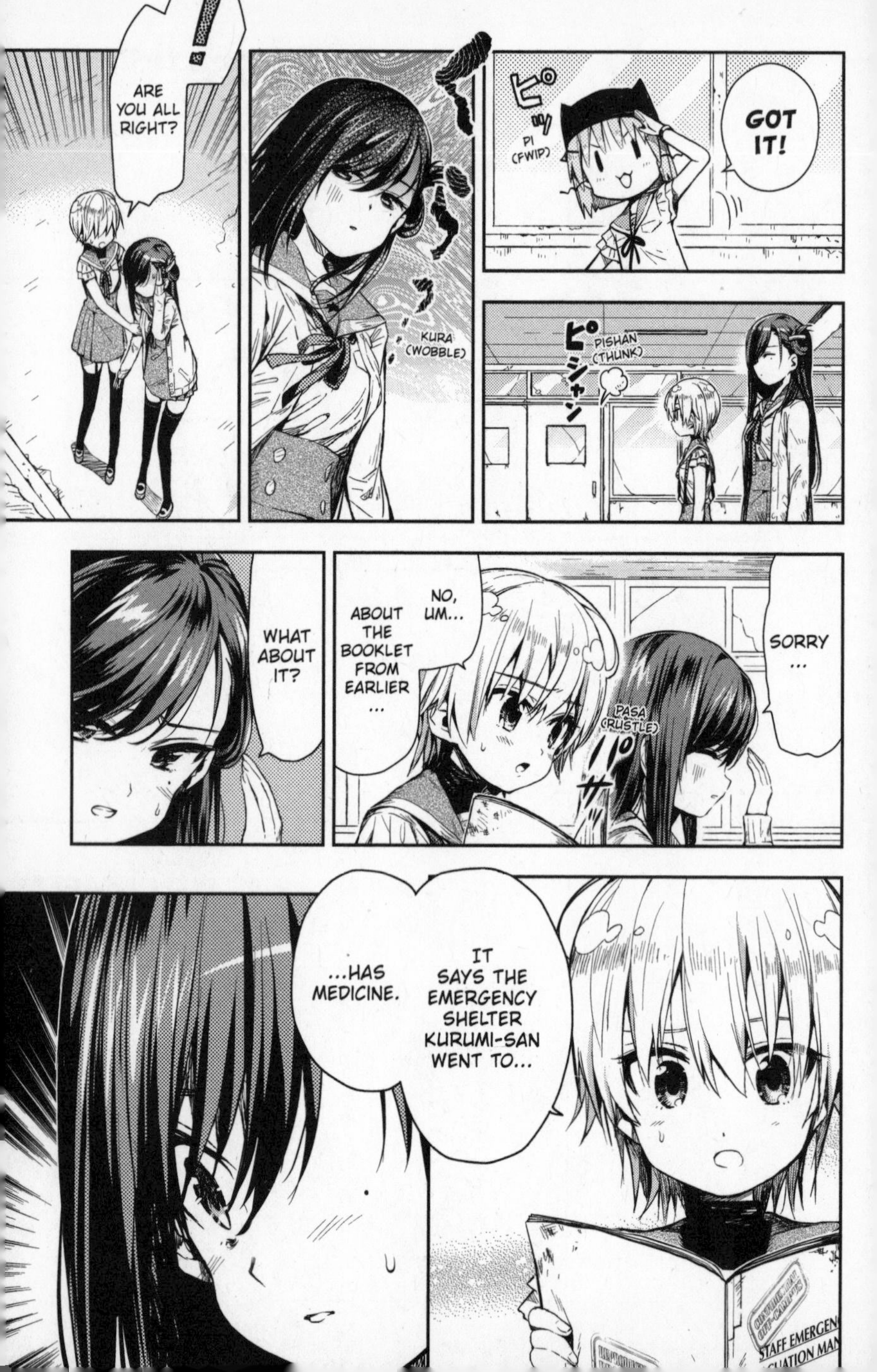
GOT IT!
ピッ
PI (FWIP)
ピシャン
PISHAN (THUNK)
KURA (WOBBLE)
!
ARE YOU ALL RIGHT?
SORRY...
パサ
PASA (RUSTLE)
NO, UM...
ABOUT THE BOOKLET FROM EARLIER...
WHAT ABOUT IT?
IT SAYS THE EMERGENCY SHELTER KURUMI-SAN WENT TO...
...HAS MEDICINE.

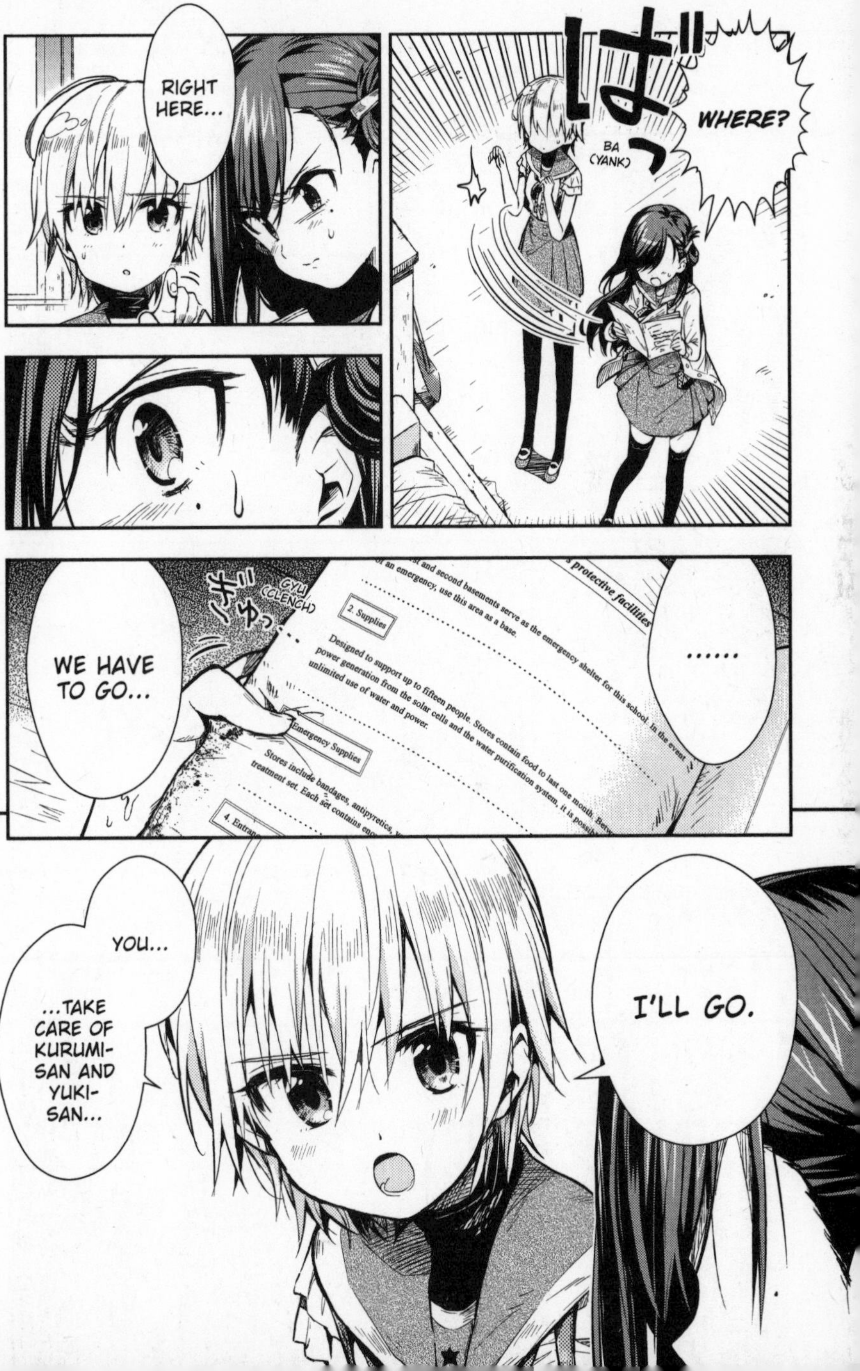
ばっ
BA (YANK)
WHERE?
RIGHT HERE...
......
protective facilities
st and second basements serve as the emergency shelter for this school. In the event
of an emergency, use this area as a base.
2. Supplies
Designed to support up to fifteen people. Stores contain food to last one month. Betw
power generation from the solar cells and the water purification system, it is possi
unlimited use of water and power.
Emergency Supplies
Stores include bandages, antipyretics,
treatment set. Each set contains eno
4. Entran
ぎゅっ
GYU (CLENCH)
WE HAVE TO GO...
I'LL GO.
YOU...
...TAKE CARE OF KURUMI-SAN AND YUKI-SAN...

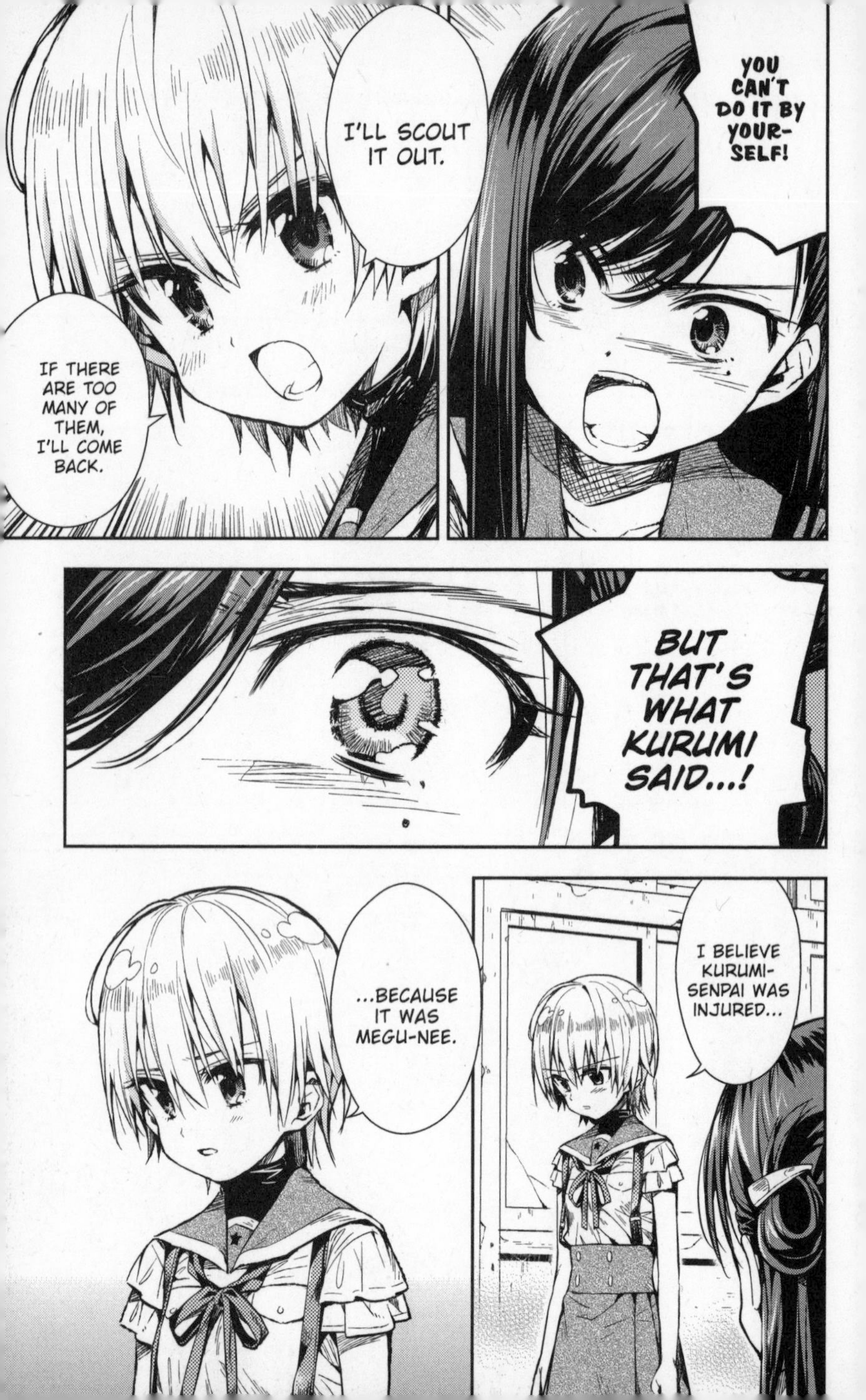
YOU CAN'T DO IT BY YOUR-SELF!
I'LL SCOUT IT OUT.
IF THERE ARE TOO MANY OF THEM, I'LL COME BACK.
BUT THAT'S WHAT KURUMI SAID...!
I BELIEVE KURUMI-SENPAI WAS INJURED...
...BECAUSE IT WAS MEGU-NEE.

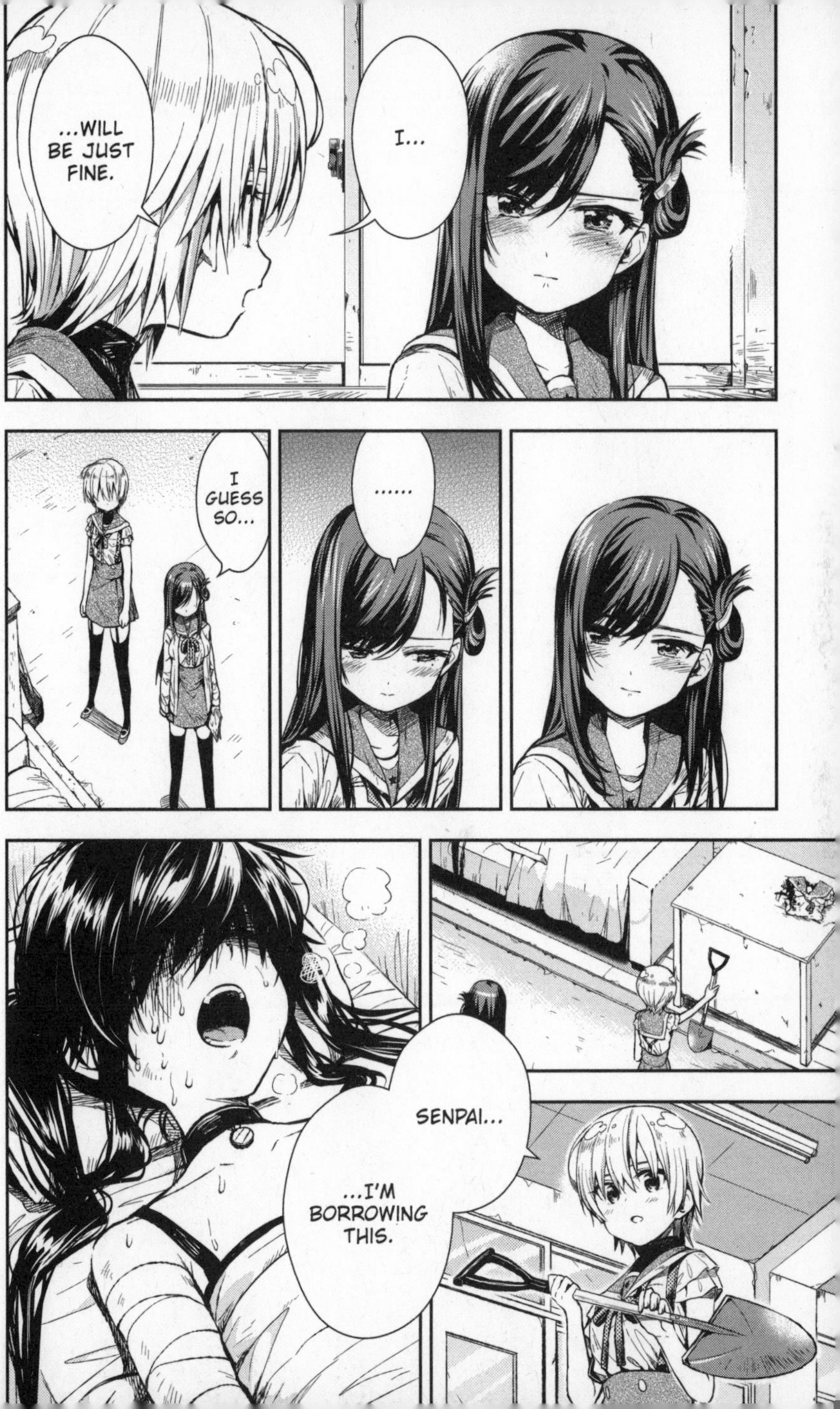
I...
...WILL BE JUST FINE.
......
I GUESS SO...
SENPAI...
...I'M BORROWING THIS.

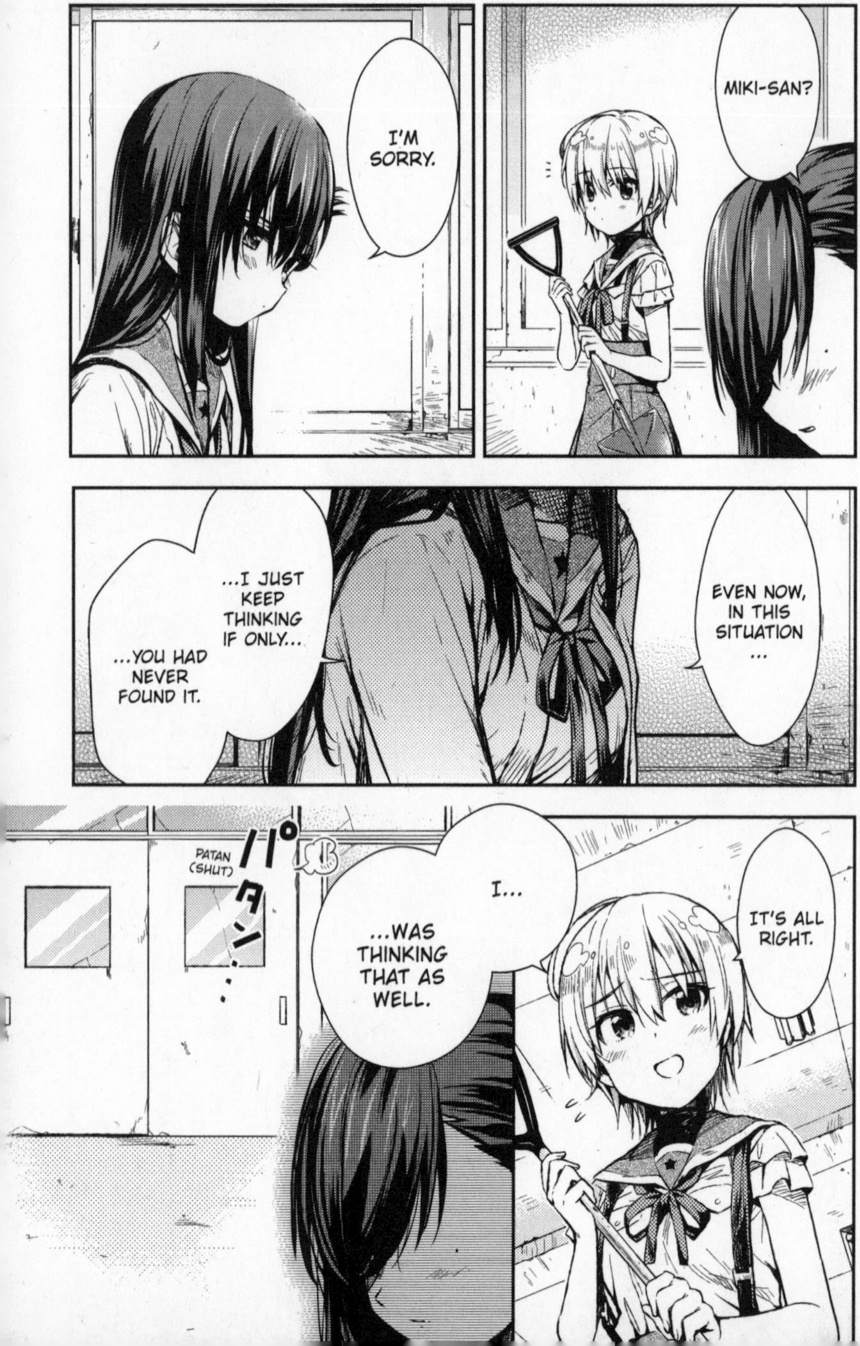
MIKI-SAN?
I'M SORRY.
EVEN NOW, IN THIS SITUATION ...
...I JUST KEEP THINKING IF ONLY...
...YOU HAD NEVER FOUND IT.
IT'S ALL RIGHT.
I...
...WAS THINKING THAT AS WELL.
パタン…
PATAN (SHUT)

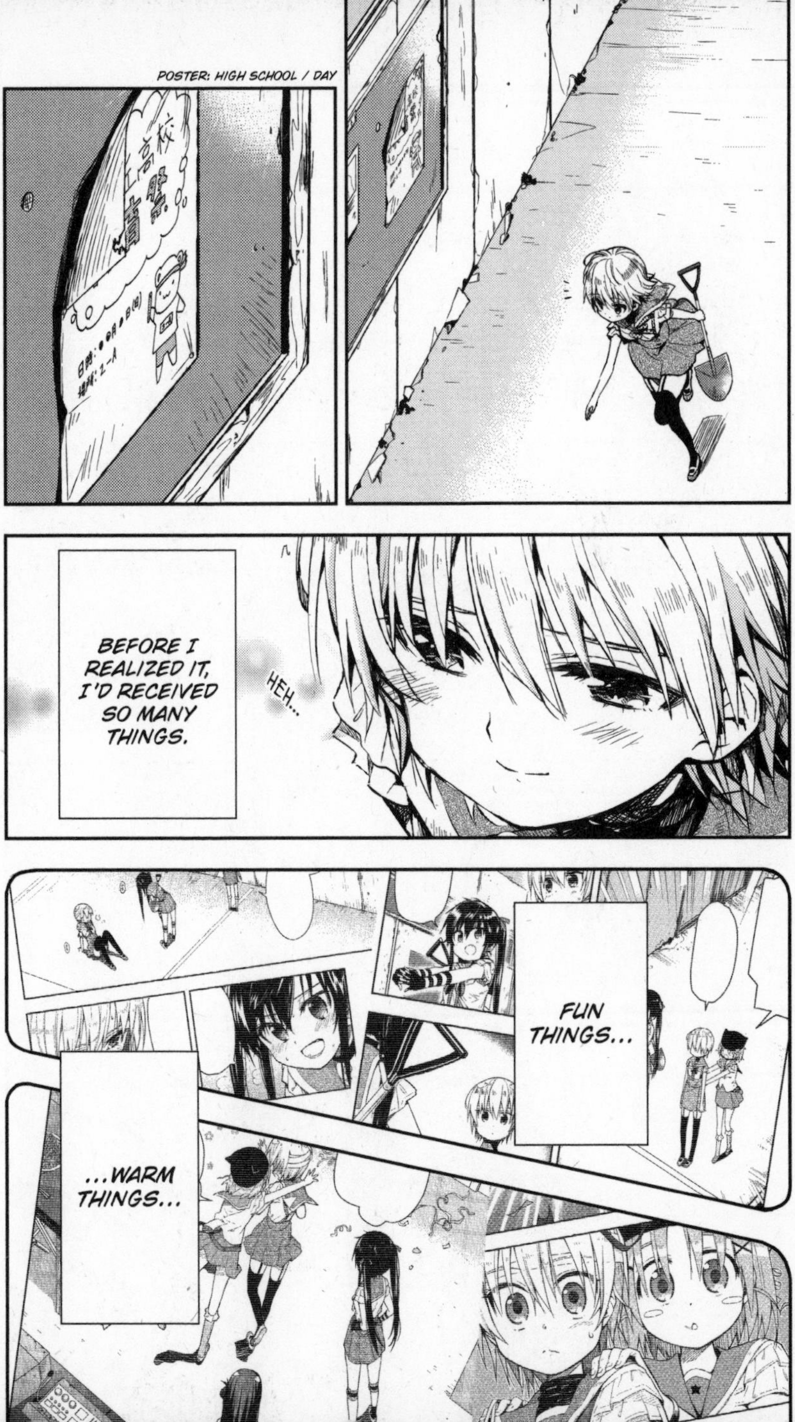
POSTER: HIGH SCHOOL / DAY
HEH...
BEFORE I REALIZED IT, I'D RECEIVED SO MANY THINGS.
FUN THINGS...
...WARM THINGS...

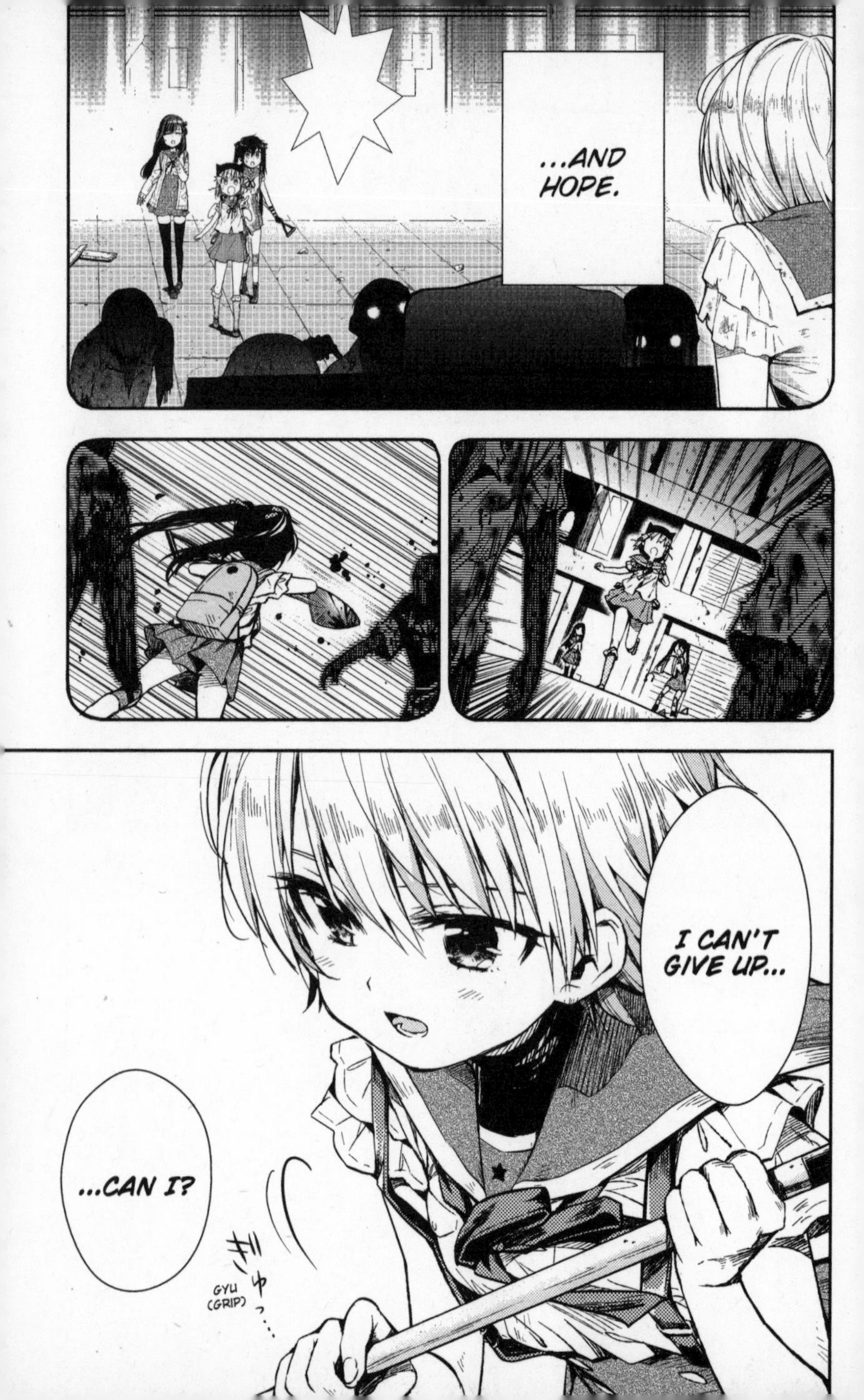
...AND HOPE.
I CAN'T GIVE UP...
...CAN I?
ぎゅっ...
GYU (GRIP)

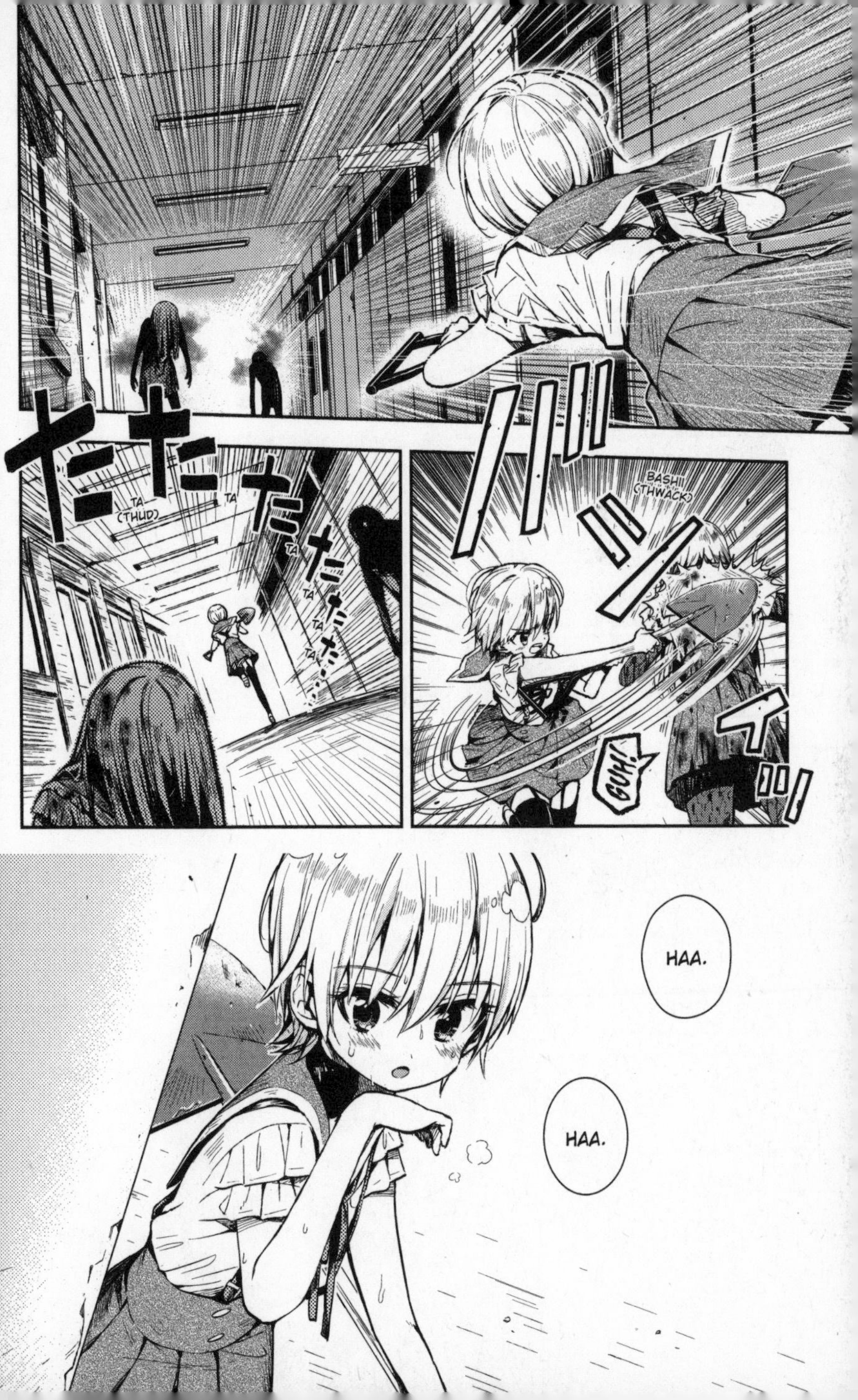
BASHI (THWACK)
GUH!
TA (THUD)
TA
TA
TA
TA
TA
HAA.
HAA.

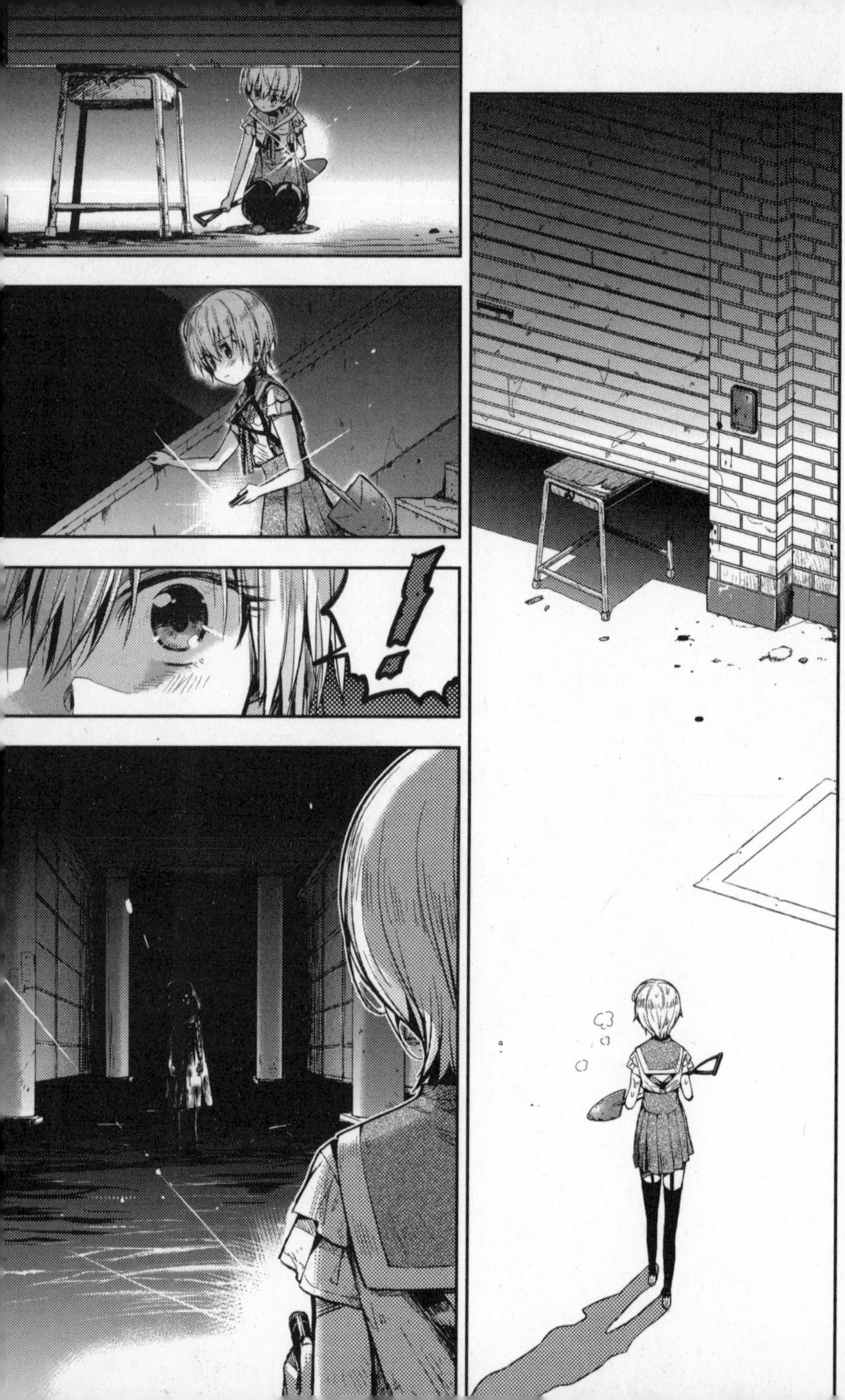
!

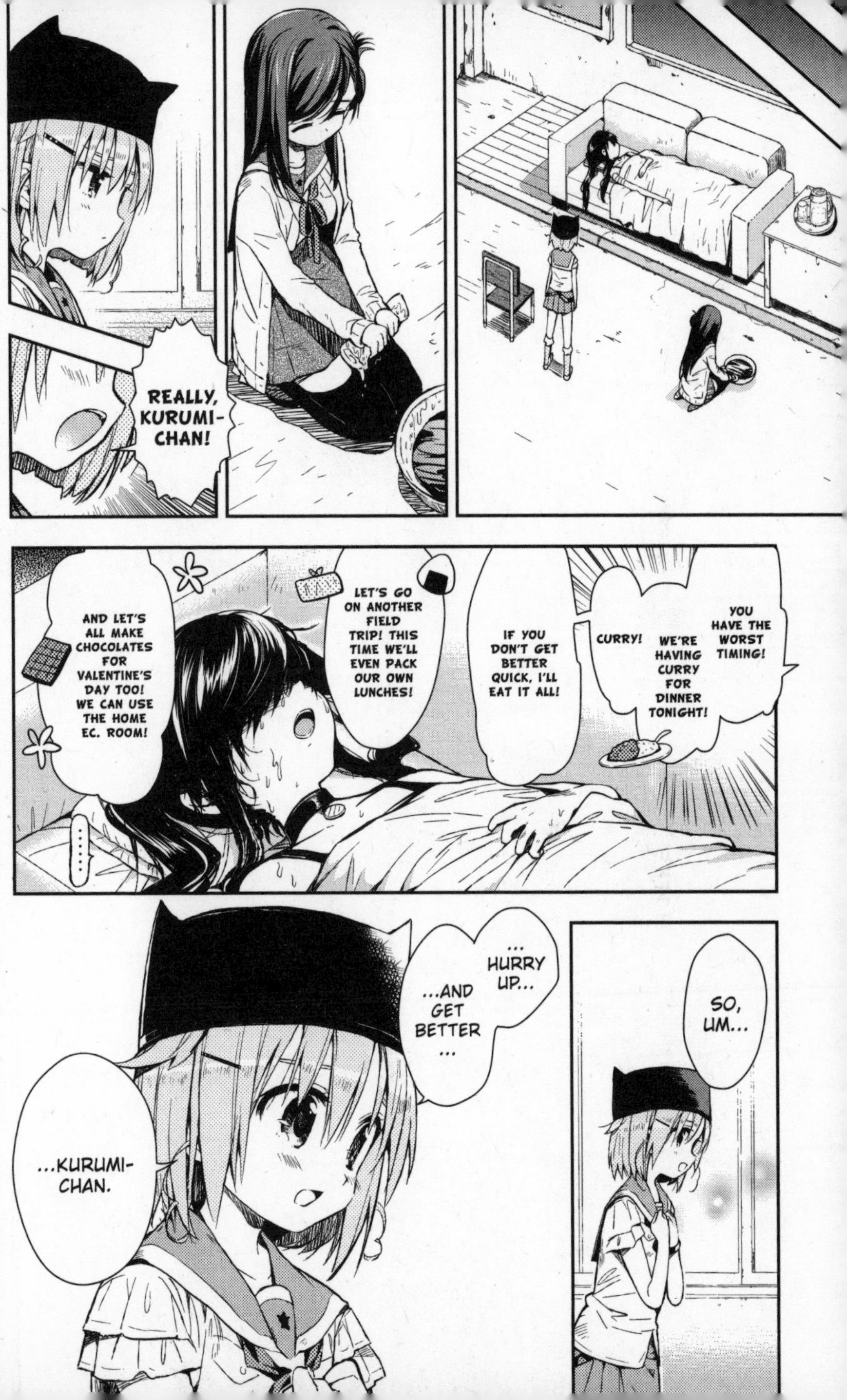
REALLY, KURUMI-CHAN!
YOU HAVE THE WORST TIMING!
WE'RE HAVING CURRY FOR DINNER TONIGHT!
CURRY!
IF YOU DON'T GET BETTER QUICK, I'LL EAT IT ALL!
LET'S GO ON ANOTHER FIELD TRIP! THIS TIME WE'LL EVEN PACK OUR OWN LUNCHES!
AND LET'S ALL MAKE CHOCOLATES FOR VALENTINE'S DAY TOO! WE CAN USE THE HOME EC. ROOM!
......
SO, UM...
... HURRY UP...
...AND GET BETTER ...
...KURUMI-CHAN.

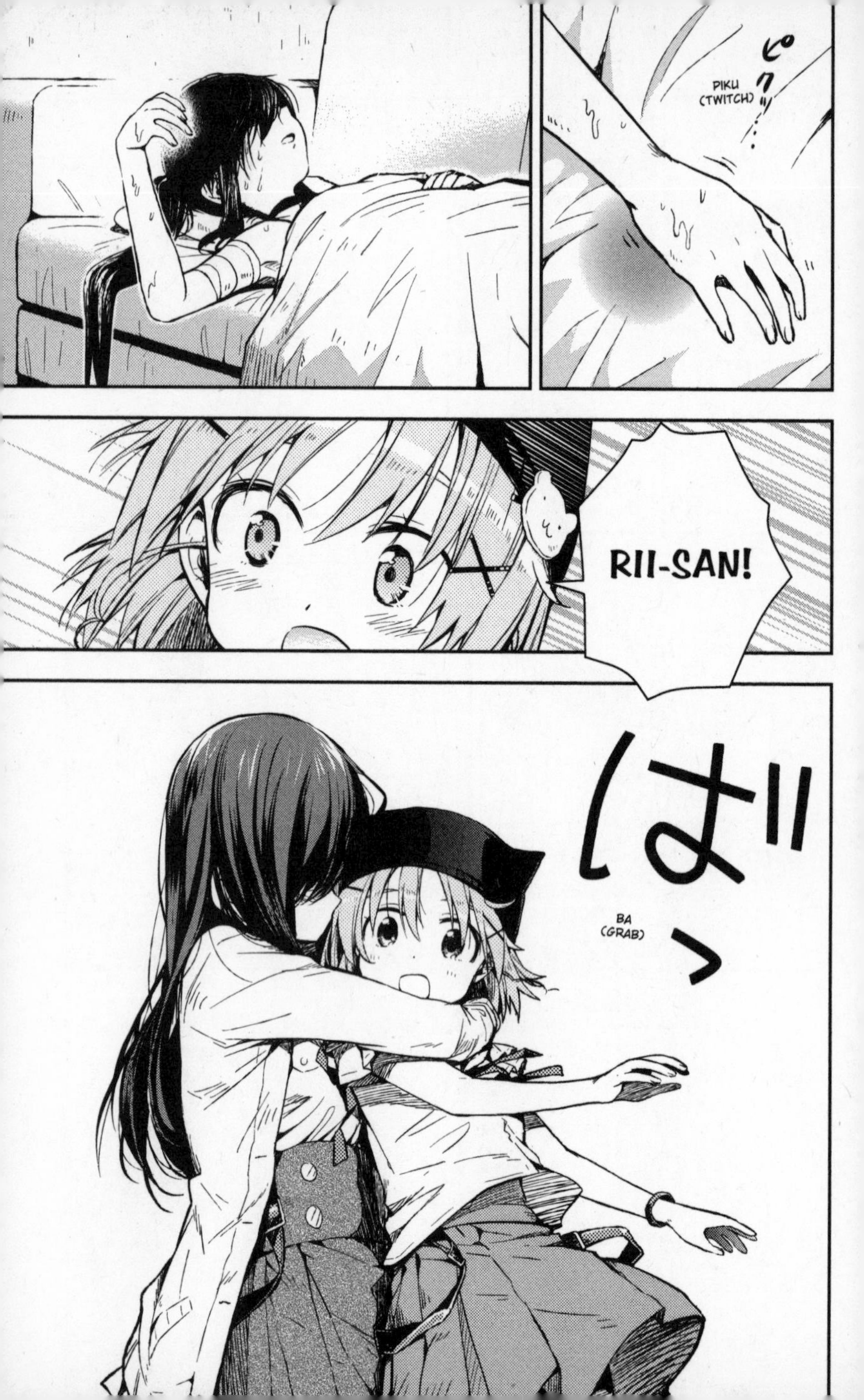
ピク…
PIKU (TWITCH)
…
RII-SAN!
はっ
BA (GRAB)

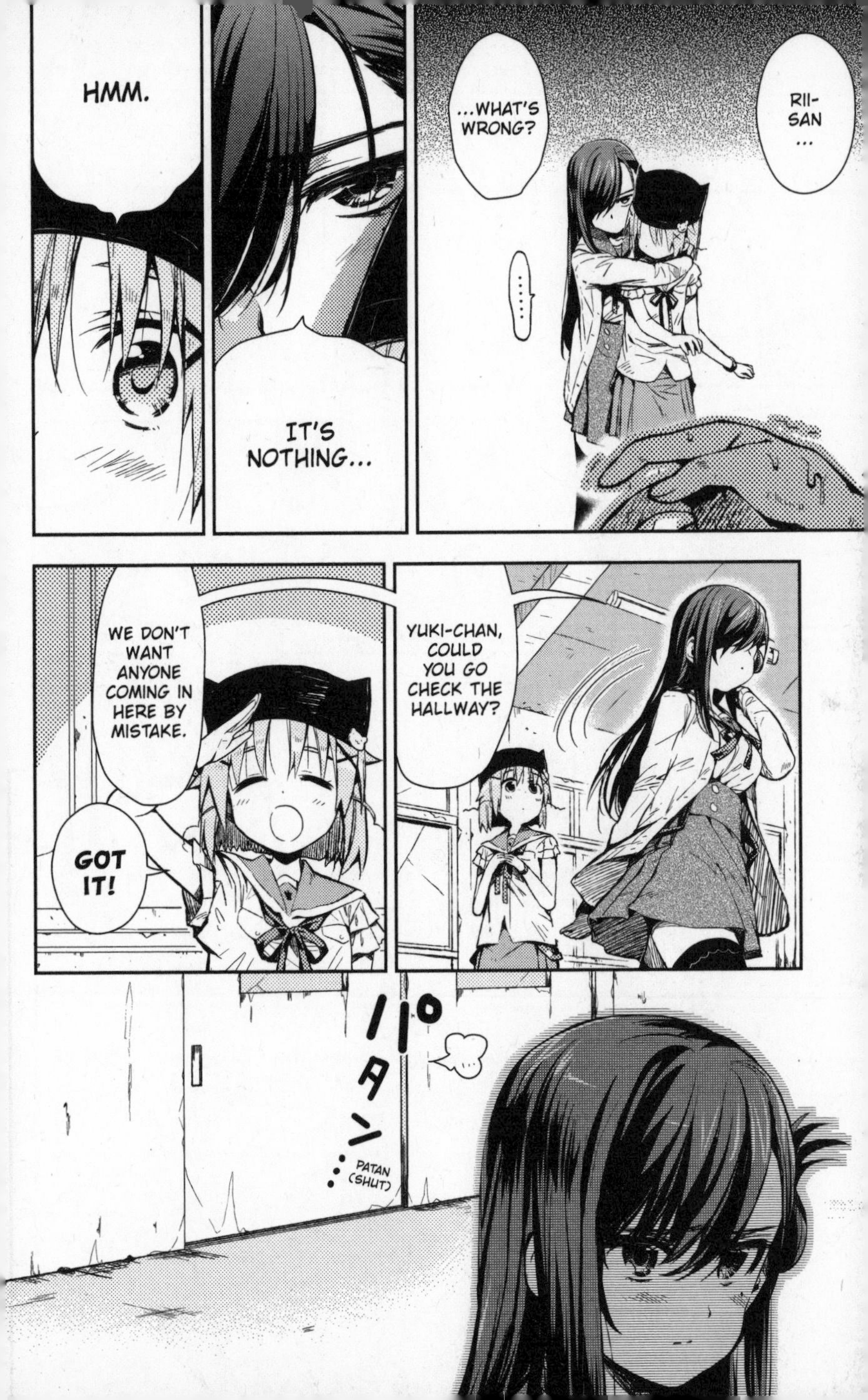
RII-SAN ...
...WHAT'S WRONG?
......
IT'S NOTHING...
HMM.
YUKI-CHAN, COULD YOU GO CHECK THE HALLWAY?
WE DON'T WANT ANYONE COMING IN HERE BY MISTAKE.
GOT IT!
...
パタン
PATAN (SHUT)

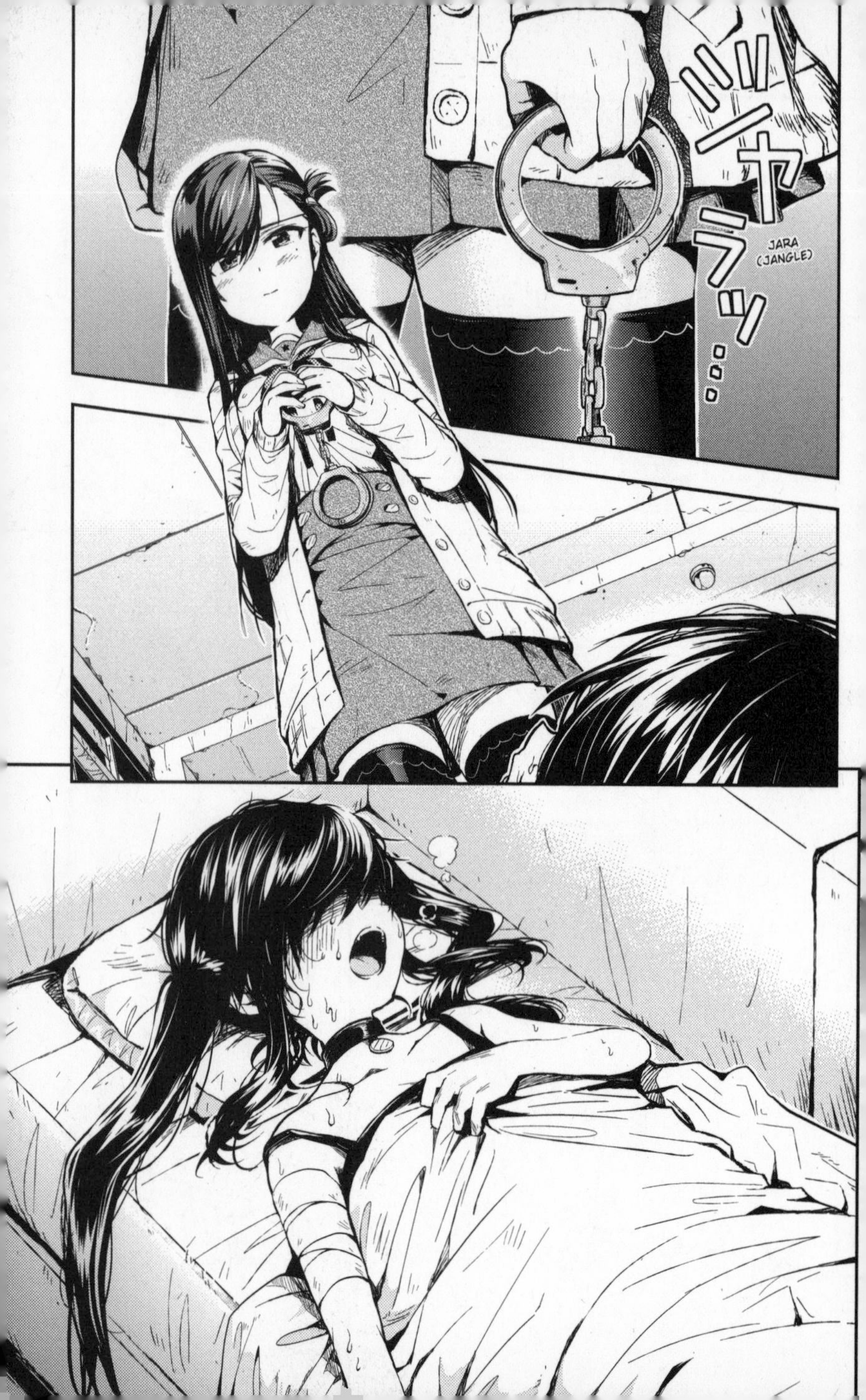
ジャラッ…
JARA
(JANGLE)

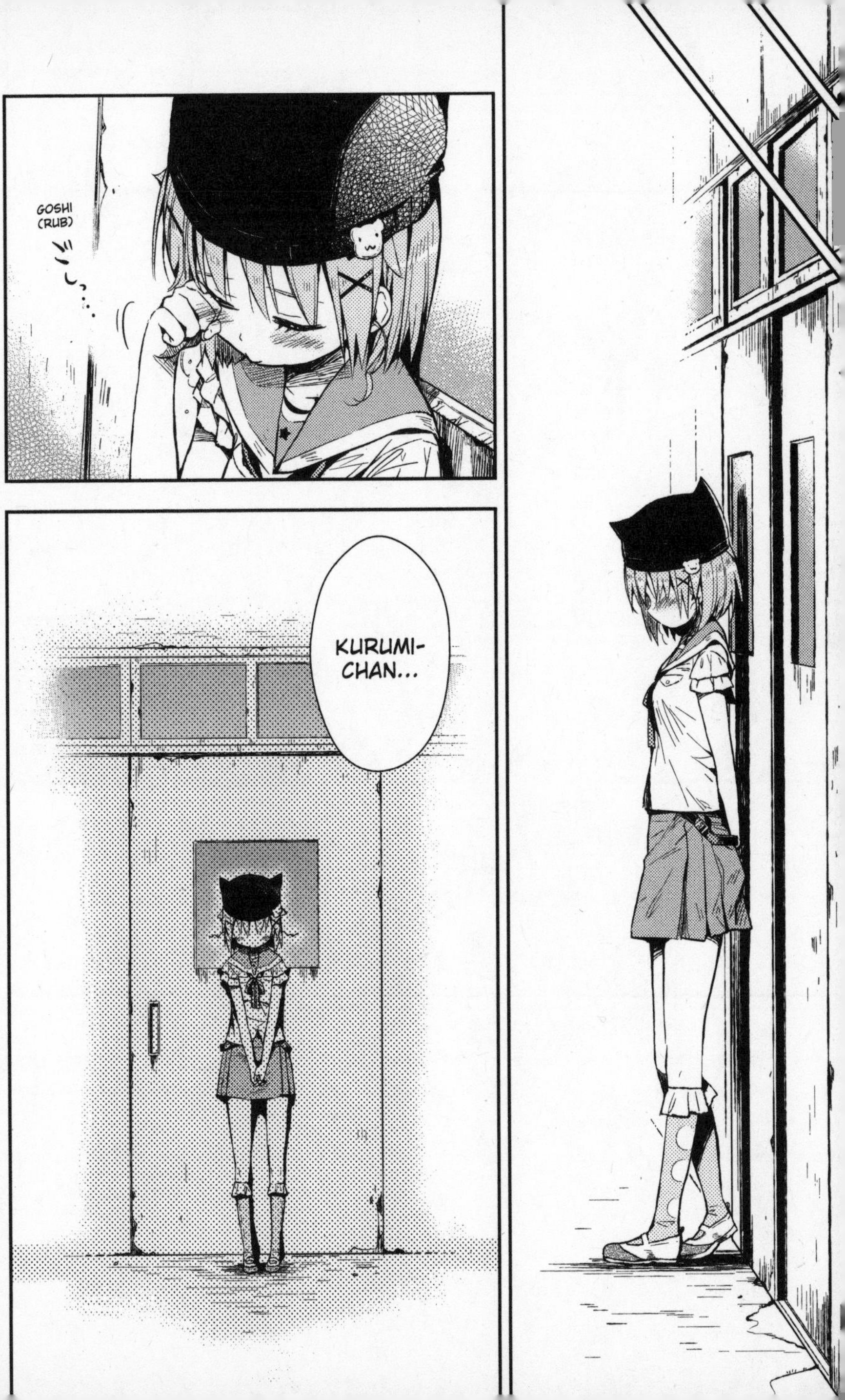
GOSHI (RUB)
ごしっ…
KURUMI-CHAN...

SCHOOL-LIVE!

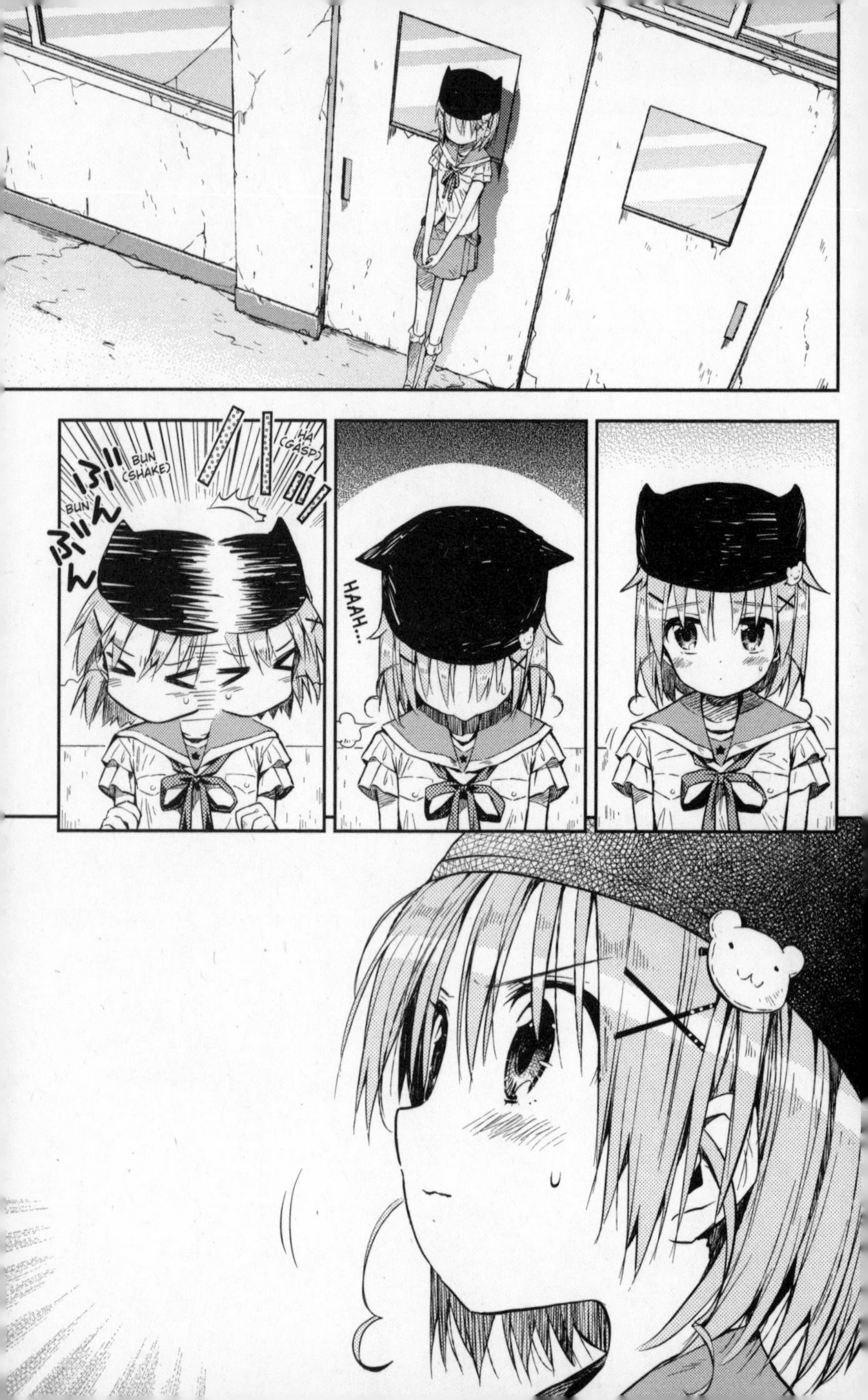
HAAH...
HA (GASP)
ぶん
BUN (SHAKE)
ぶん
BUN

Chapter 20

Sensei

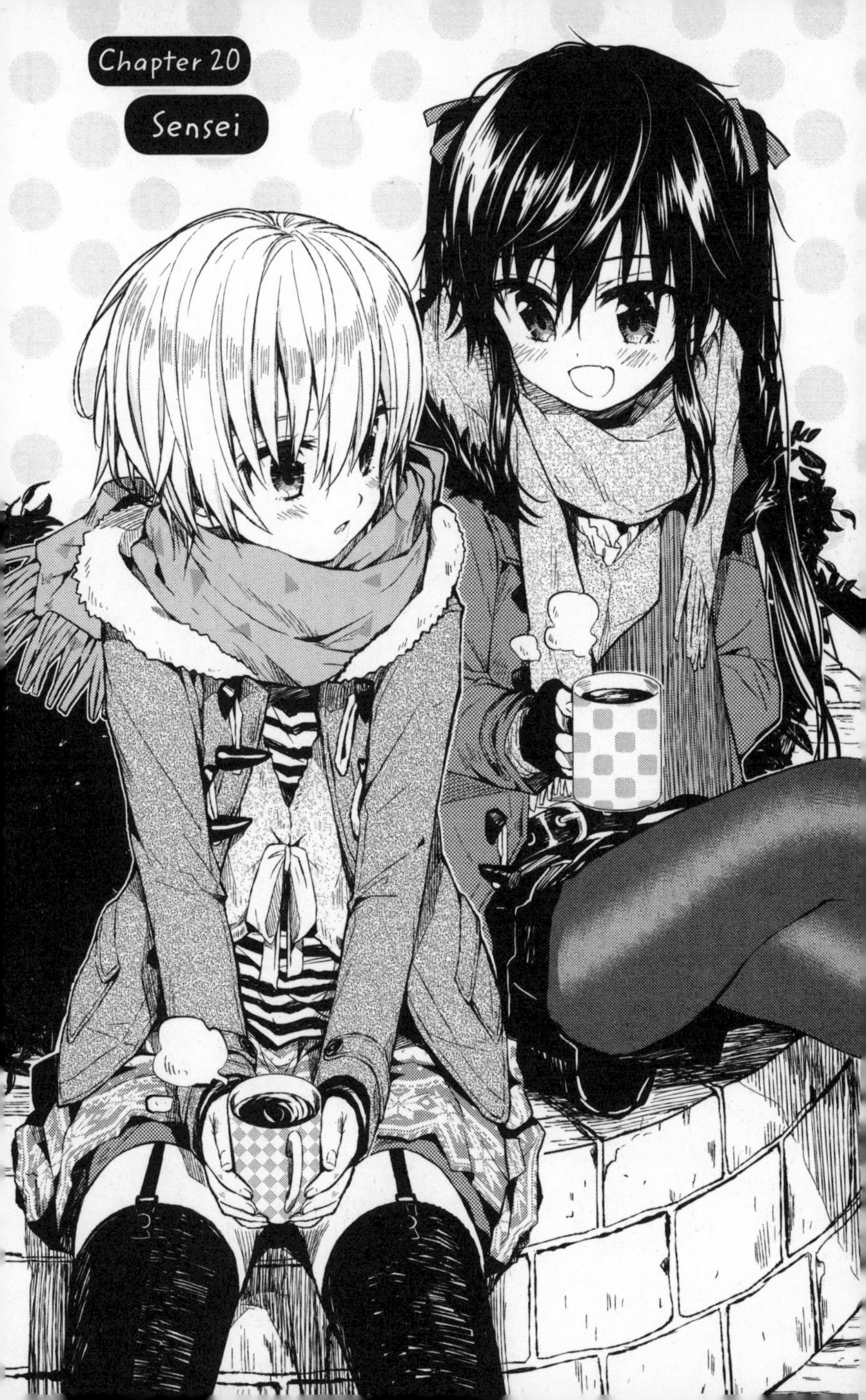

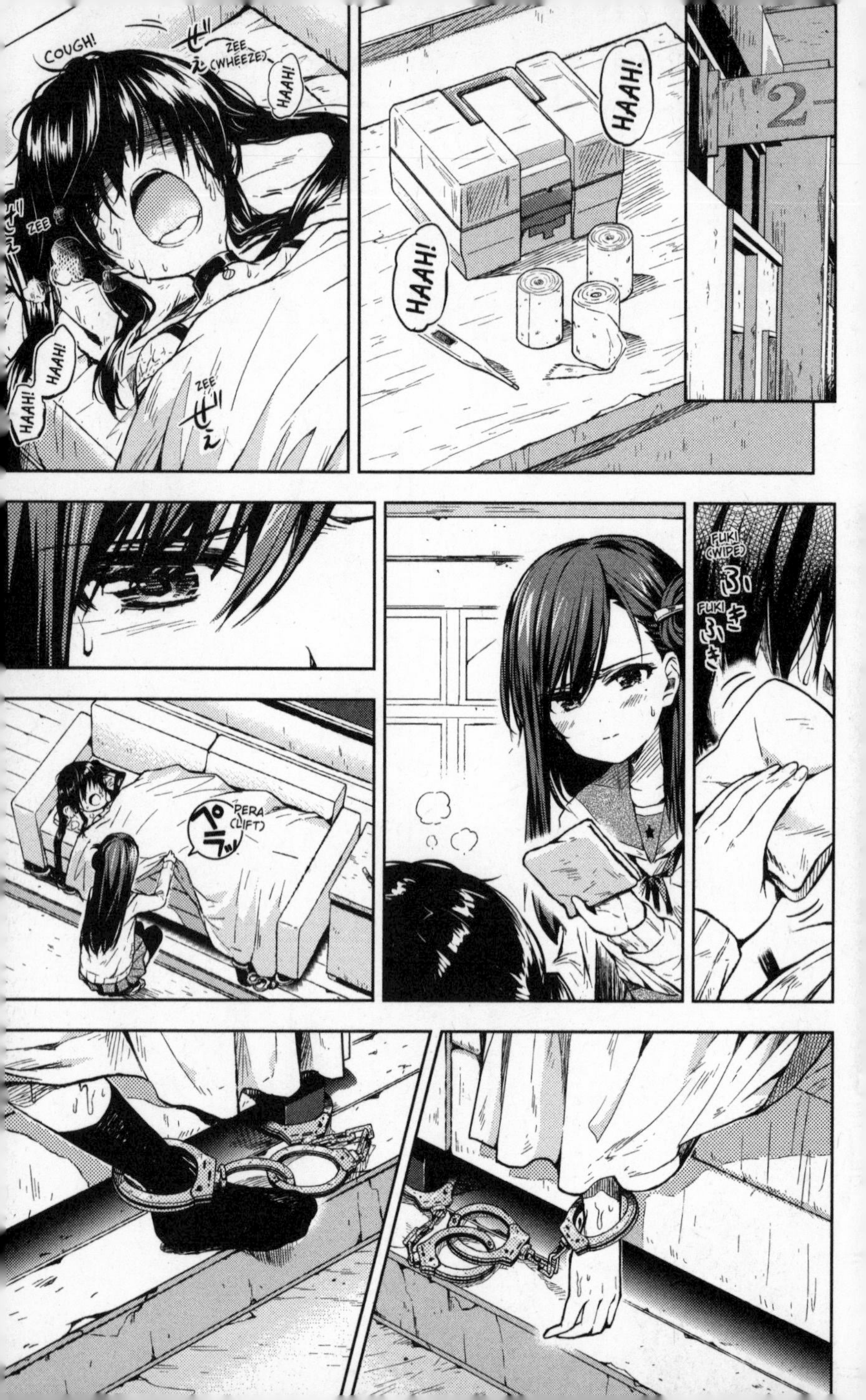
HAAH!
HAAH!
COUGH!
ぜぇ
ZEE (WHEEZE)
HAAH!
ぜぇ
ZEE
HAAH!
HAAH!
HAAH!
ZEE
ぜぇ
ふき
FUKI (WIPE)
ふき
FUKI
ペラッ
PERA (LIFT)

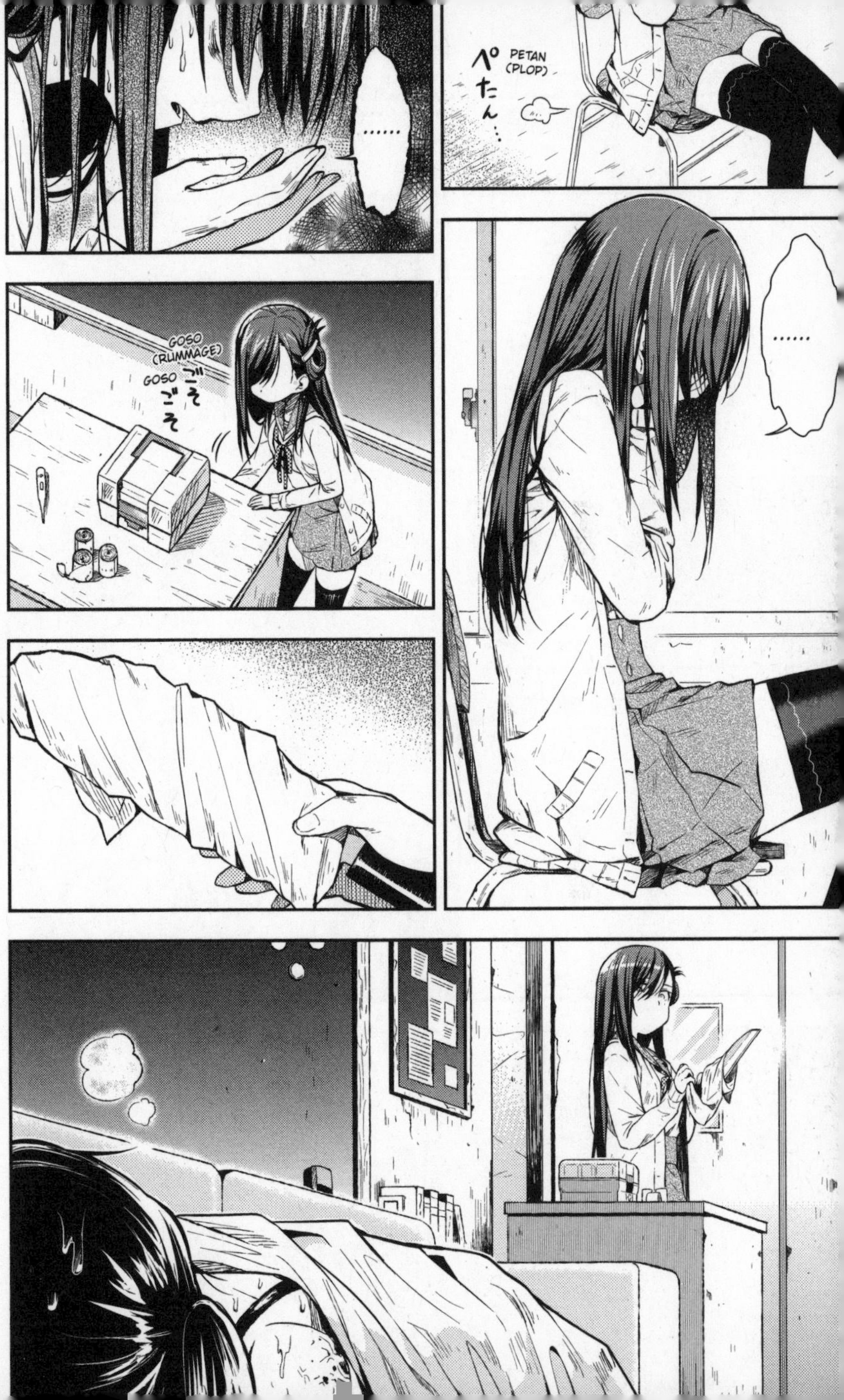
PETAN (PLOP)
ぺたん…
……
……
GOSO (RUMMAGE) GOSO
ごそごそ

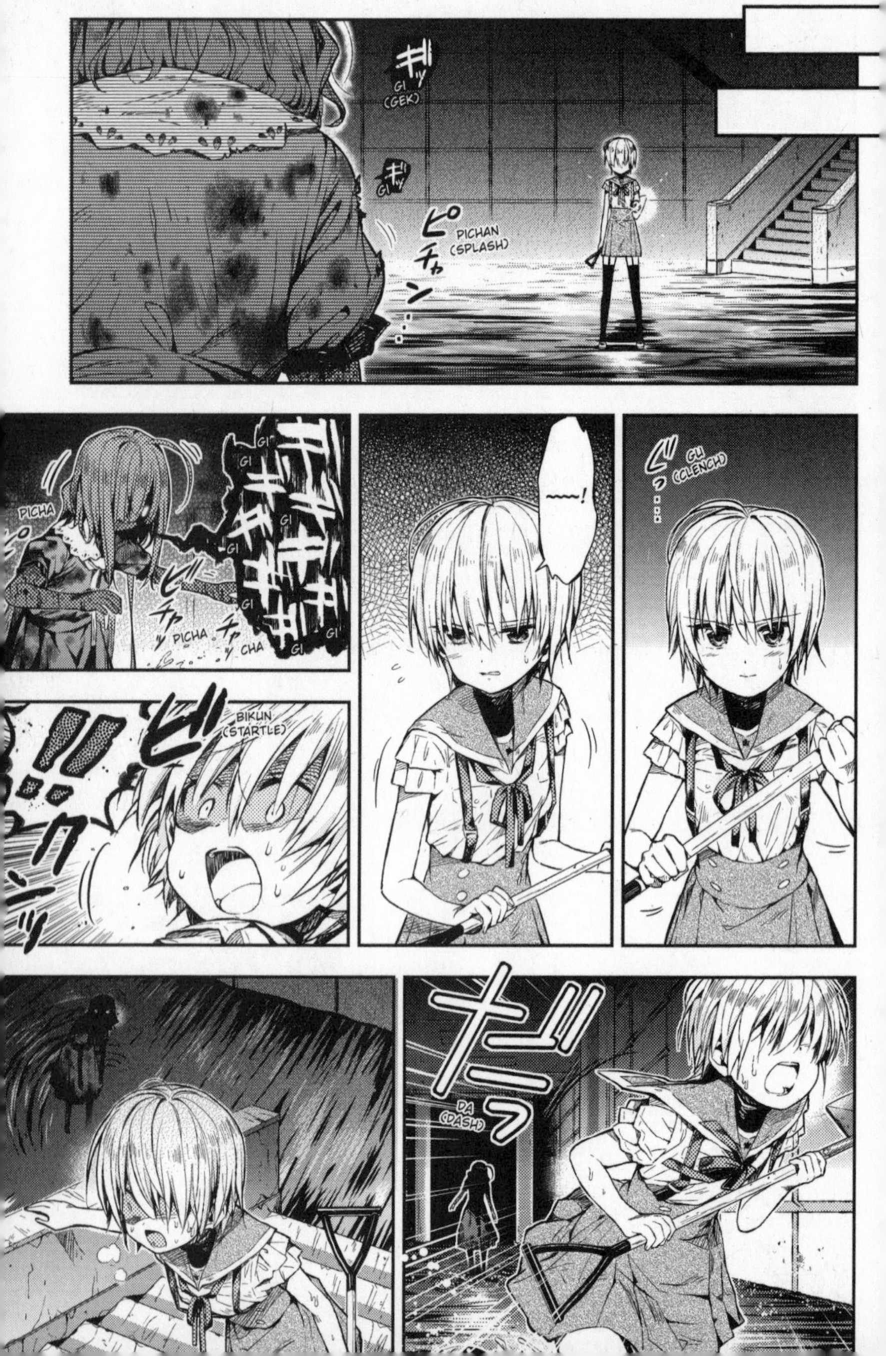
GI (GEK)
GI
PICHAN (SPLASH)
GU (CLENCH)
——!
GI GI GI GI GI GI
PICHA
PICHA CHA
BIKUN (STARTLE)
!!
DA (DASH)

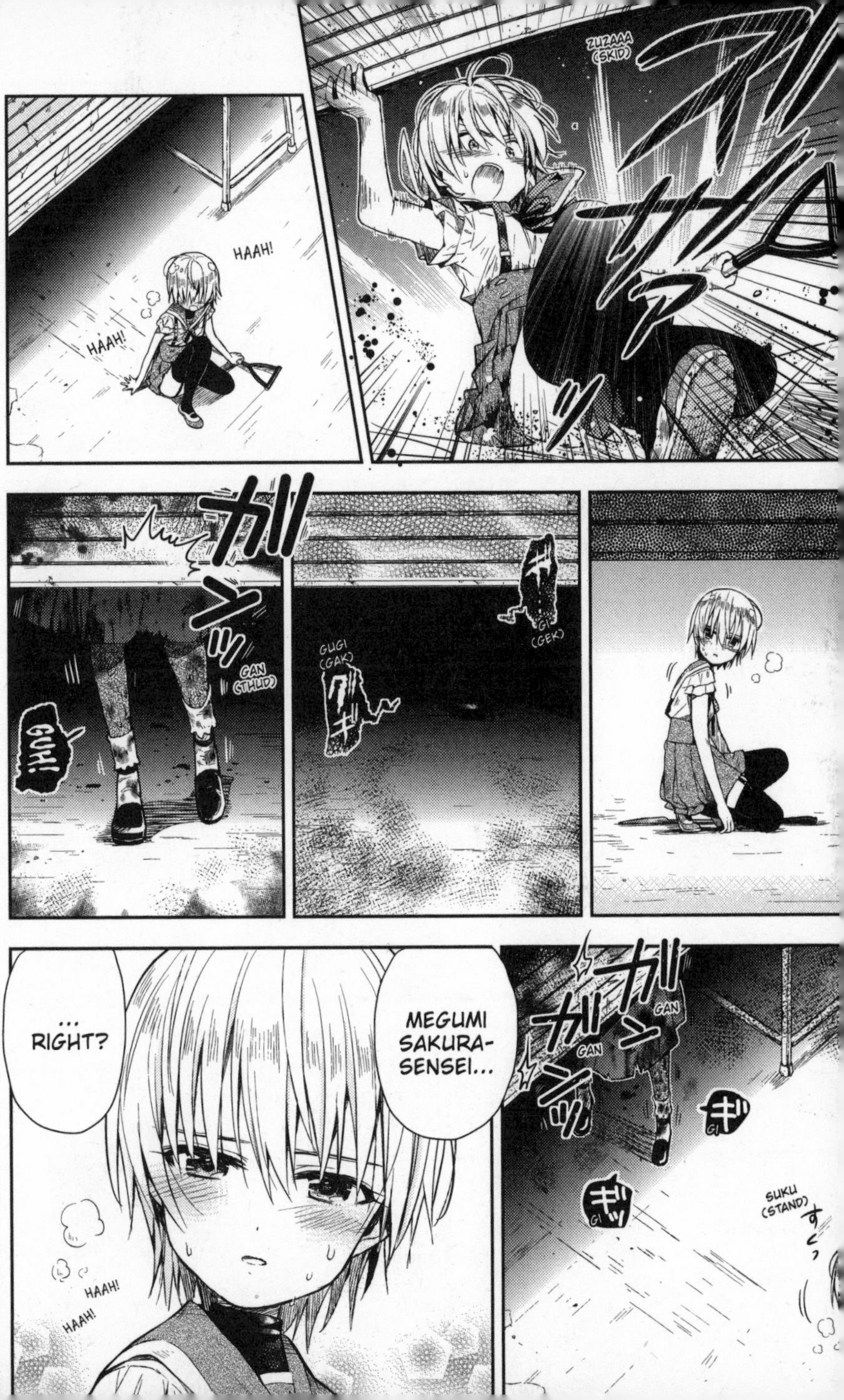
ZUZAAA (SKID)
HAAH!
HAAH!
GI (GEK)
GUGI (GAK)
GAN (THUD)
GUH!
GAN
GAN
GI
GI
SUKU (STAND)
MEGUMI SAKURA-SENSEI...
... RIGHT?
HAAH!
HAAH!

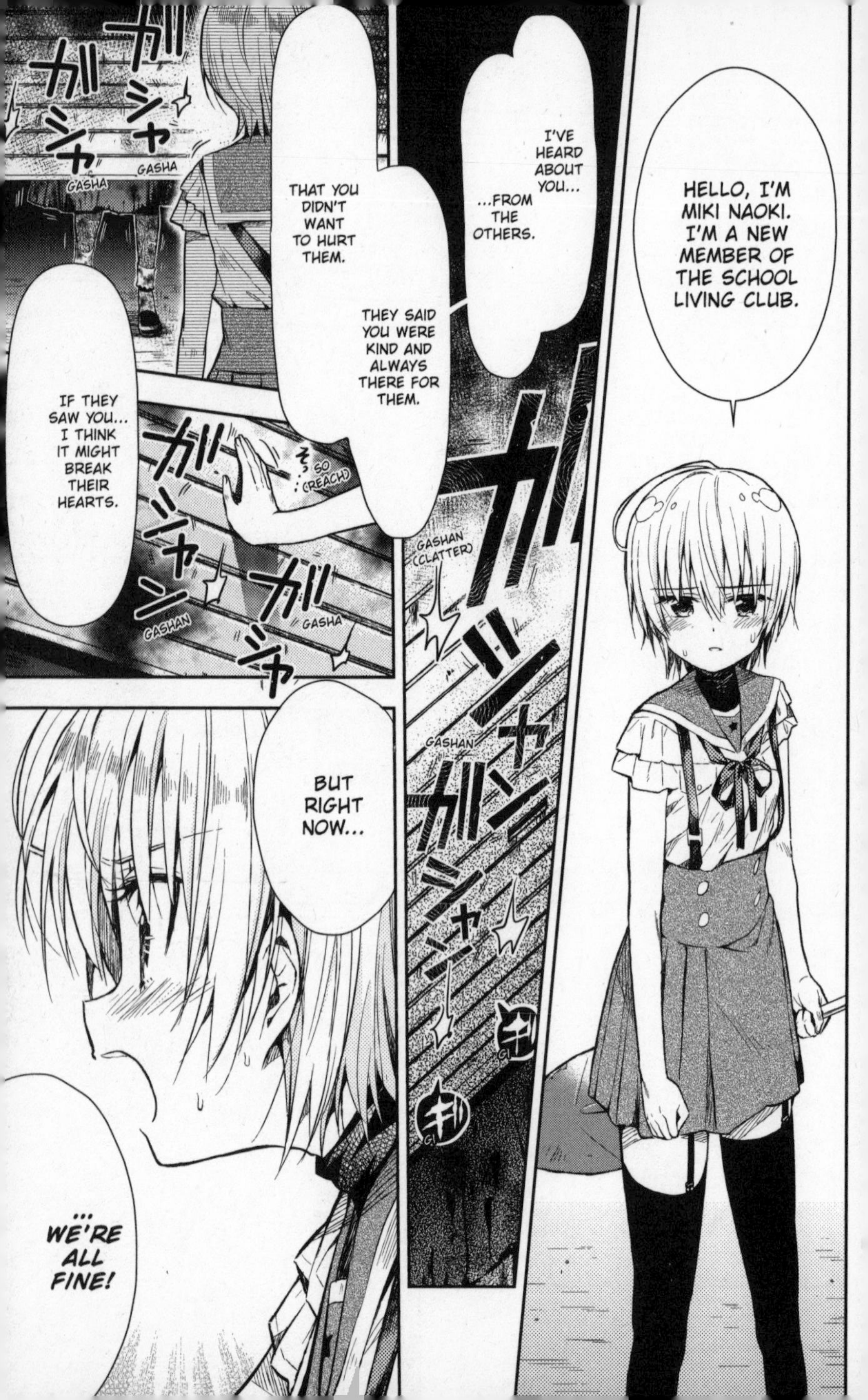
HELLO, I'M MIKI NAOKI. I'M A NEW MEMBER OF THE SCHOOL LIVING CLUB.
I'VE HEARD ABOUT YOU...
...FROM THE OTHERS.
GASHAN (CLATTER)
GASHAN
GI
GI
THAT YOU DIDN'T WANT TO HURT THEM.
THEY SAID YOU WERE KIND AND ALWAYS THERE FOR THEM.
GASHA
GASHA
SO (REACH)
IF THEY SAW YOU... I THINK IT MIGHT BREAK THEIR HEARTS.
GASHA
GASHAN
BUT RIGHT NOW...
...WE'RE ALL FINE!

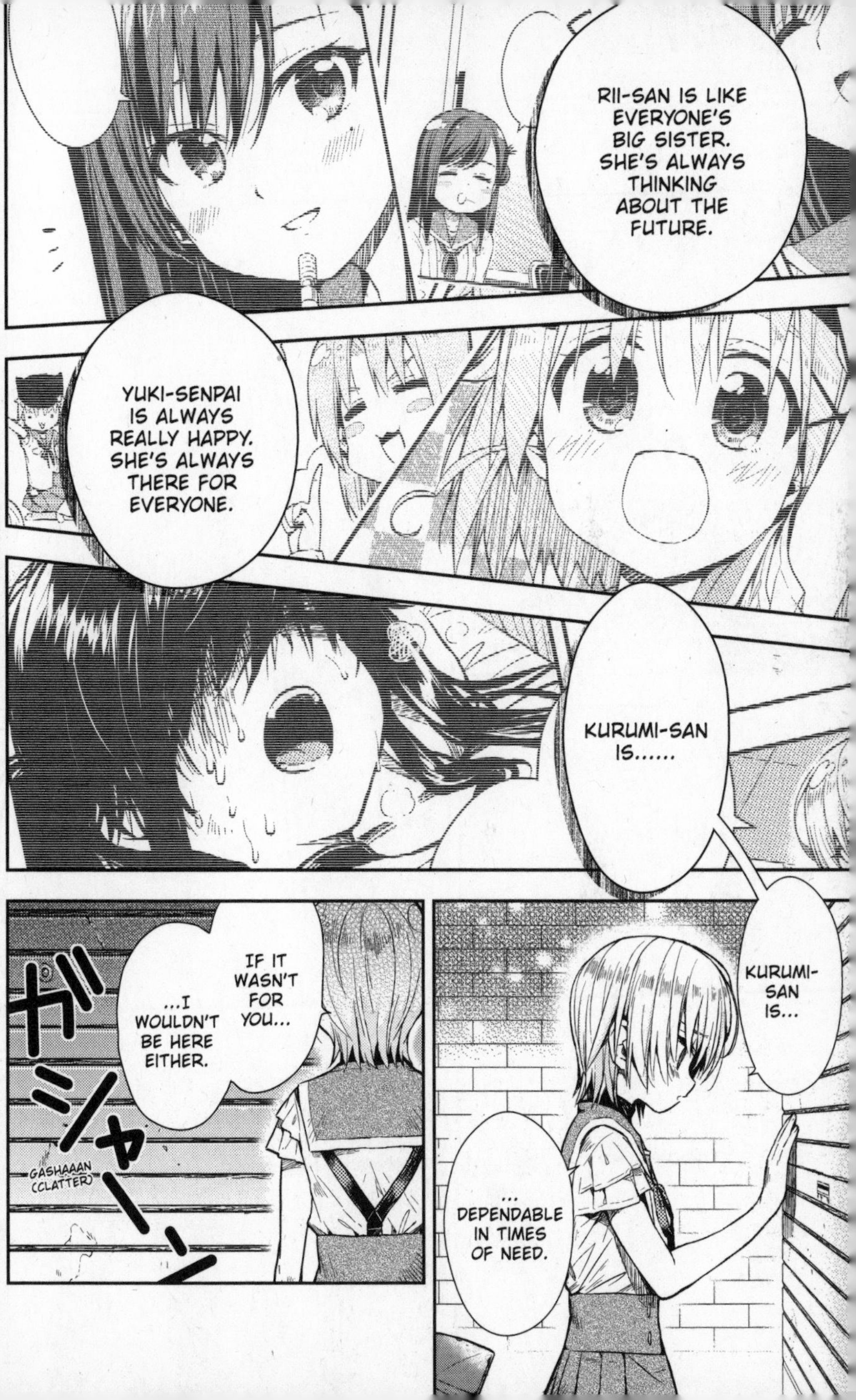
RII-SAN IS LIKE EVERYONE'S BIG SISTER. SHE'S ALWAYS THINKING ABOUT THE FUTURE.
YUKI-SENPAI IS ALWAYS REALLY HAPPY. SHE'S ALWAYS THERE FOR EVERYONE.
KURUMI-SAN IS......
KURUMI-SAN IS...
...DEPENDABLE IN TIMES OF NEED.
IF IT WASN'T FOR YOU...
...I WOULDN'T BE HERE EITHER.
GASHAAAN (CLATTER)

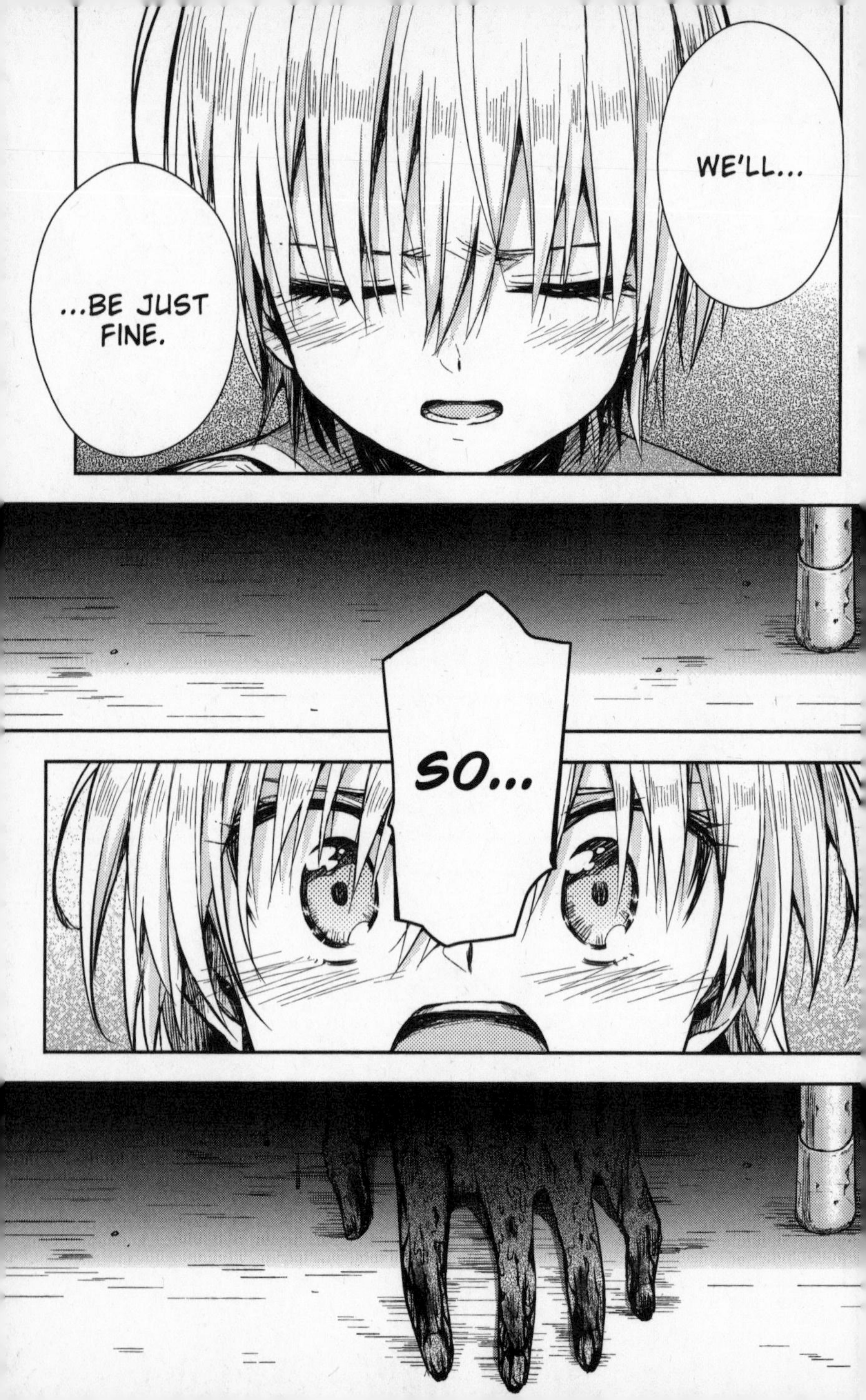
WE'LL...
...BE JUST FINE.
SO...

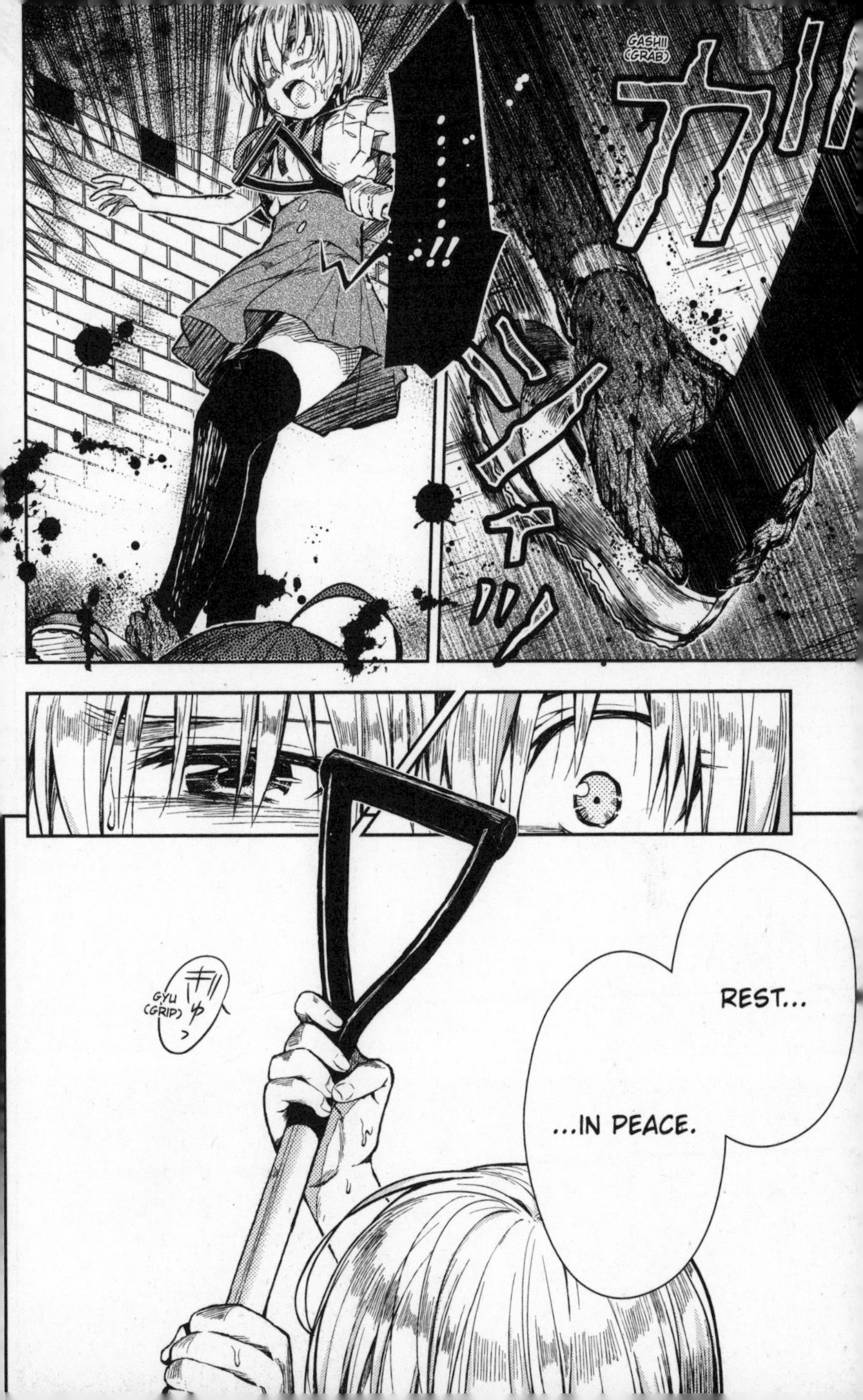
GASHI! (GRAB)
...!!
GYU (GRIP)
REST...
...IN PEACE.

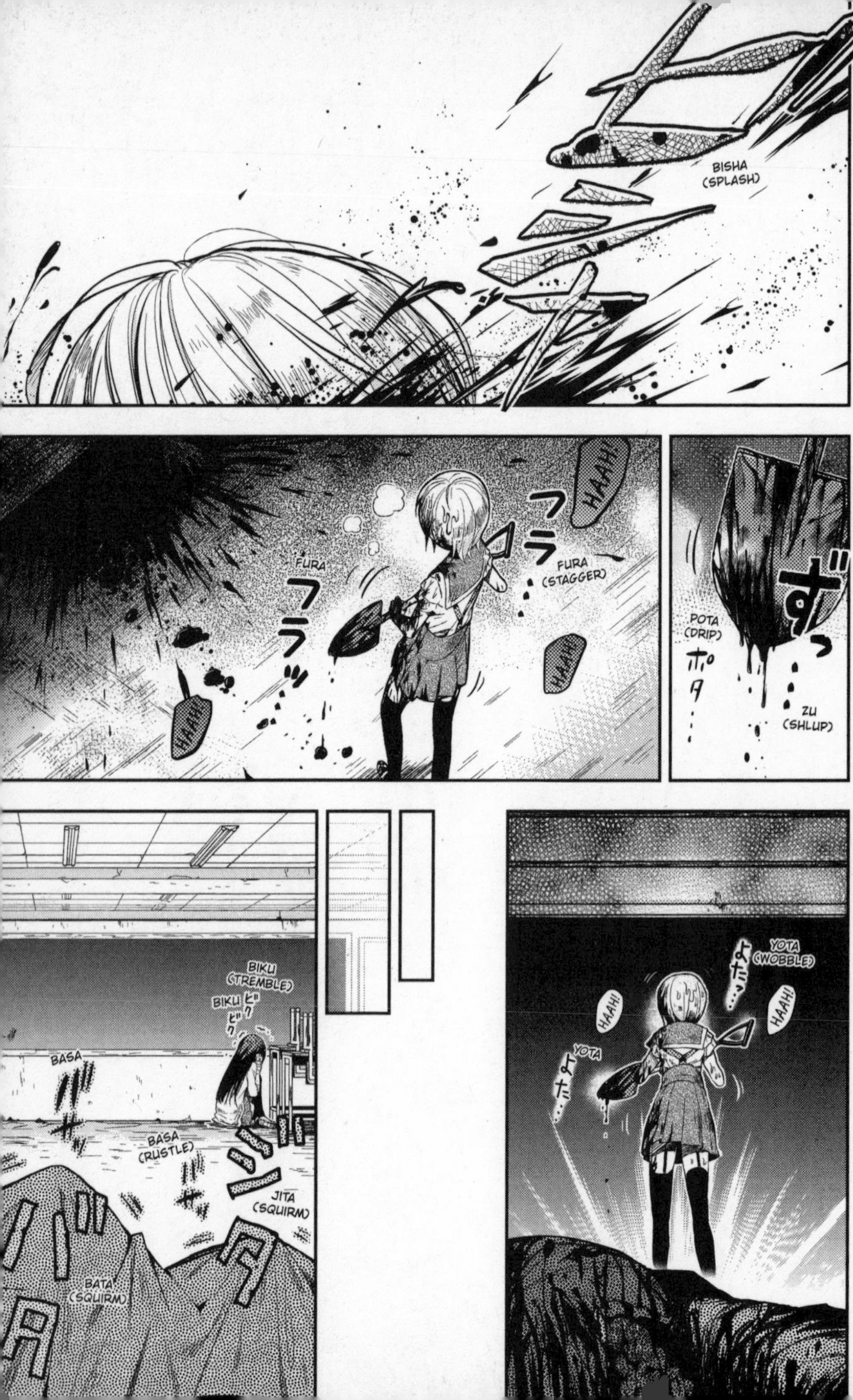
BISHA (SPLASH)
ずっ
ZU (SHLUP)
ポタ…
POTA (DRIP)
HAAH!
フラ
FURA (STAGGER)
HAAH!
フラッ
FURA
HAAH!
よたっ…
YOTA (WOBBLE)
HAAH!
HAAH!
よた…
YOTA
ビクビク
BIKU (TREMBLE)
BIKU
BASA
BASA (RUSTLE)
JITA (SQUIRM)
BATA (SQUIRM)

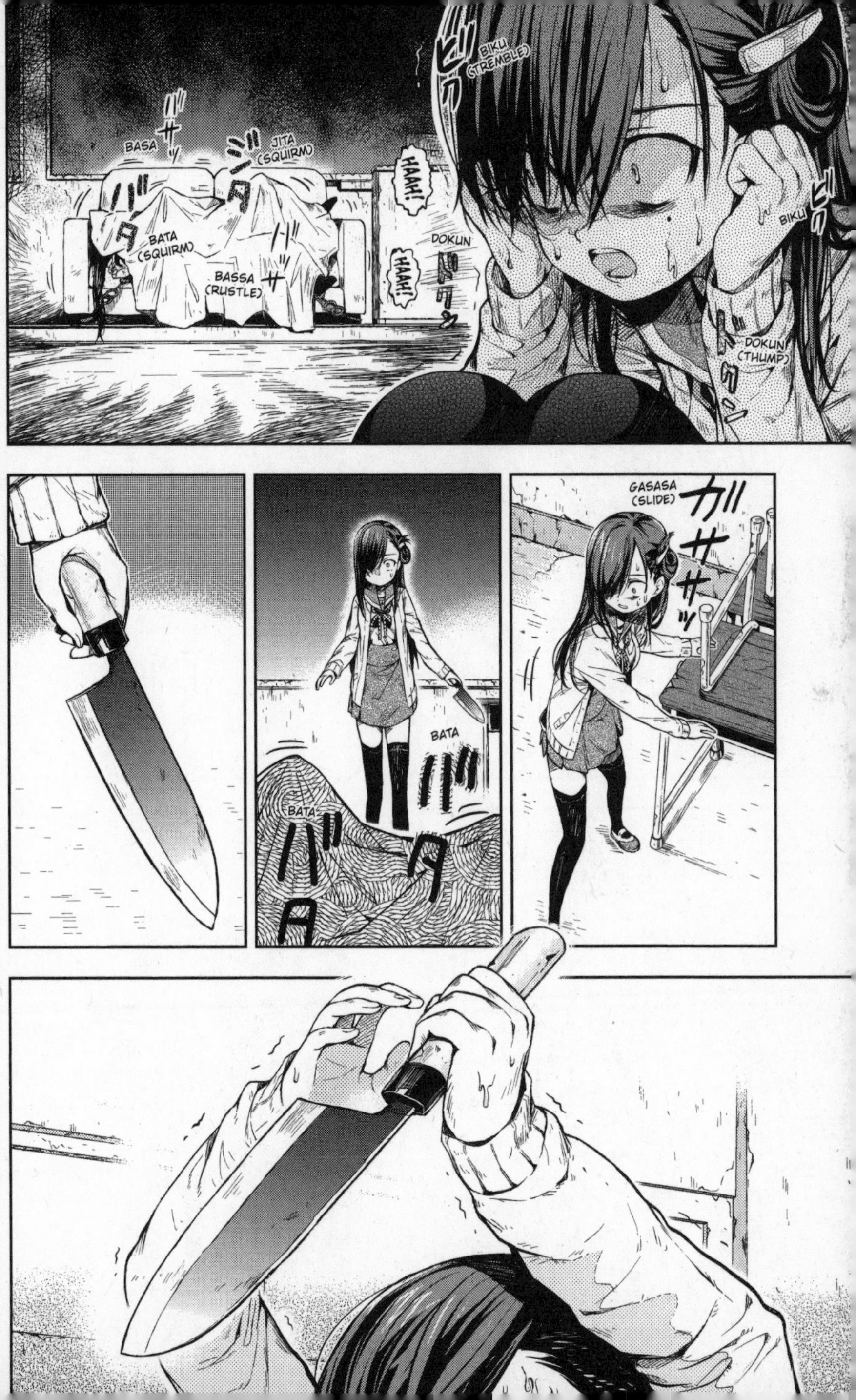
BIKU (TREMBLE)
BIKU
DOKUN (THUMP)
HAAH!
HAAH!
DOKUN
JITA (SQUIRM)
BASA
BATA (SQUIRM)
BASSA (RUSTLE)
GASASA (SLIDE)
BATA
BATA

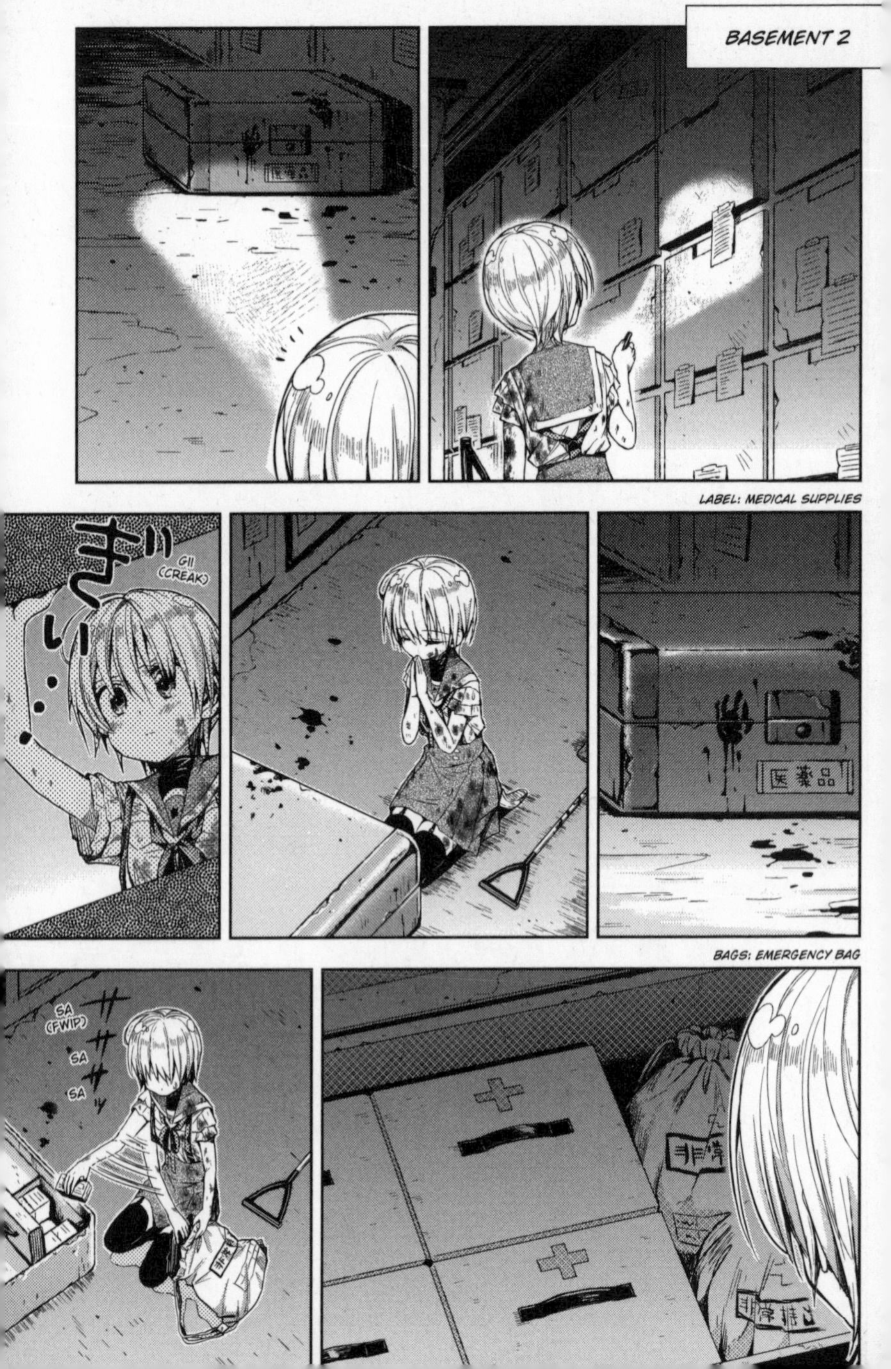

BASEMENT 2
LABEL: MEDICAL SUPPLIES
医薬品
きぃ…
GII (CREAK)
BAGS: EMERGENCY BAG
サ
SA (FWIP)
サ
SA
サ
SA

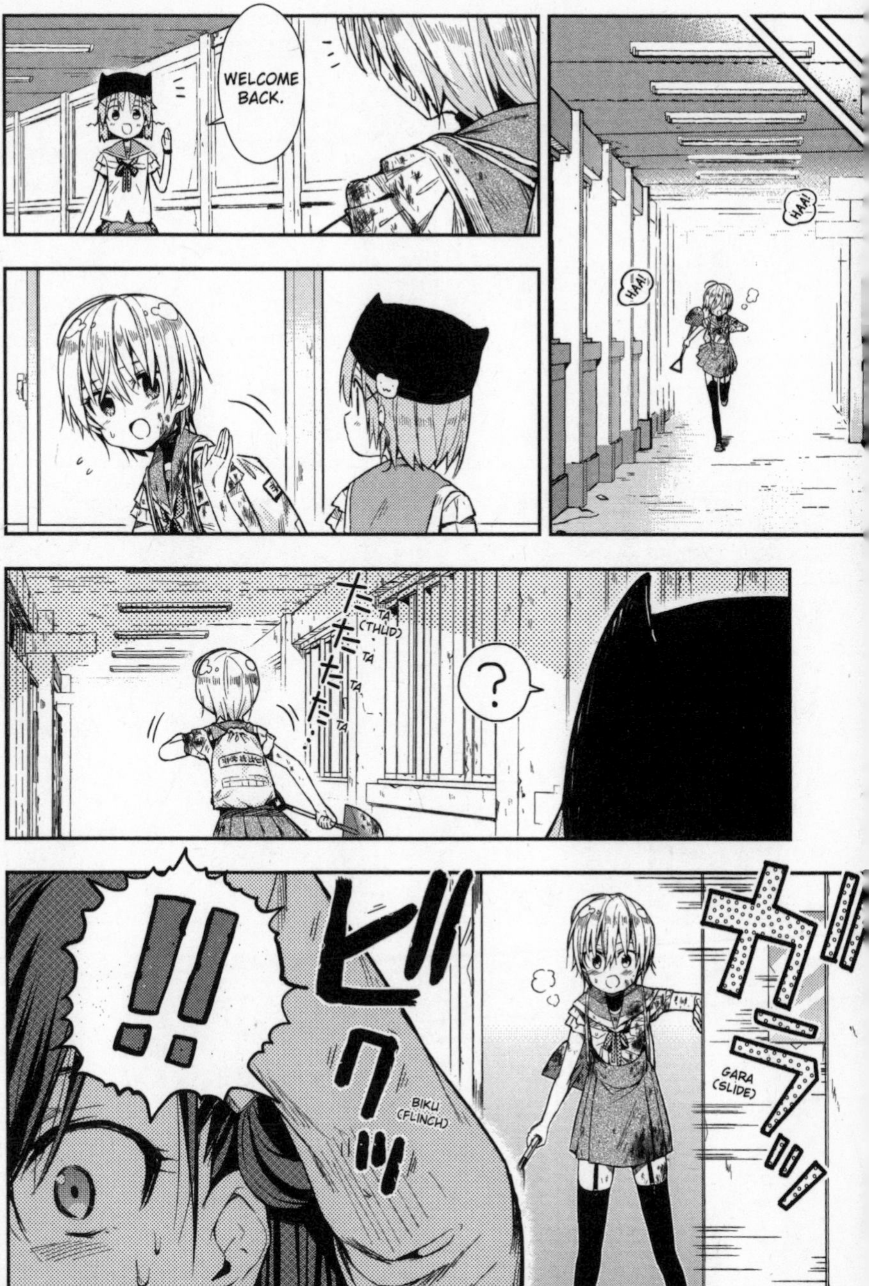
HAA!
HAA!
WELCOME BACK.
たたたた
TA (THUD) TA TA TA
?
ガラッ
GARA (SLIDE)
!!
ビクッ
BIKU (FLINCH)

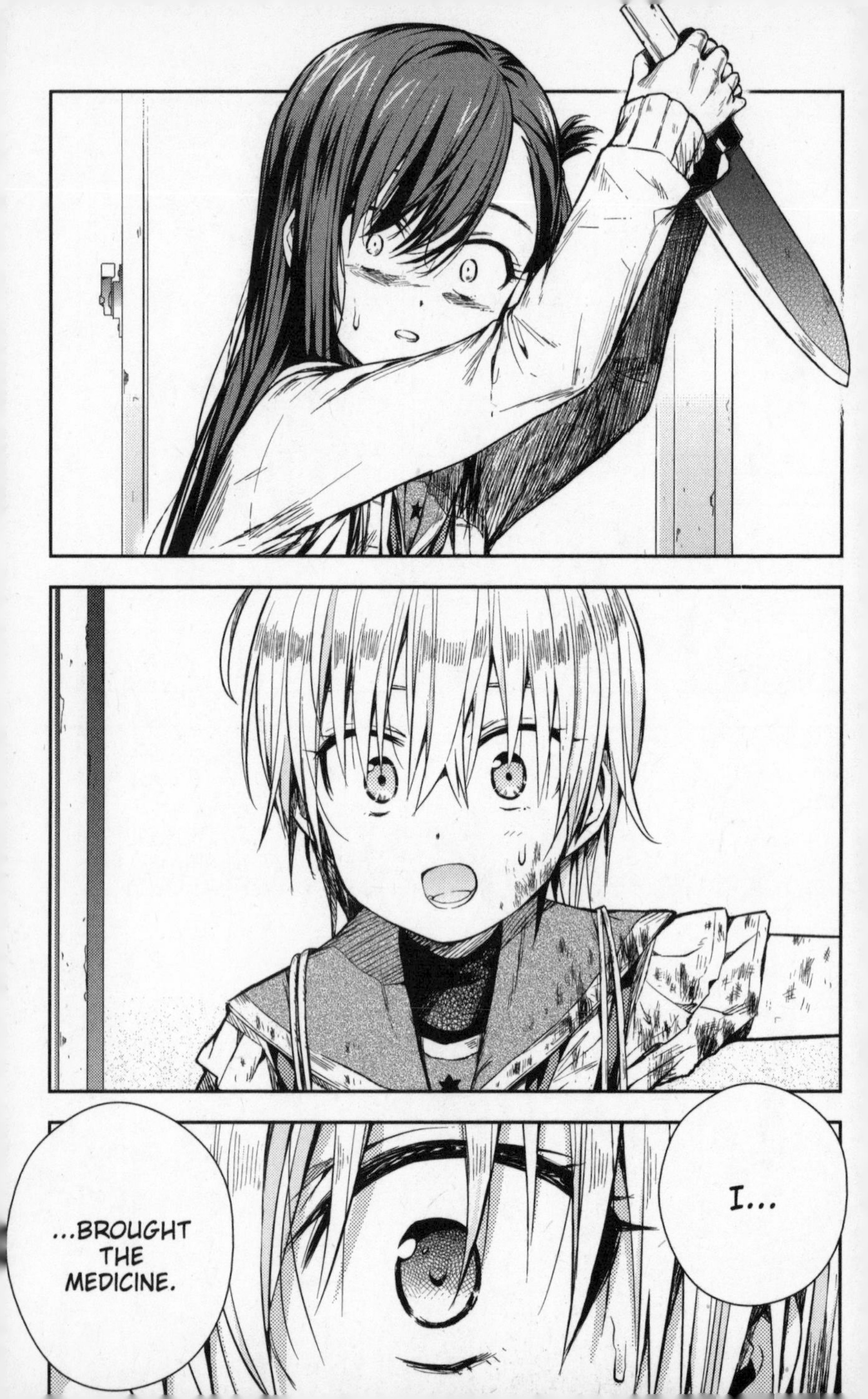
I...
...BROUGHT THE MEDICINE.

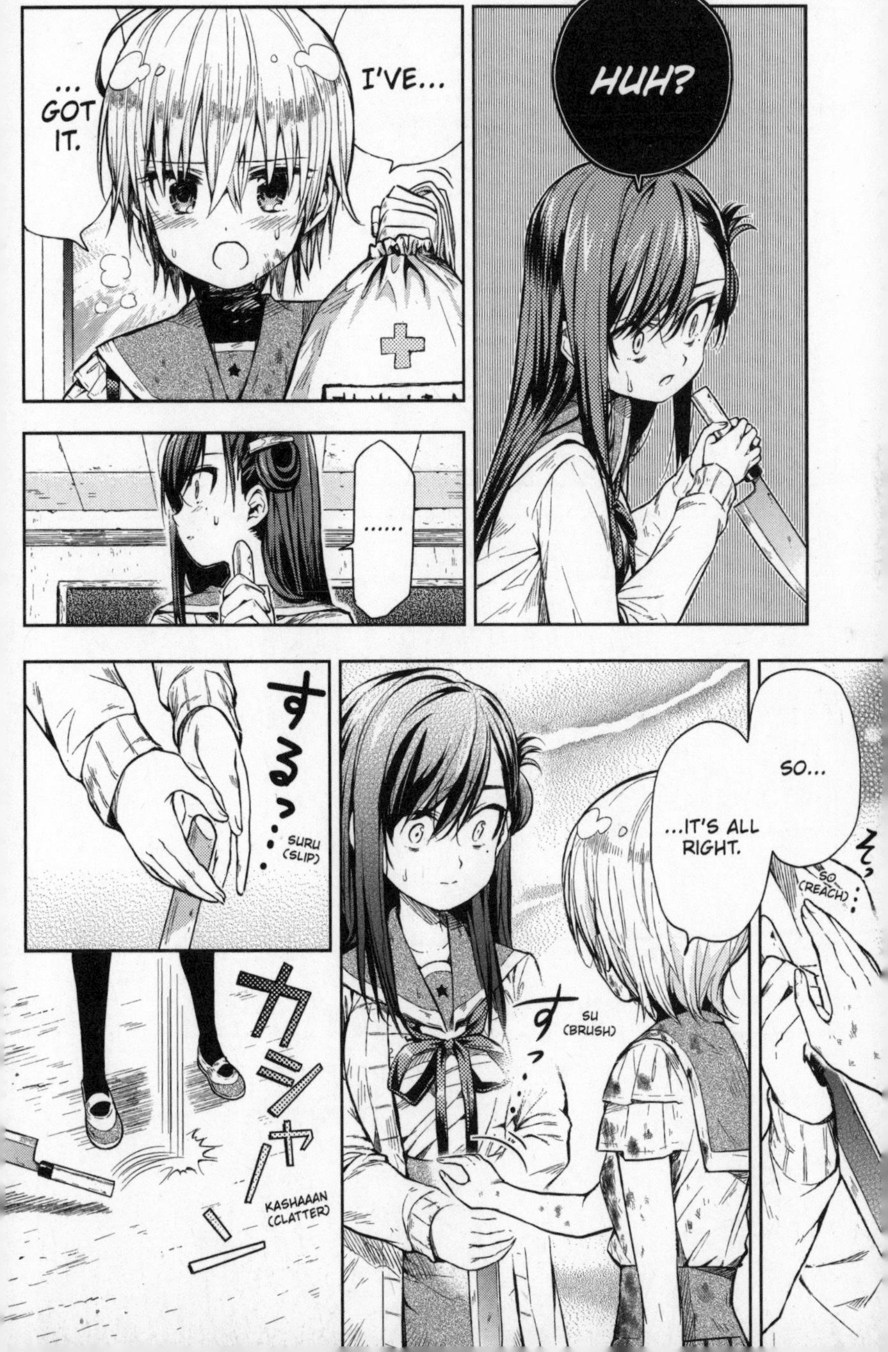
HUH?
I'VE...
... GOT IT.
......
SO...
...IT'S ALL RIGHT.
SO (REACH)
すっ
SU (BRUSH)
するっ…
SURU (SLIP)
KASHAAAN (CLATTER)

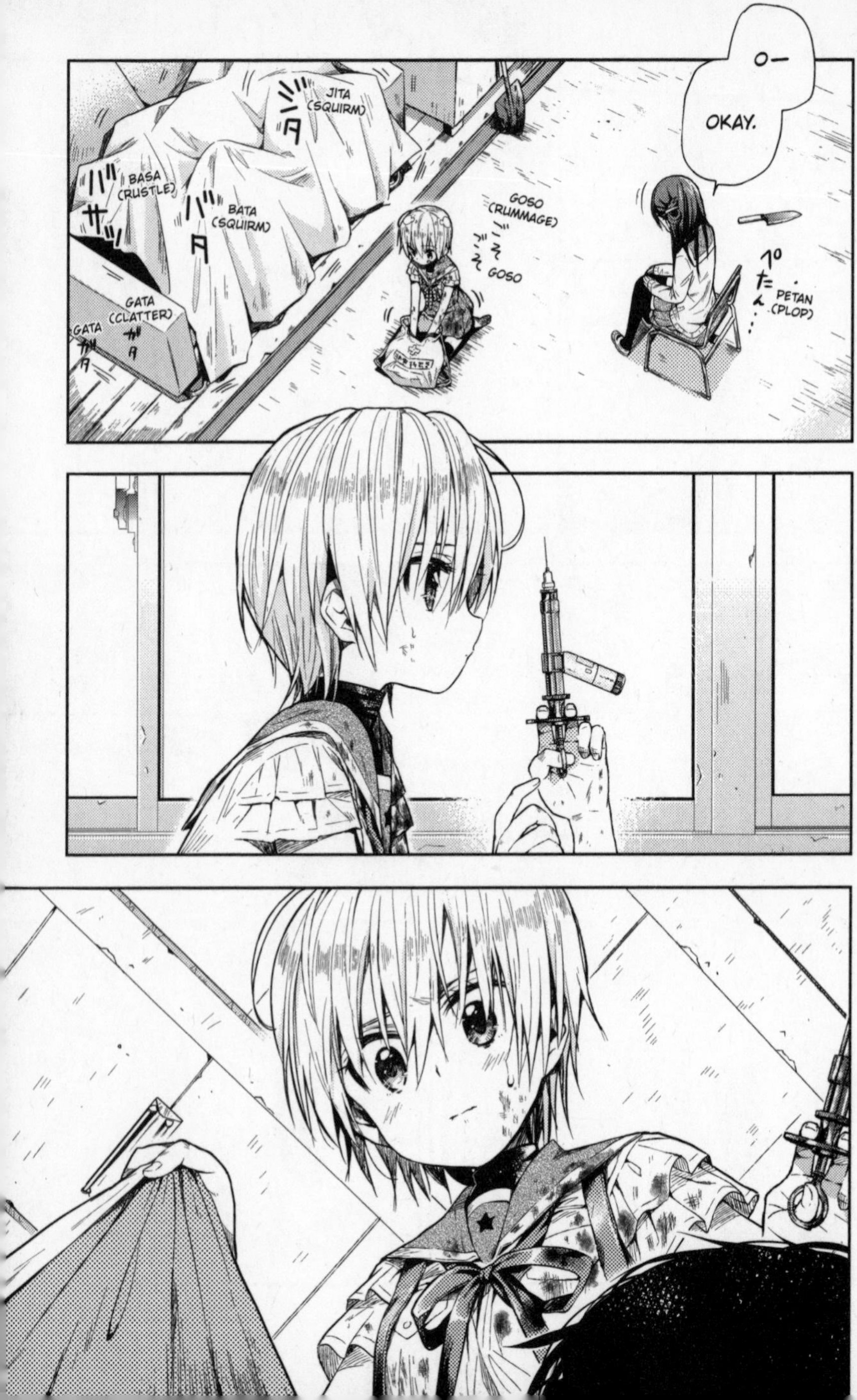
O—
OKAY.
PETAN (PLOP)
GOSO (RUMMAGE)
GOSO
JITA (SQUIRM)
BASA (RUSTLE)
BATA (SQUIRM)
GATA (CLATTER)
GATA

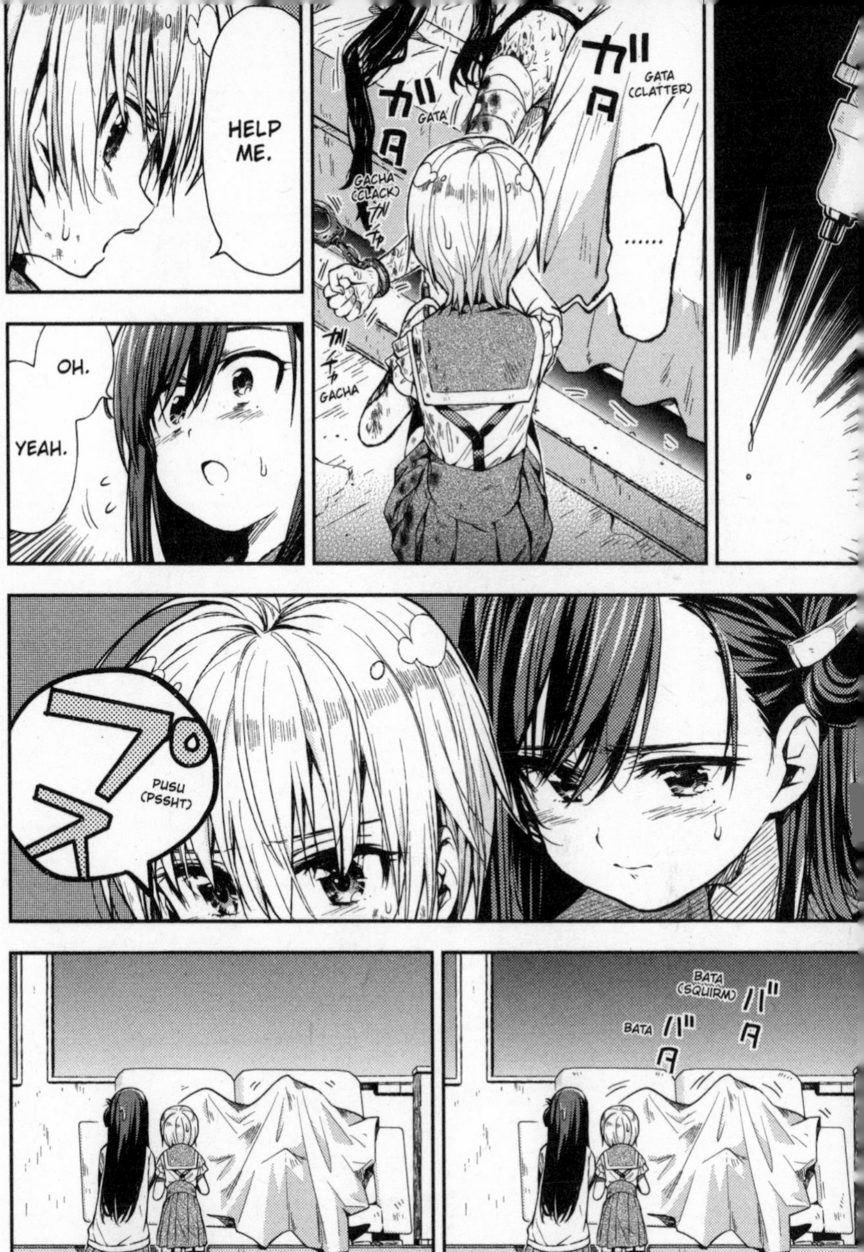
GATA (CLATTER)
......
GATA
GACHA (CLACK)
GACHA
HELP ME.
OH.
YEAH.
PUSU (PSSHT)
BATA (SQUIRM)
BATA

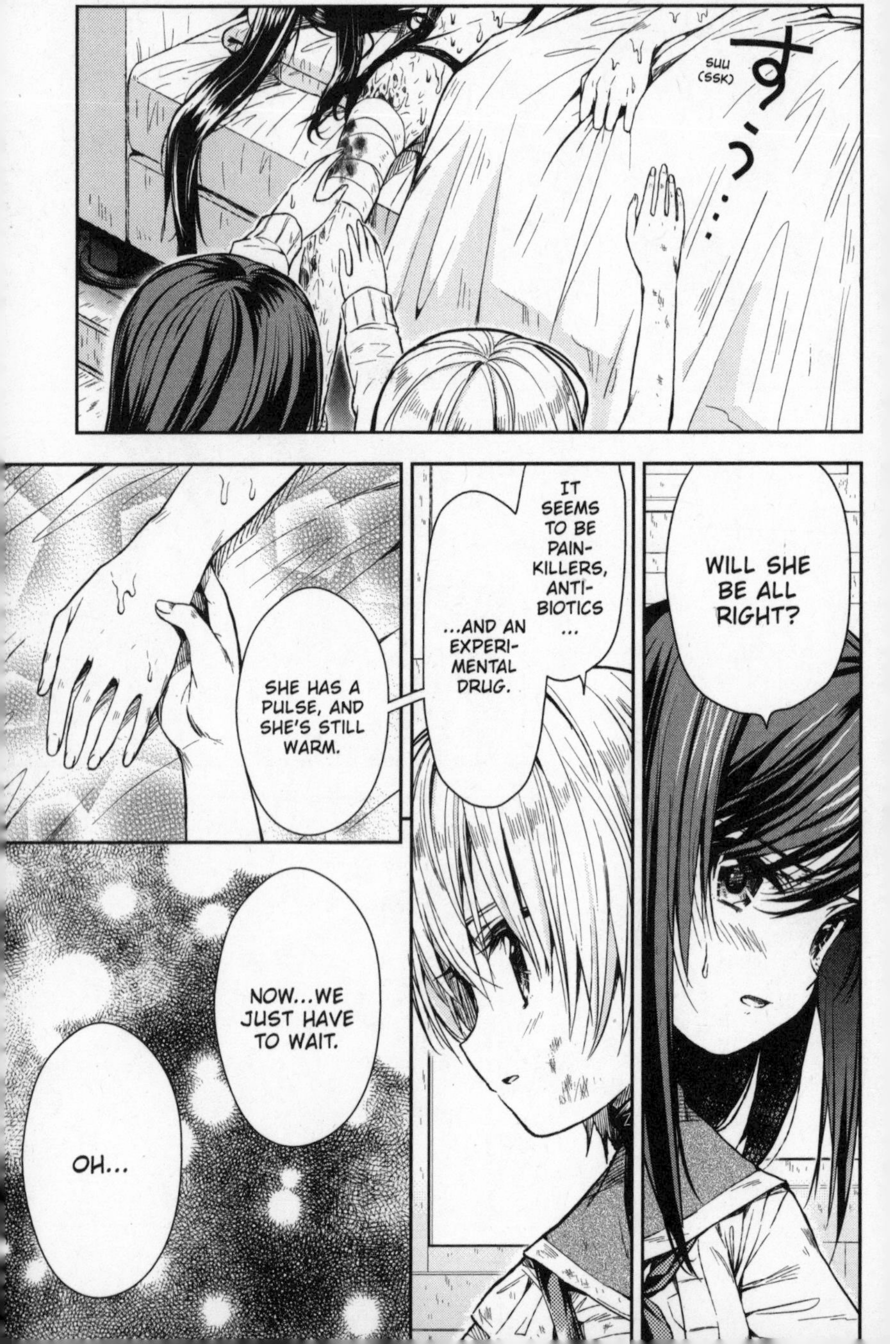
すう…
SUU (SSK)
WILL SHE BE ALL RIGHT?
IT SEEMS TO BE PAIN-KILLERS, ANTI-BIOTICS ...
...AND AN EXPERI-MENTAL DRUG.
SHE HAS A PULSE, AND SHE'S STILL WARM.
NOW...WE JUST HAVE TO WAIT.
OH...

PON
(PAT)

HANG IN
THERE...

...

KURUMI.

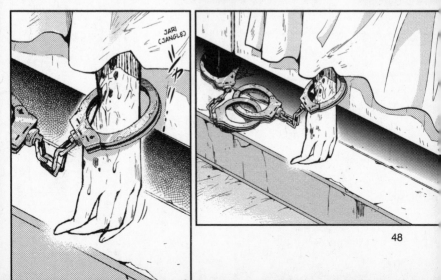

JARI
(JANGLE)

48

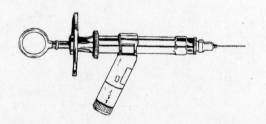

SCHOOL-LIVE!

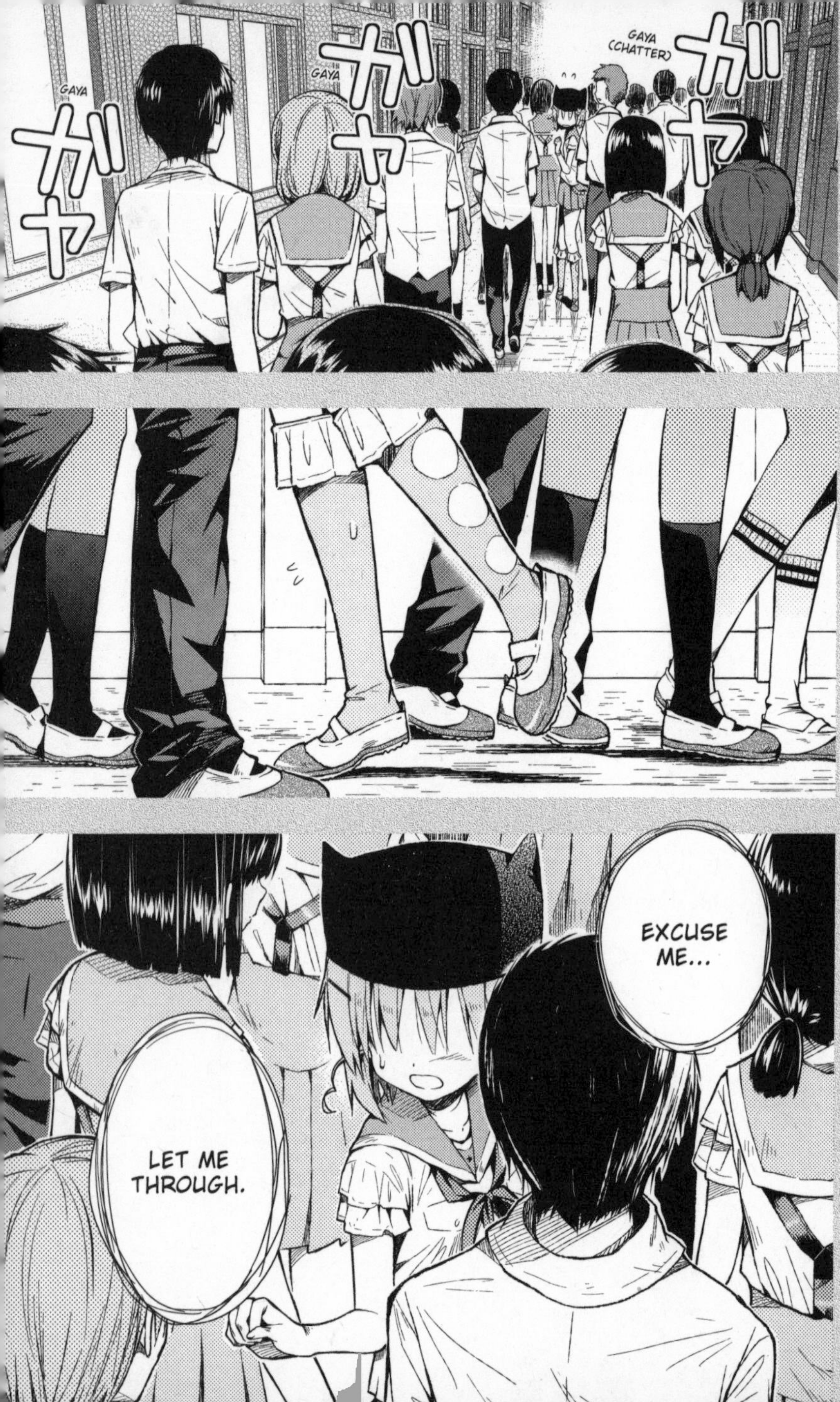
GAYA
(CHATTER)
ガヤ
GAYA
ガヤ
GAYA
ガヤ
EXCUSE ME...
LET ME THROUGH.

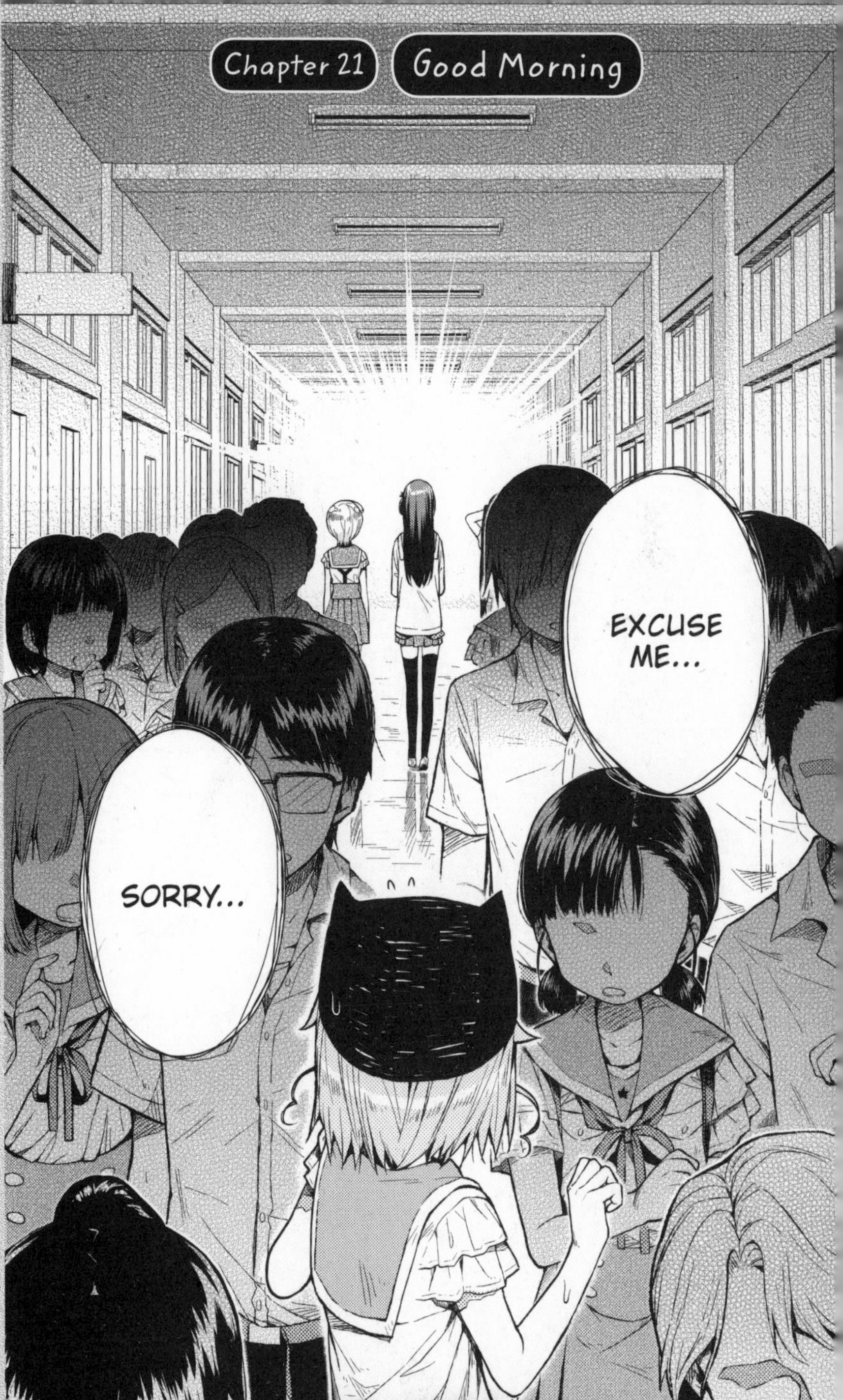
Chapter 21
Good Morning
EXCUSE ME...
SORRY...

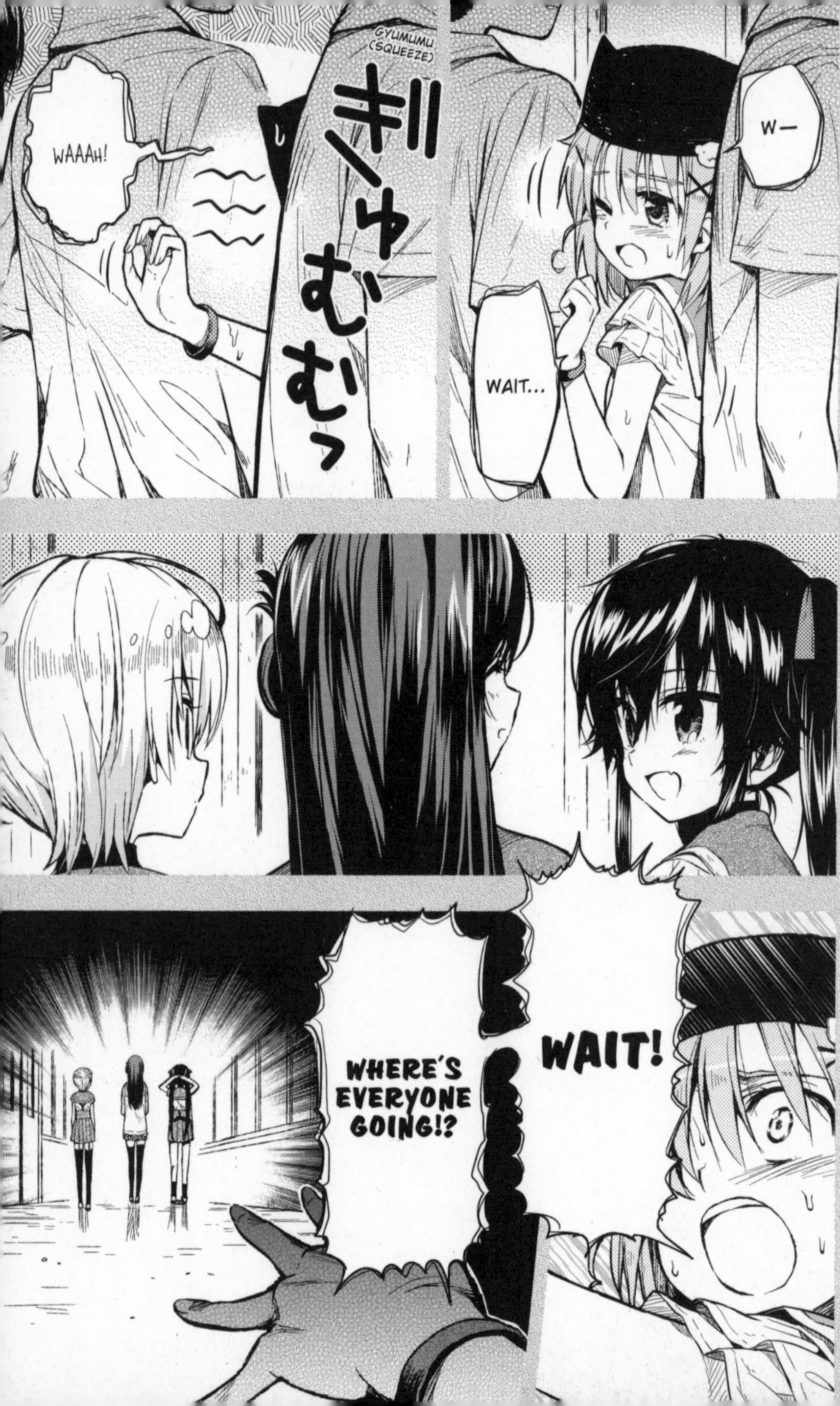
W—
WAIT...
GYUMUMU (SQUEEZE)
ぎゅむむっ
WAAAH!
WAIT!
WHERE'S EVERYONE GOING!?

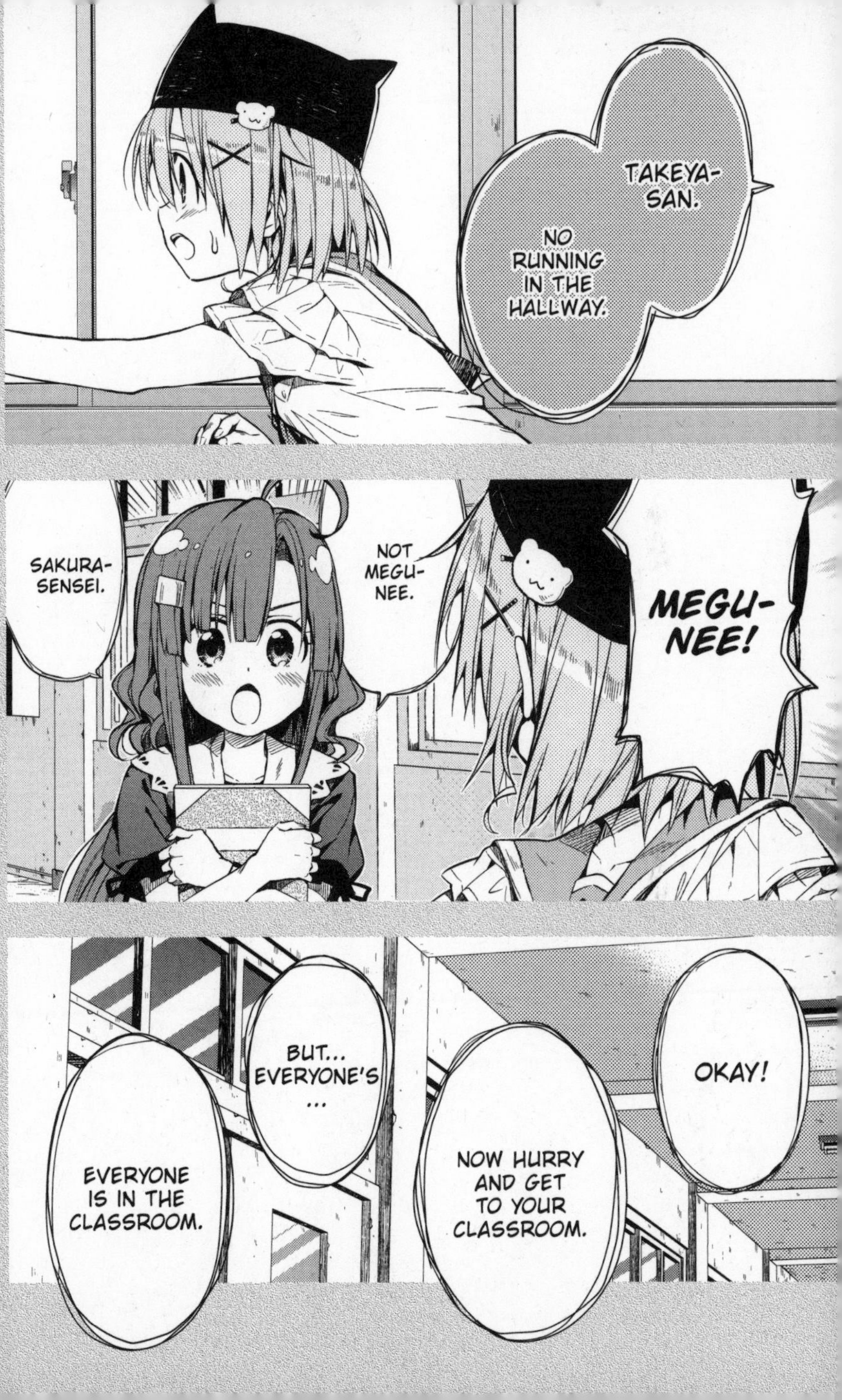
TAKEYA-SAN.
NO RUNNING IN THE HALLWAY.
MEGU-NEE!
NOT MEGU-NEE.
SAKURA-SENSEI.
OKAY!
NOW HURRY AND GET TO YOUR CLASSROOM.
BUT... EVERYONE'S ...
EVERYONE IS IN THE CLASSROOM.

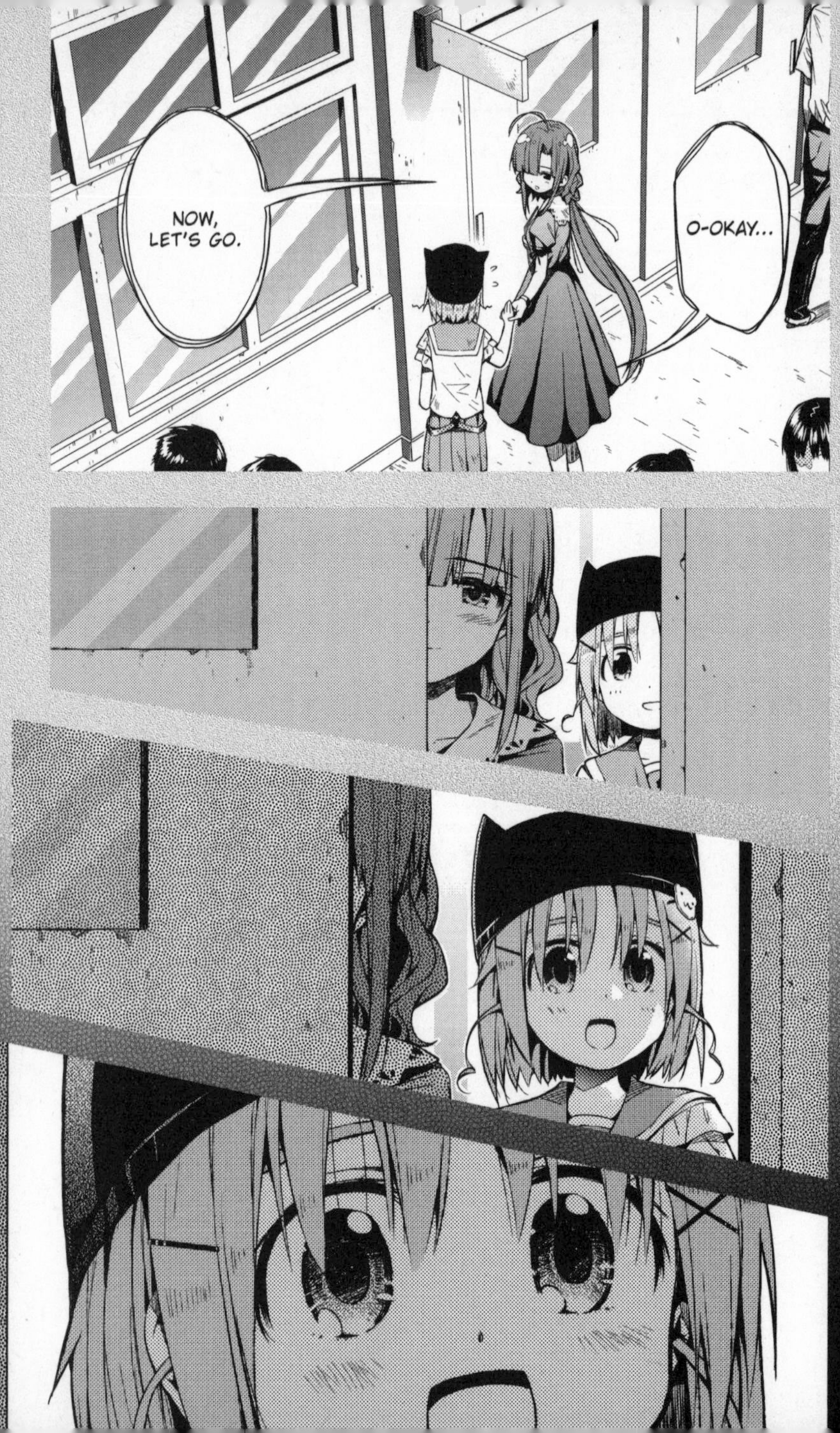
O-OKAY...
NOW, LET'S GO.

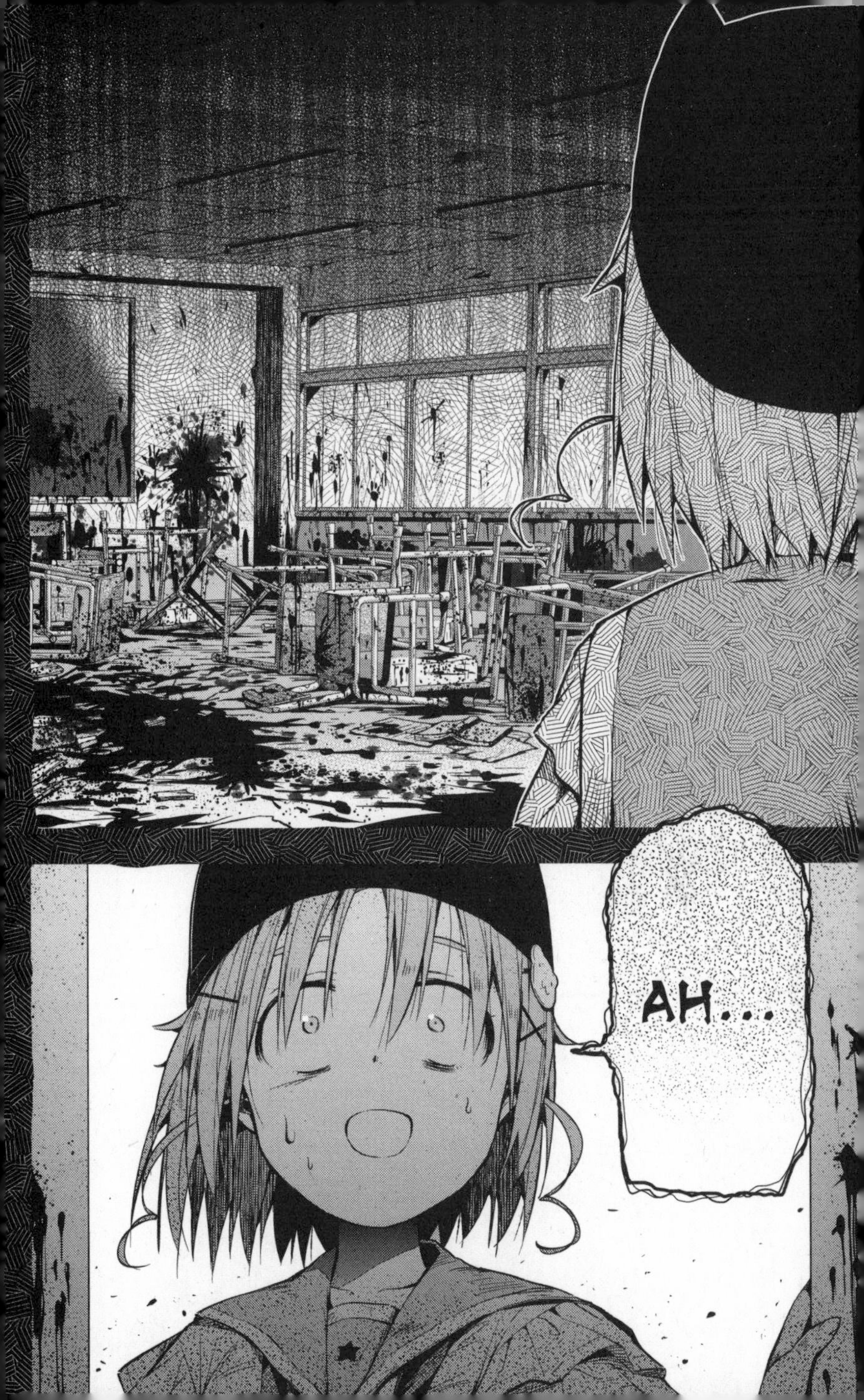
AH...

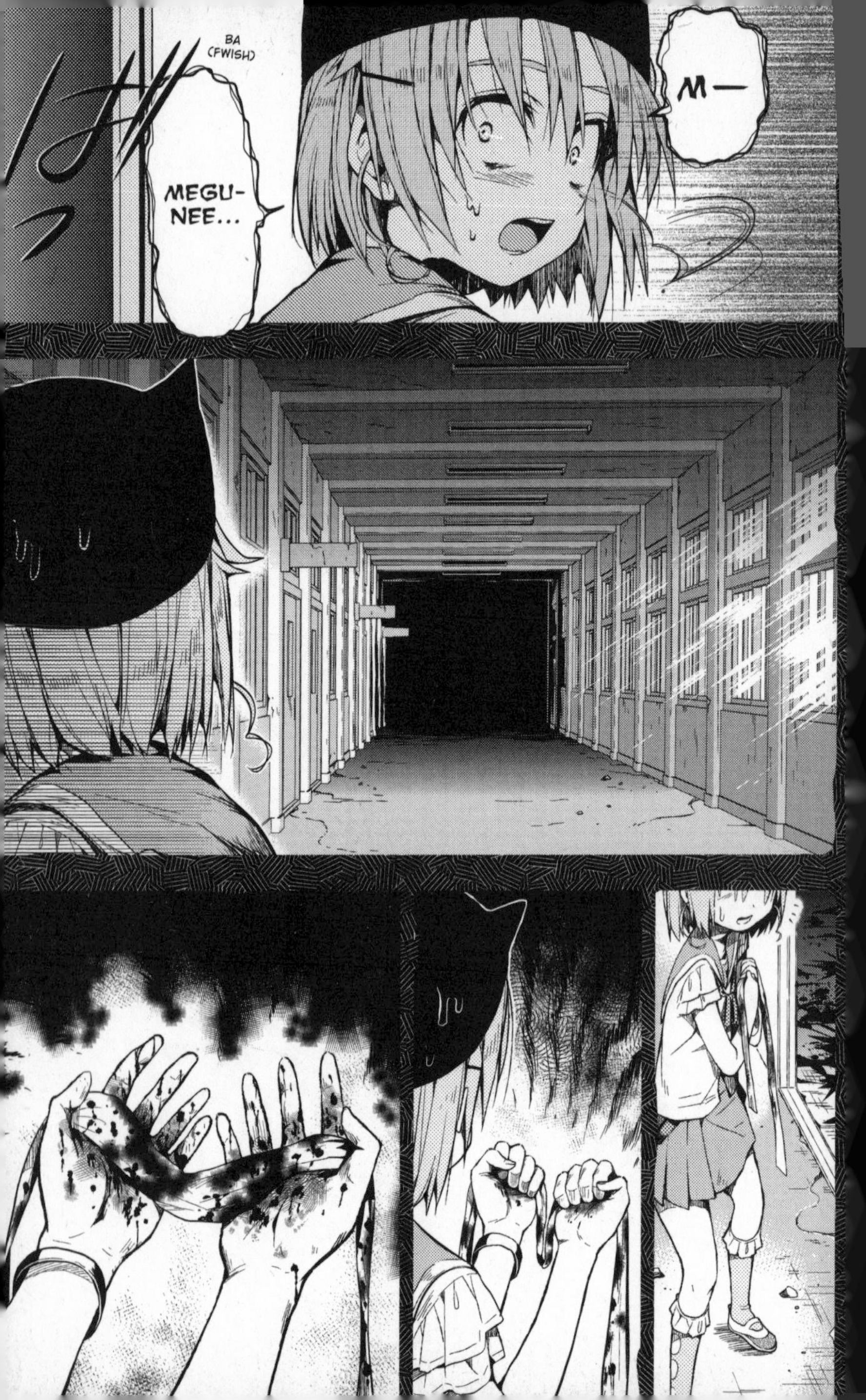
M—
BA (FWISH)
MEGU-NEE...

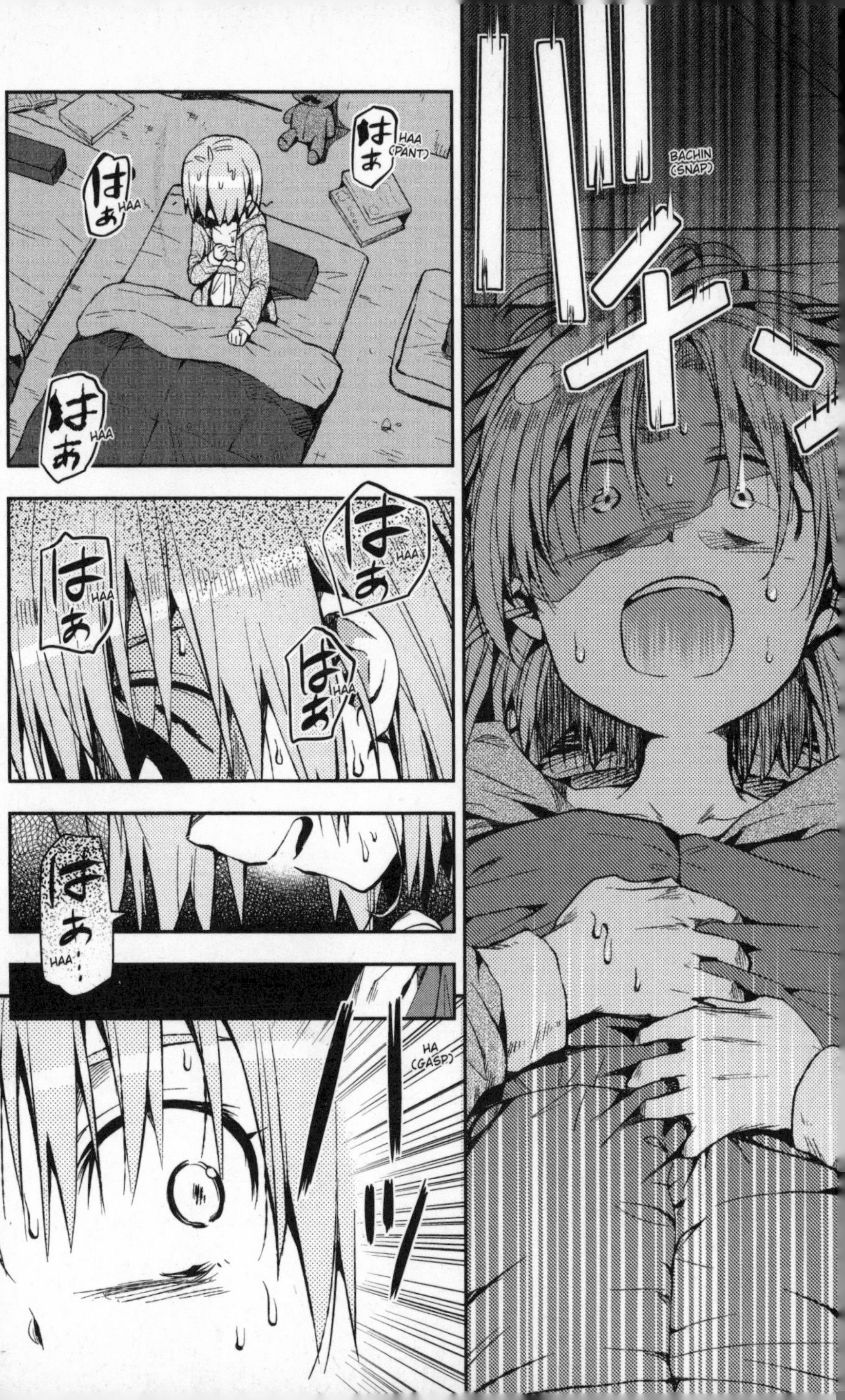
BACHIN (SNAP)
はぁ
HAA (PANT)
はぁ
HAA
はぁ
HAA
はぁ
HAA
はぁ
HAA
はぁ
HAA
はぁ…
HAA...
HA (GASP)

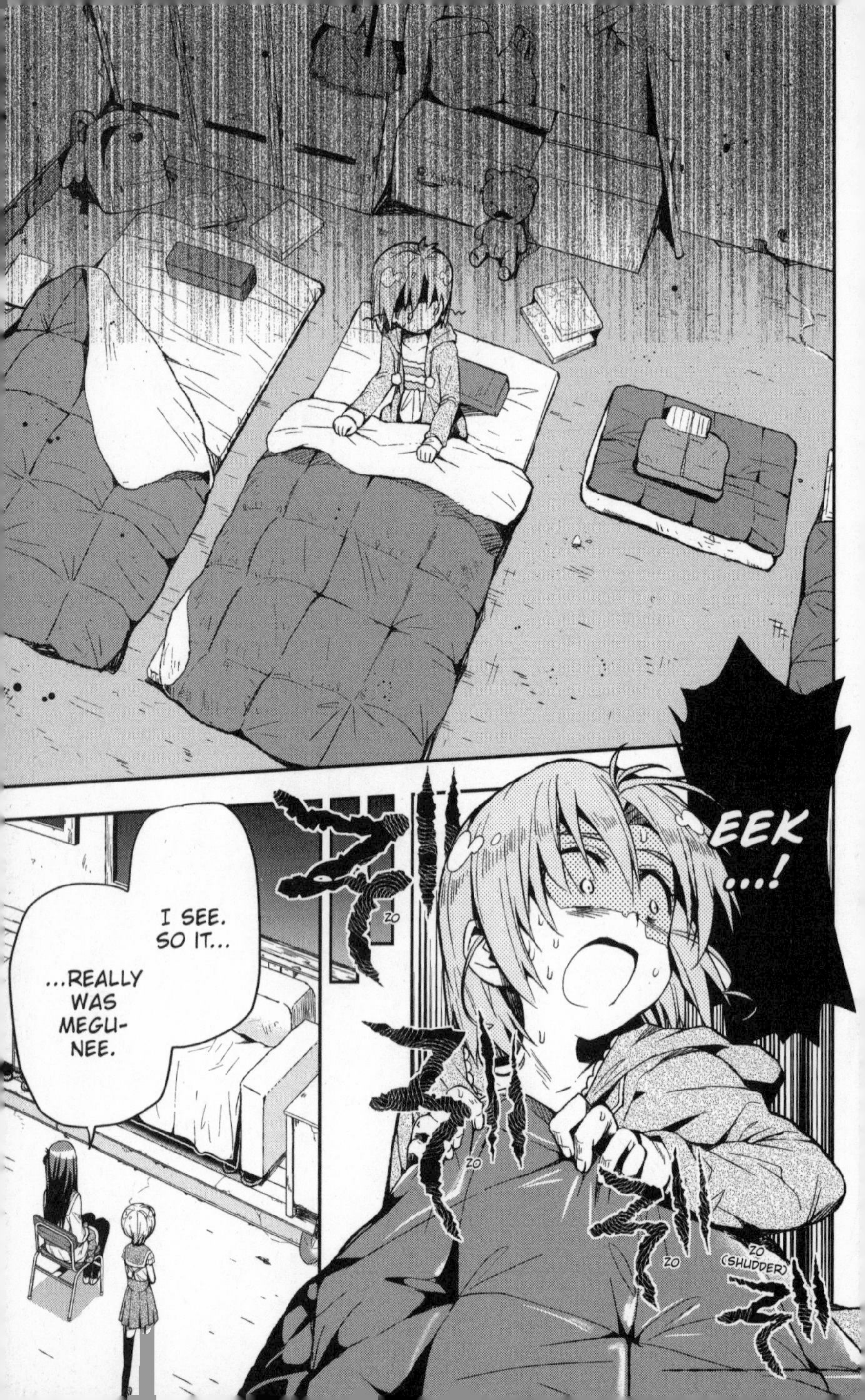
EEK...!
ZO
ZO
ZO (SHUDDER)
ZO
I SEE. SO IT...
...REALLY WAS MEGU-NEE.

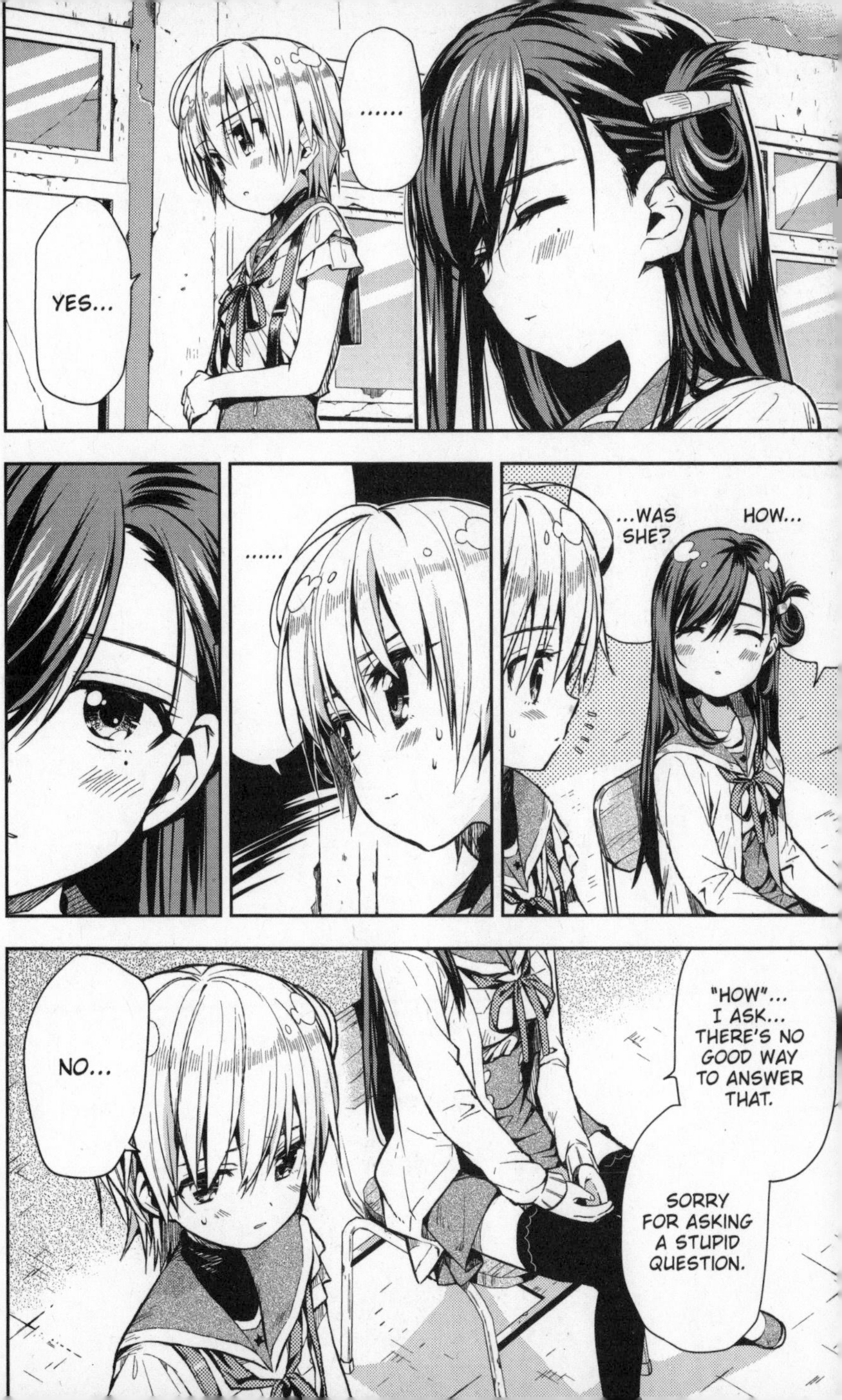
......
YES...
HOW...
...WAS SHE?
......
"HOW"... I ASK... THERE'S NO GOOD WAY TO ANSWER THAT.
SORRY FOR ASKING A STUPID QUESTION.
NO...

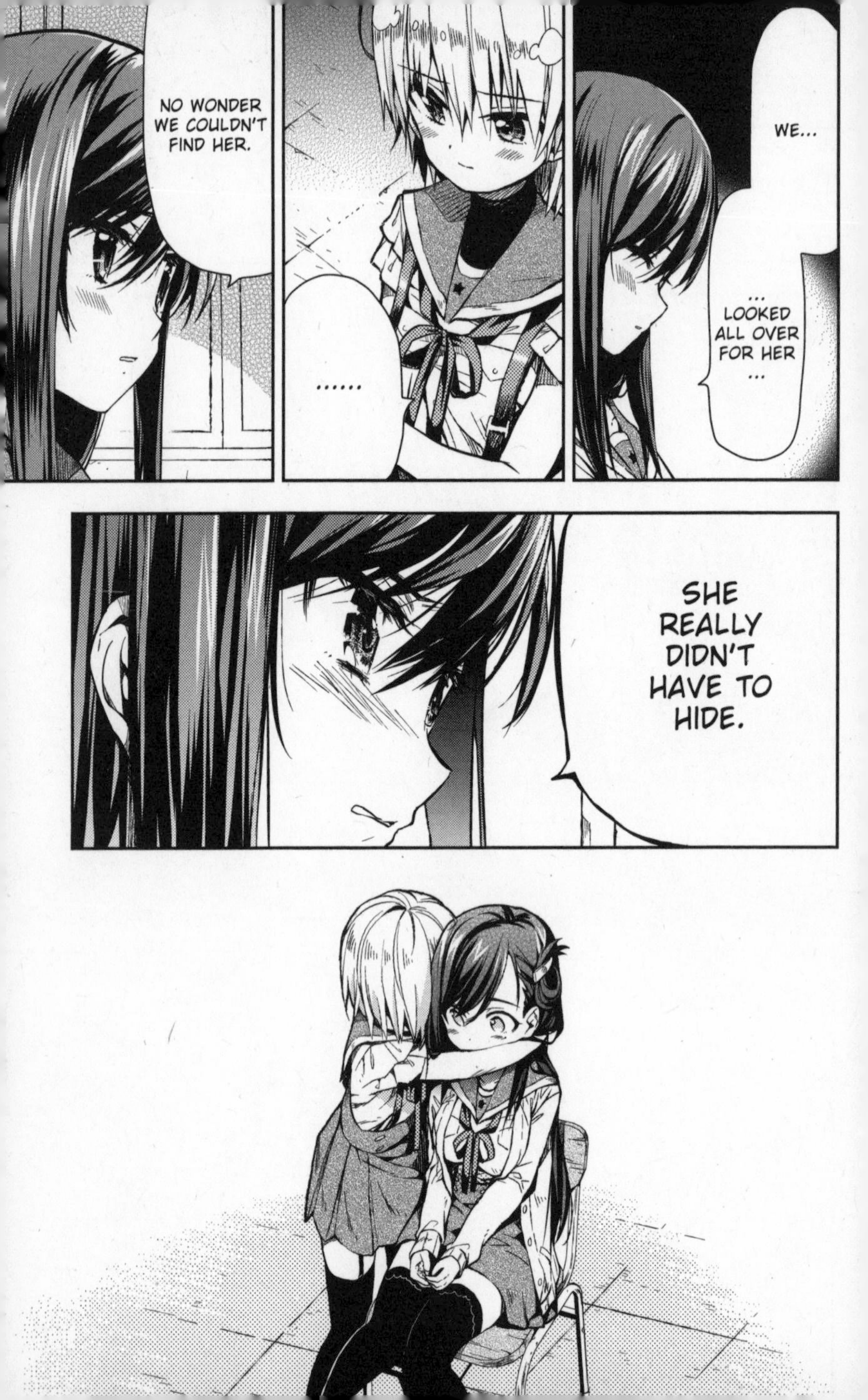
WE...
... LOOKED ALL OVER FOR HER ...
......
NO WONDER WE COULDN'T FIND HER.
SHE REALLY DIDN'T HAVE TO HIDE.

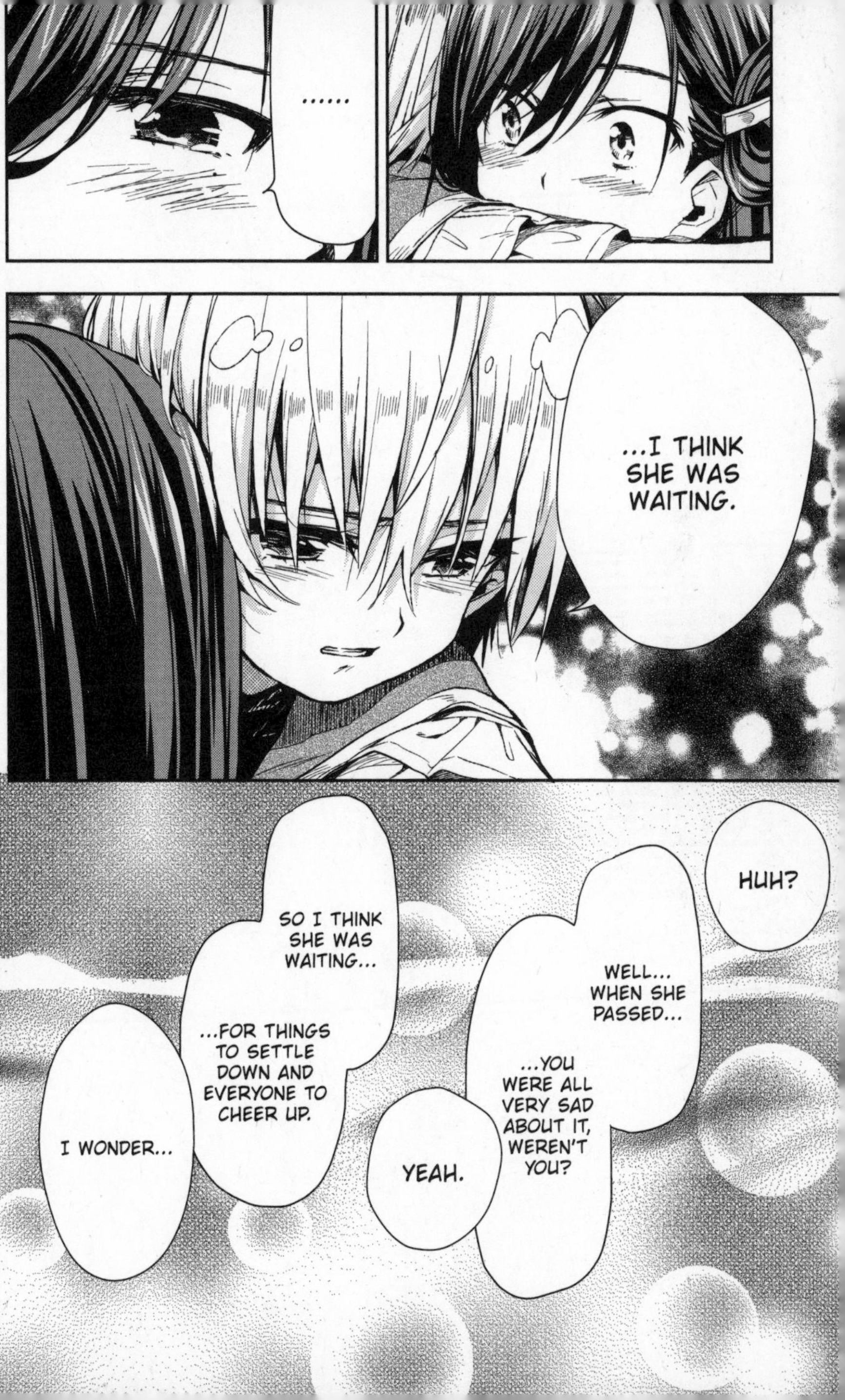
......
...I THINK SHE WAS WAITING.
HUH?
WELL... WHEN SHE PASSED...
...YOU WERE ALL VERY SAD ABOUT IT, WEREN'T YOU?
YEAH.
SO I THINK SHE WAS WAITING...
...FOR THINGS TO SETTLE DOWN AND EVERYONE TO CHEER UP.
I WONDER...

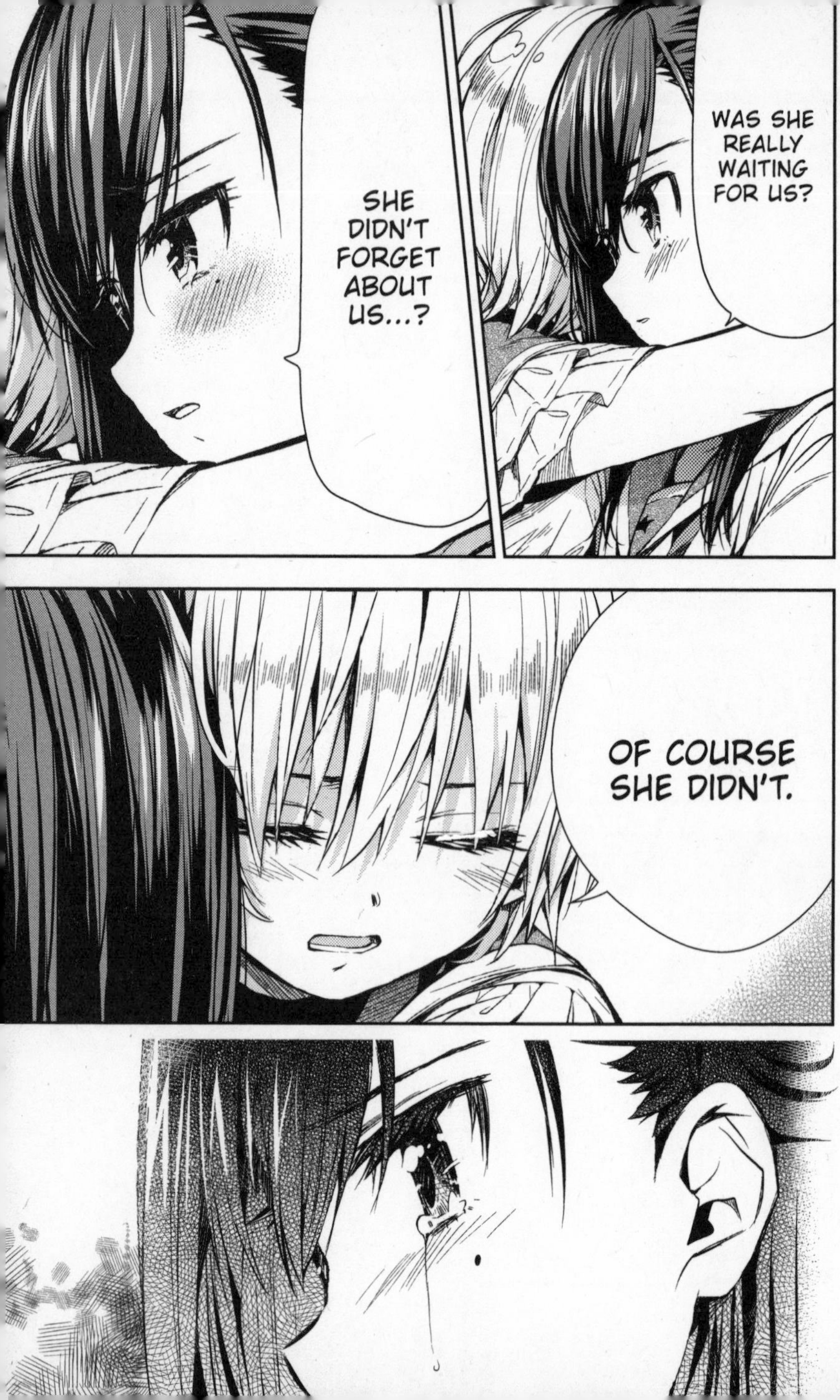
WAS SHE REALLY WAITING FOR US?
SHE DIDN'T FORGET ABOUT US...?
OF COURSE SHE DIDN'T.

SIGN: ANNOUNCEMENT ROOM

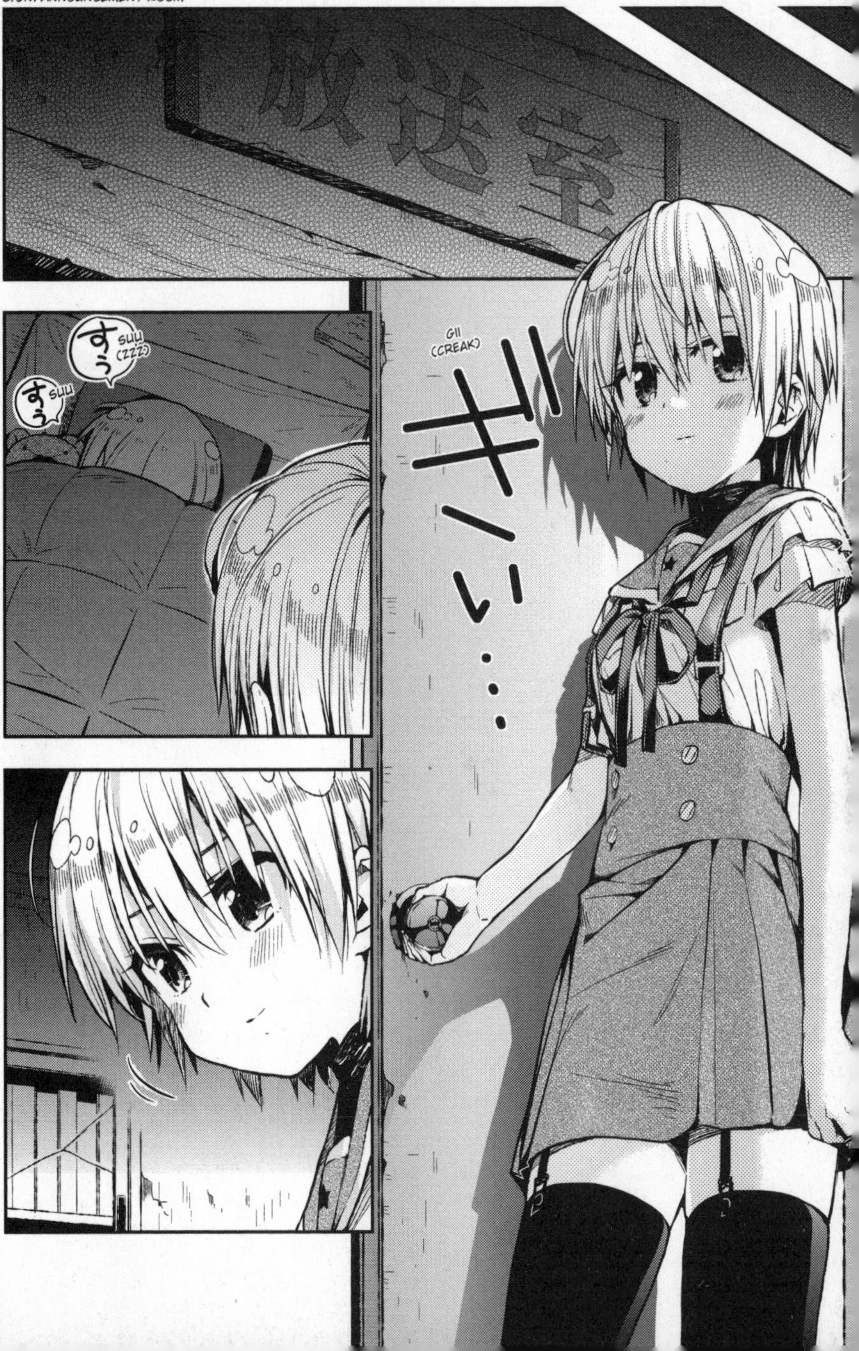
放送室
ギぃ…
GII (CREAK)
すぅ
SUU (ZZZ)
すぅ
SUU

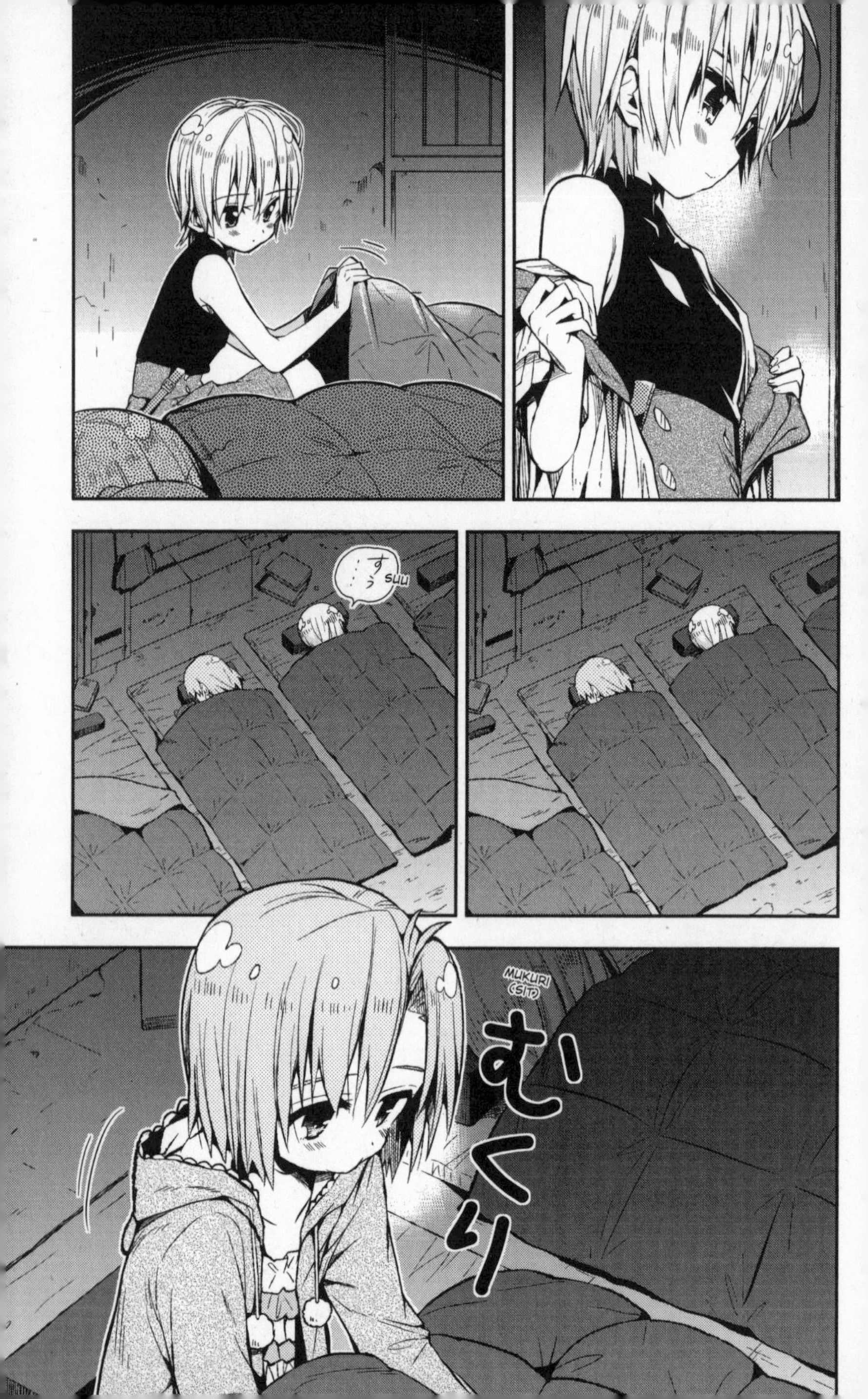
すぅ
SUU
MUKURI (SIT)
むくり

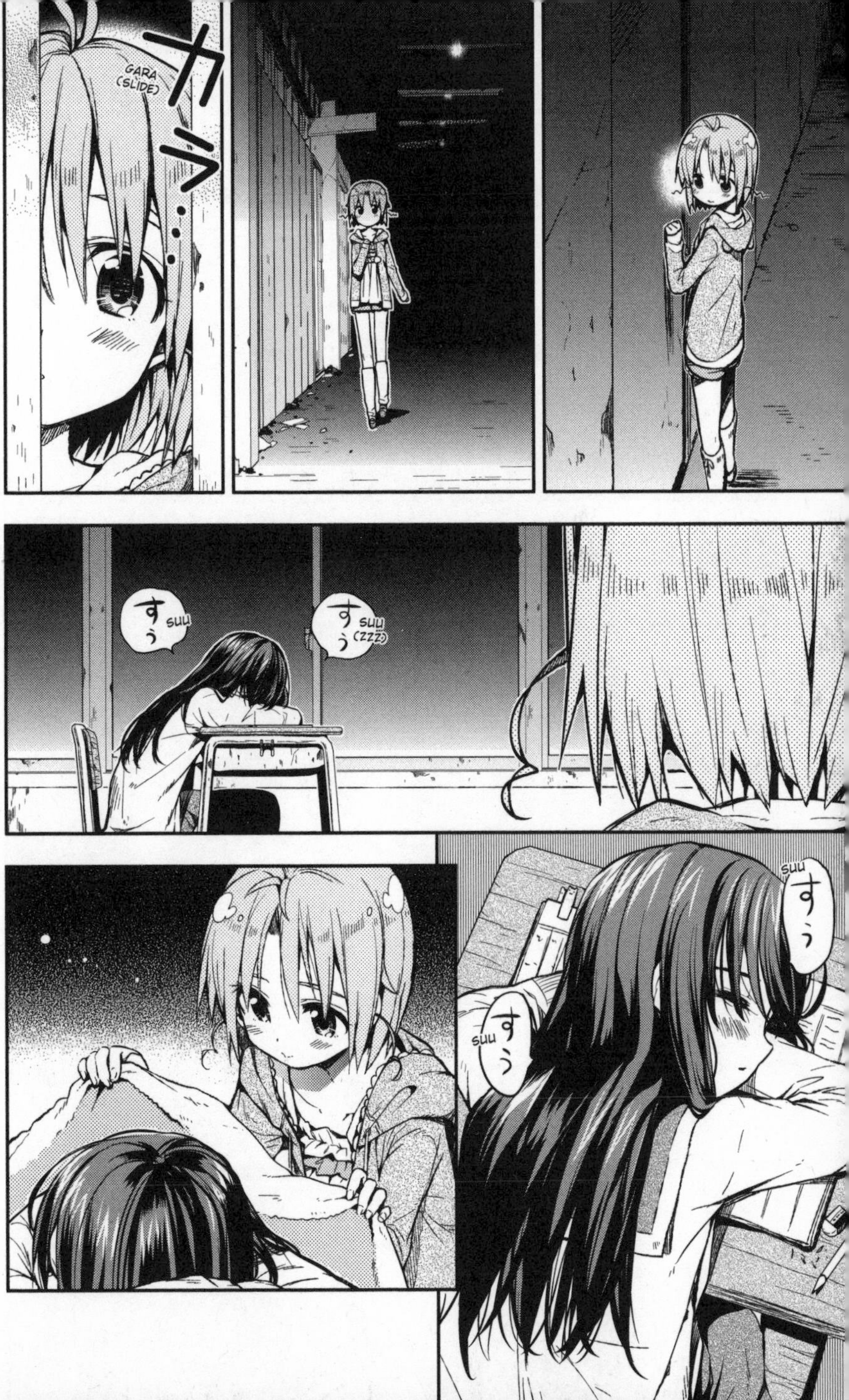
カラ…
GARA (SLIDE)
すぅ
SUU (ZZZ)
すぅ
SUU
すぅ
SUU
すぅ
SUU

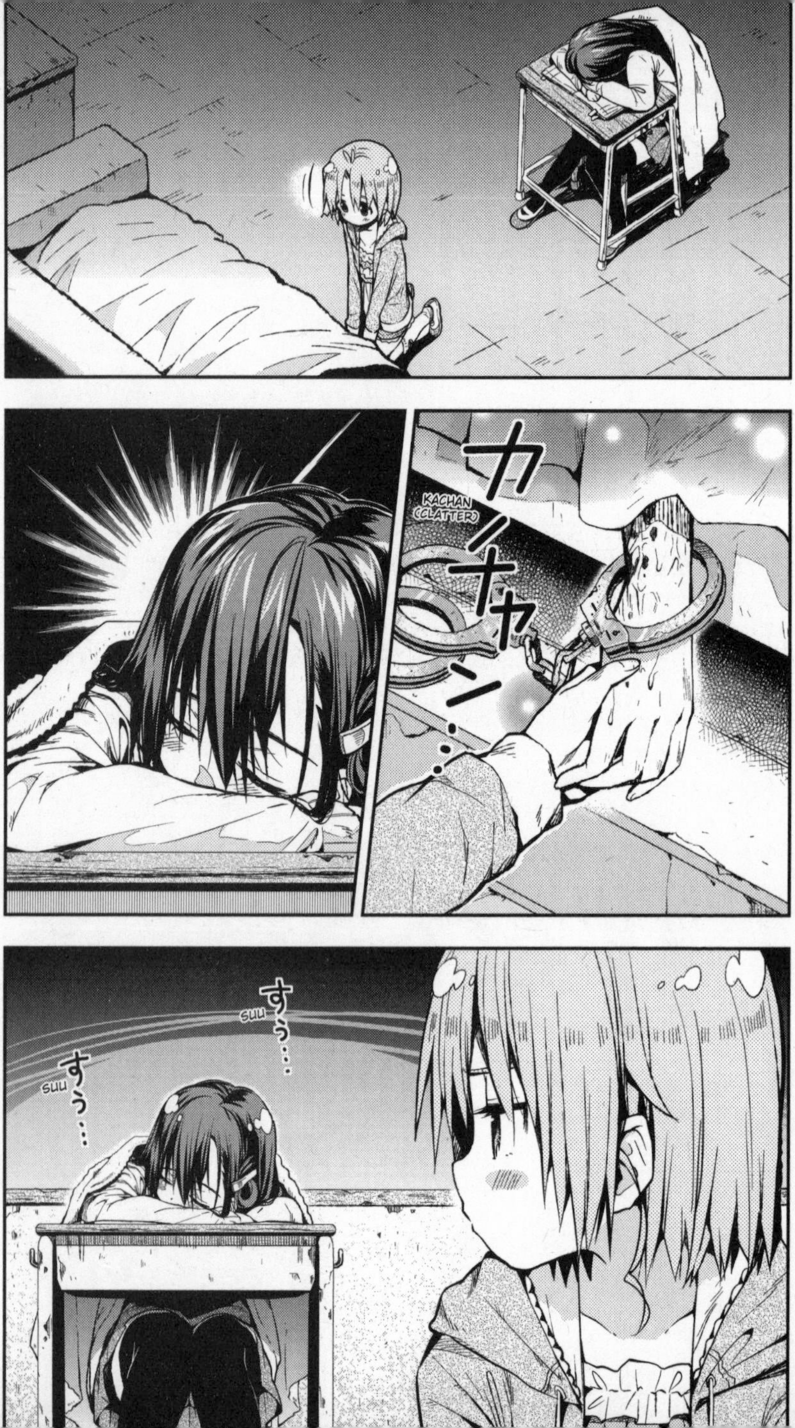

カチャン・・・
KACHAN (CLATTER)
すう・・・
SUU
すう・・・
SUU

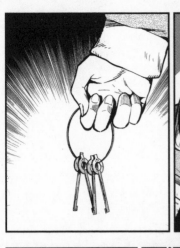

GOSO
(RUMMAGE)
ゴソ
ゴソ
GOSO

KACHA
カチャ
KACHA
カチャ
SUU
(ZZZ)
すぅ
すぅ
suu

KACHA
(CLACK)
カ
チャ
カ
チャ

TO
(TROT)
とと
と…
TO
TO

KACHIN
(CLICK)
カ
チ
ン
…

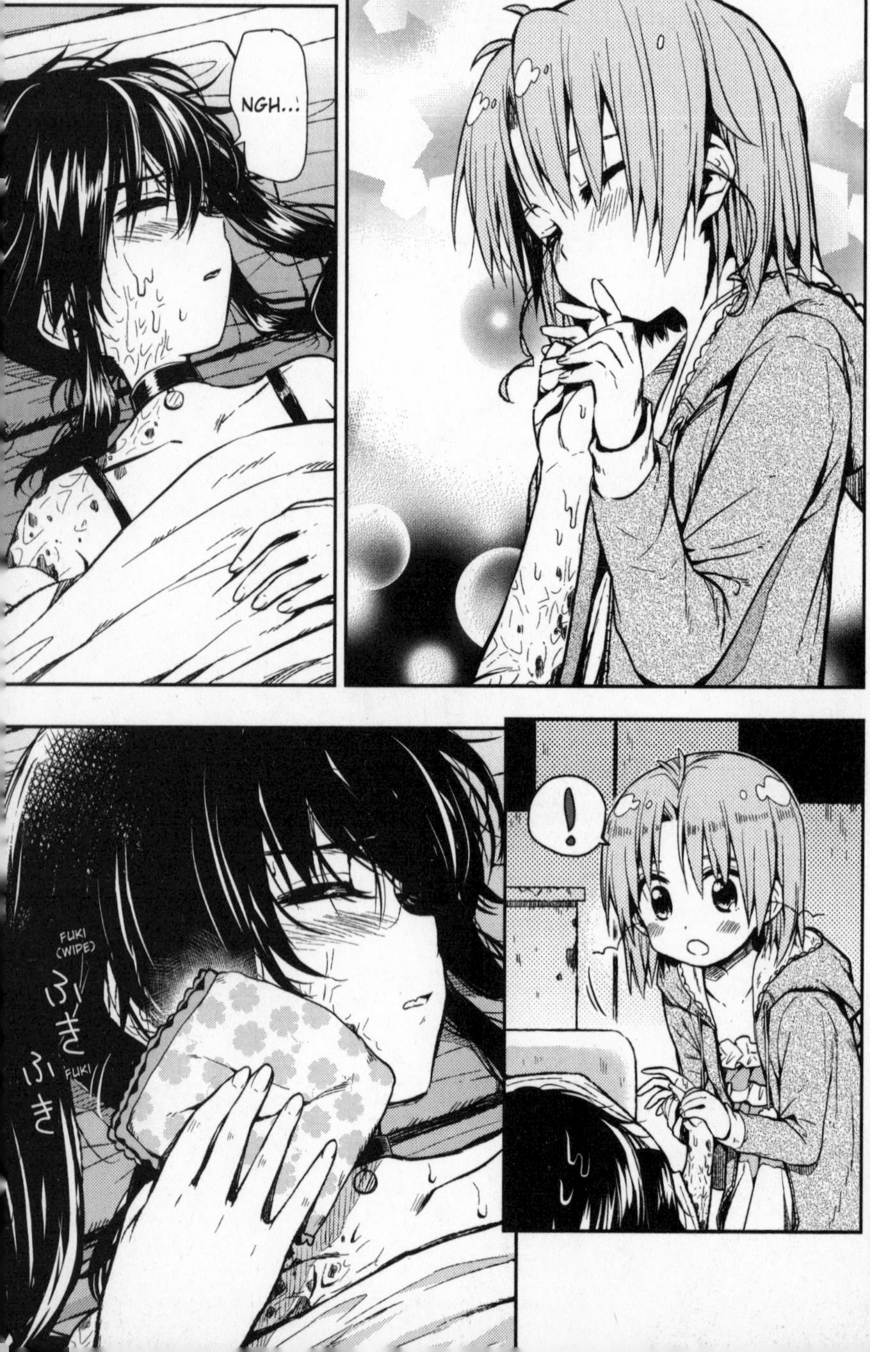
NGH...!
!
ふき
FUKI (WIPE)
ふき
FUKI

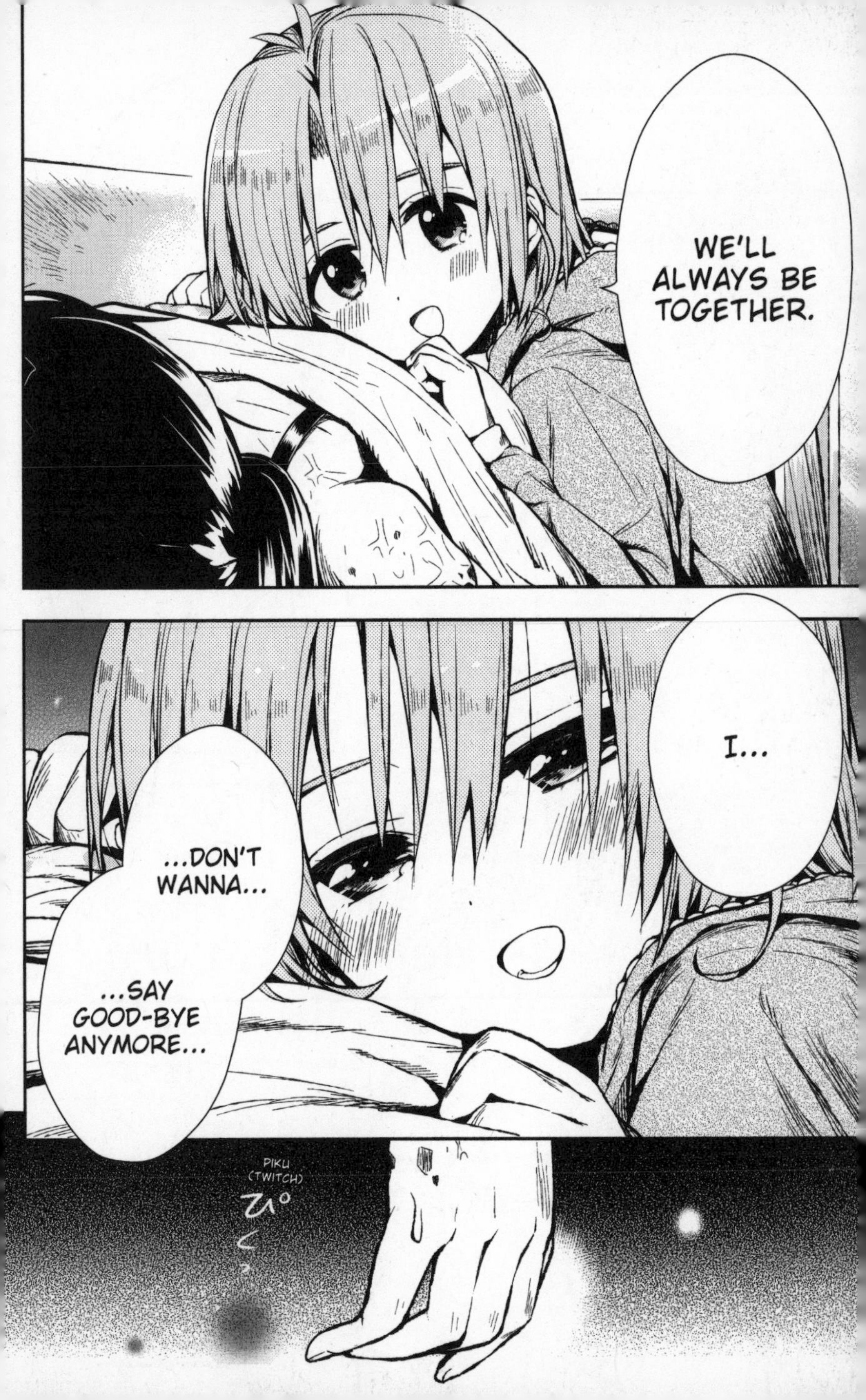
WE'LL ALWAYS BE TOGETHER.
I...
...DON'T WANNA...
...SAY GOOD-BYE ANYMORE...
PIKU (TWITCH)
ぴく

!!

ハ° PACHI (BLINK)
イチ

U-UHHN
...

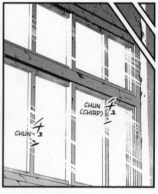

チュン
CHUN (CHIRP)

チュン
CHUN

ガ
タ
ッ
GATA (CLATTER)

は
っ
HA (GASP)

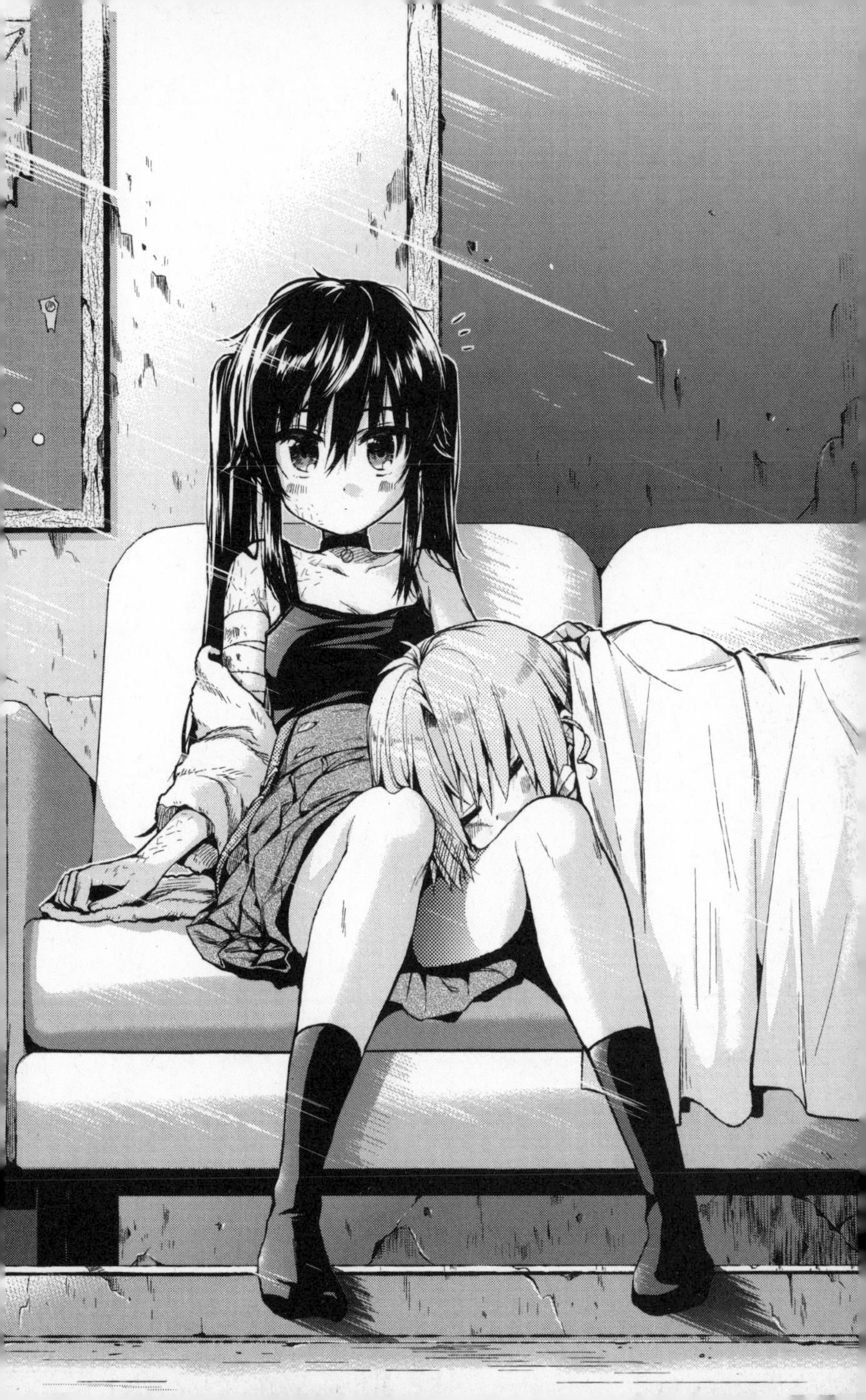

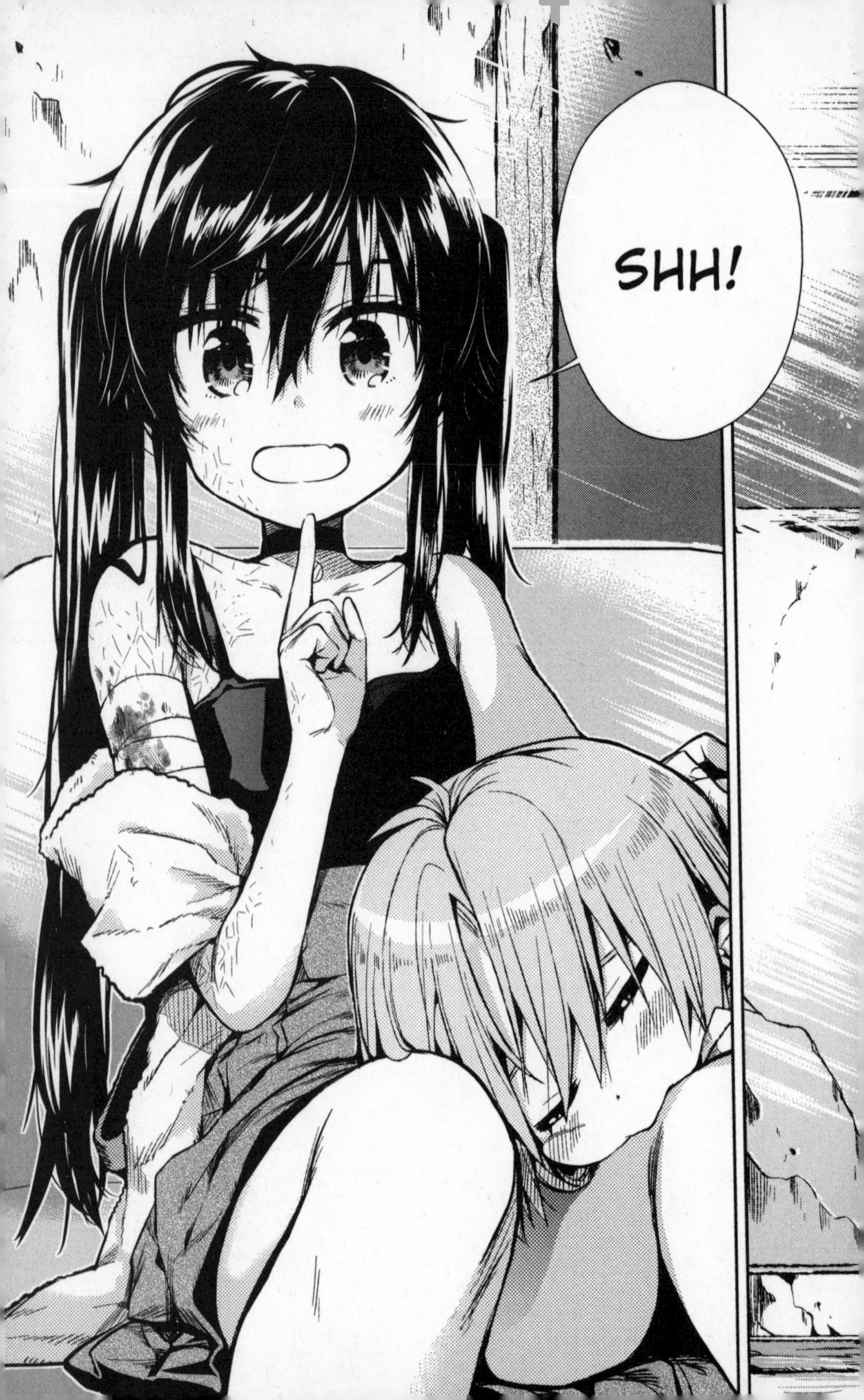
SHH!

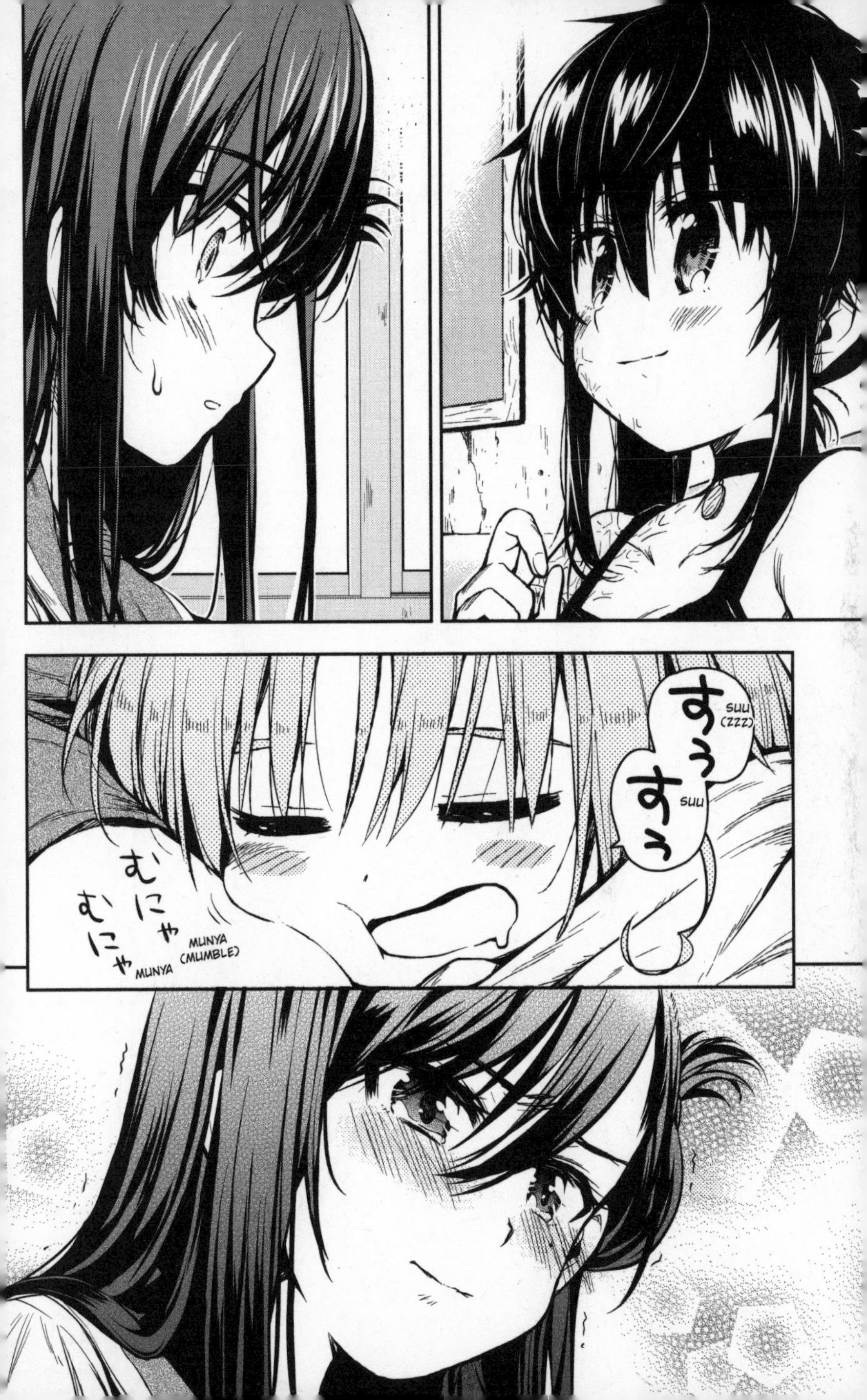
すぅ
SUU (ZZZ)
すぅ
SUU
むにゃ
MUNYA (MUMBLE)
むにゃ
MUNYA

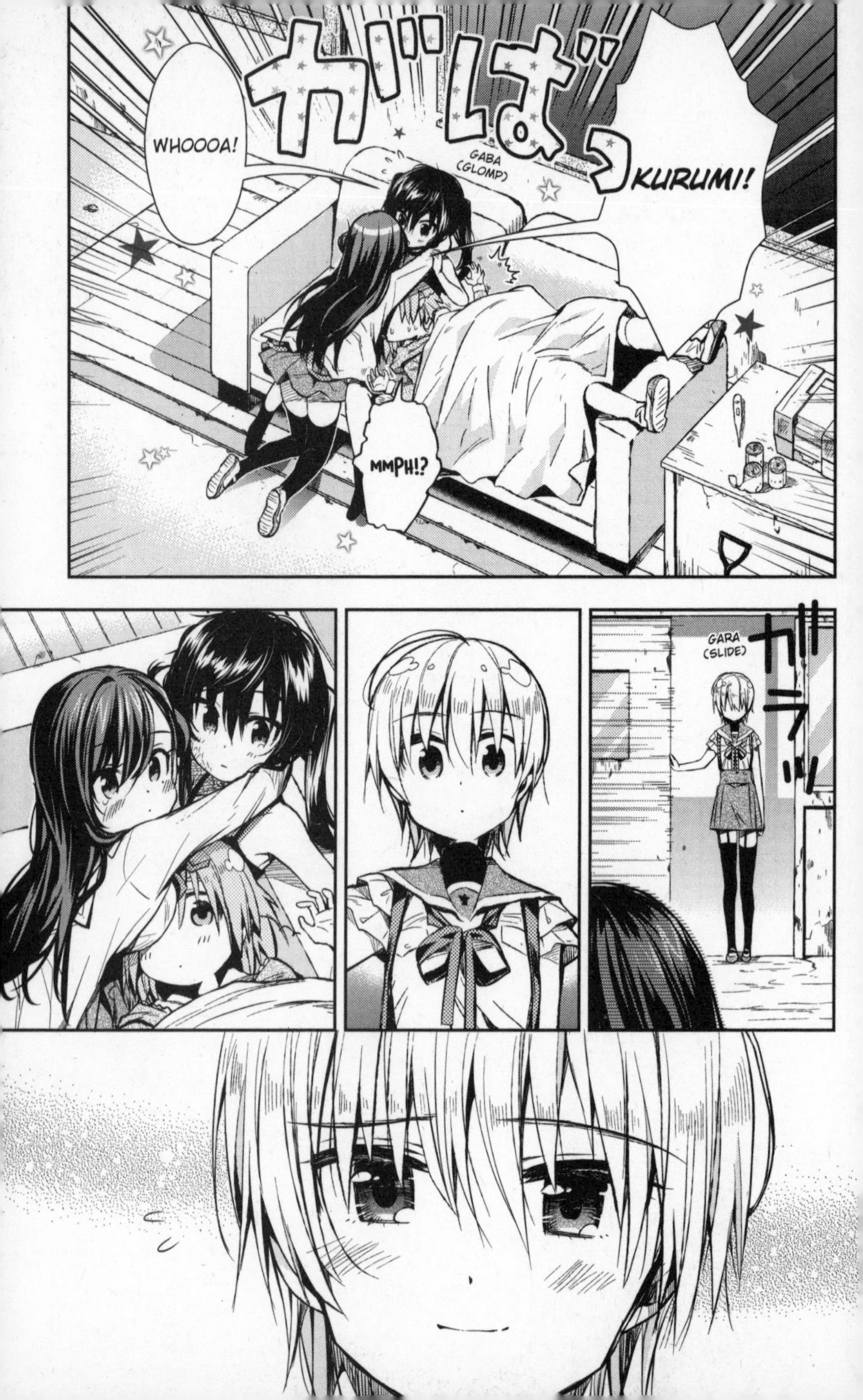
KURUMI!
GABA (GLOMP)
WHOOOA!
MMPH!?
GARA (SLIDE)

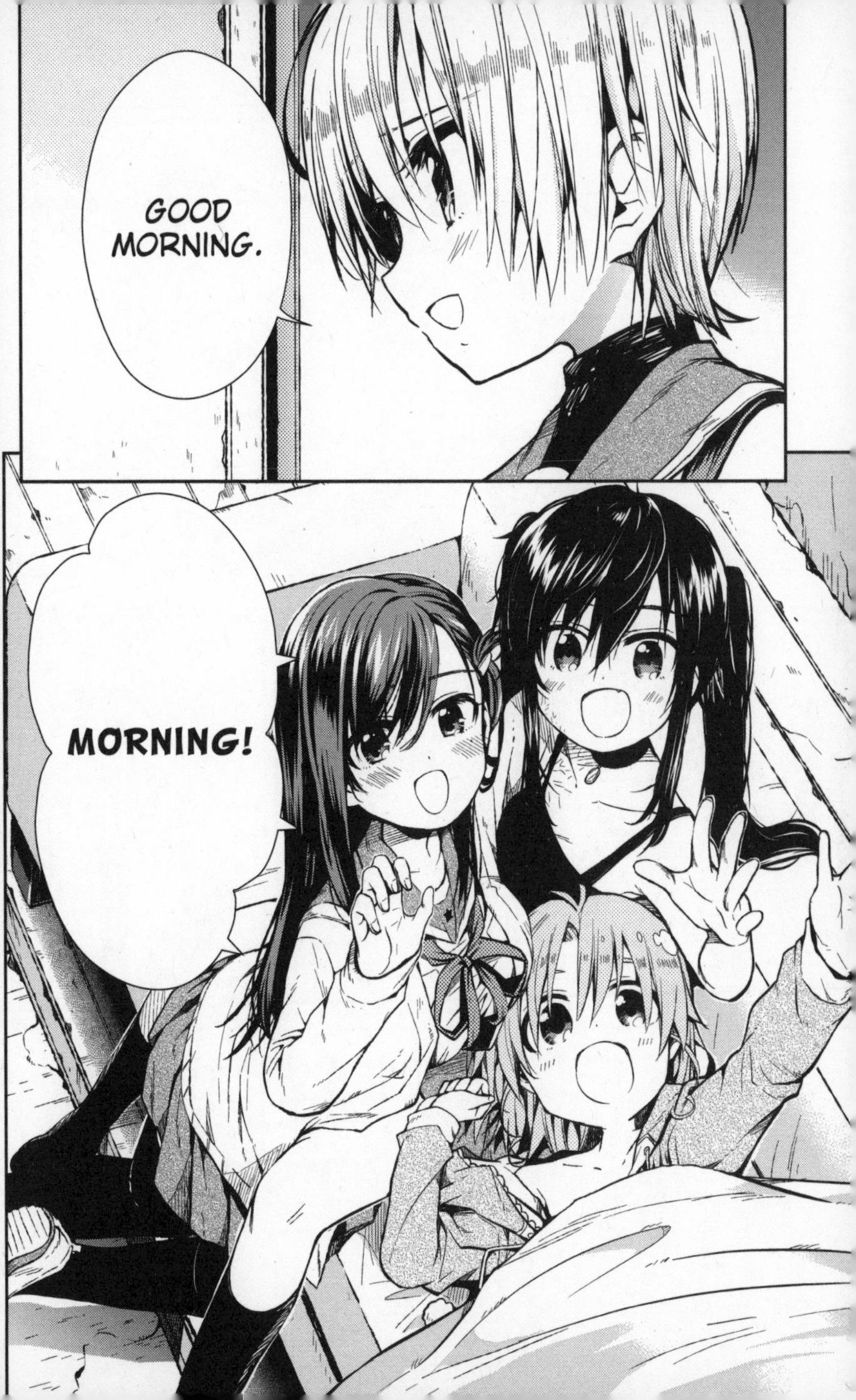
GOOD MORNING.
MORNING!

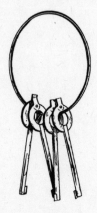

SCHOOL-LIVE!

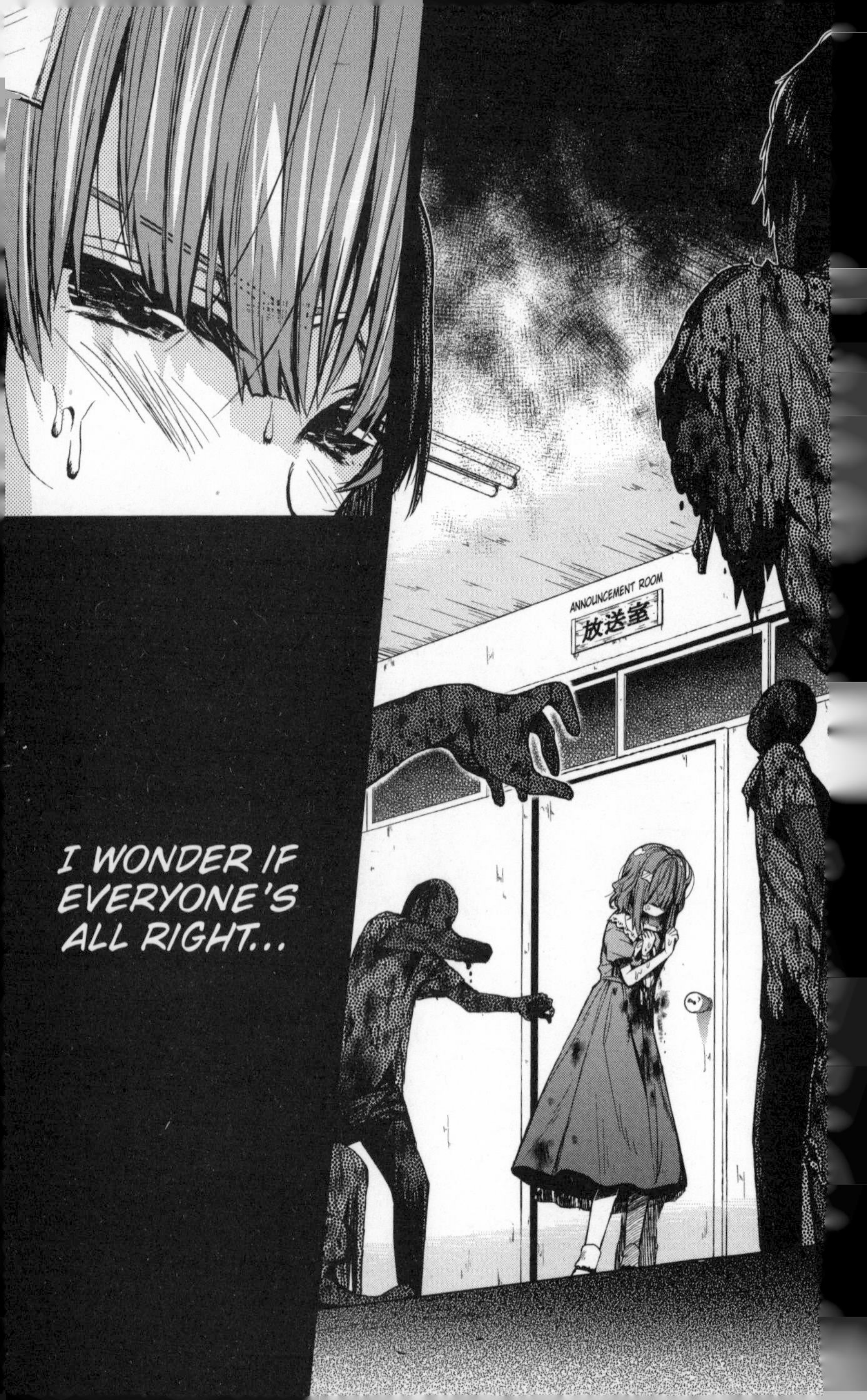
ANNOUNCEMENT ROOM
放送室
I WONDER IF EVERYONE'S ALL RIGHT...

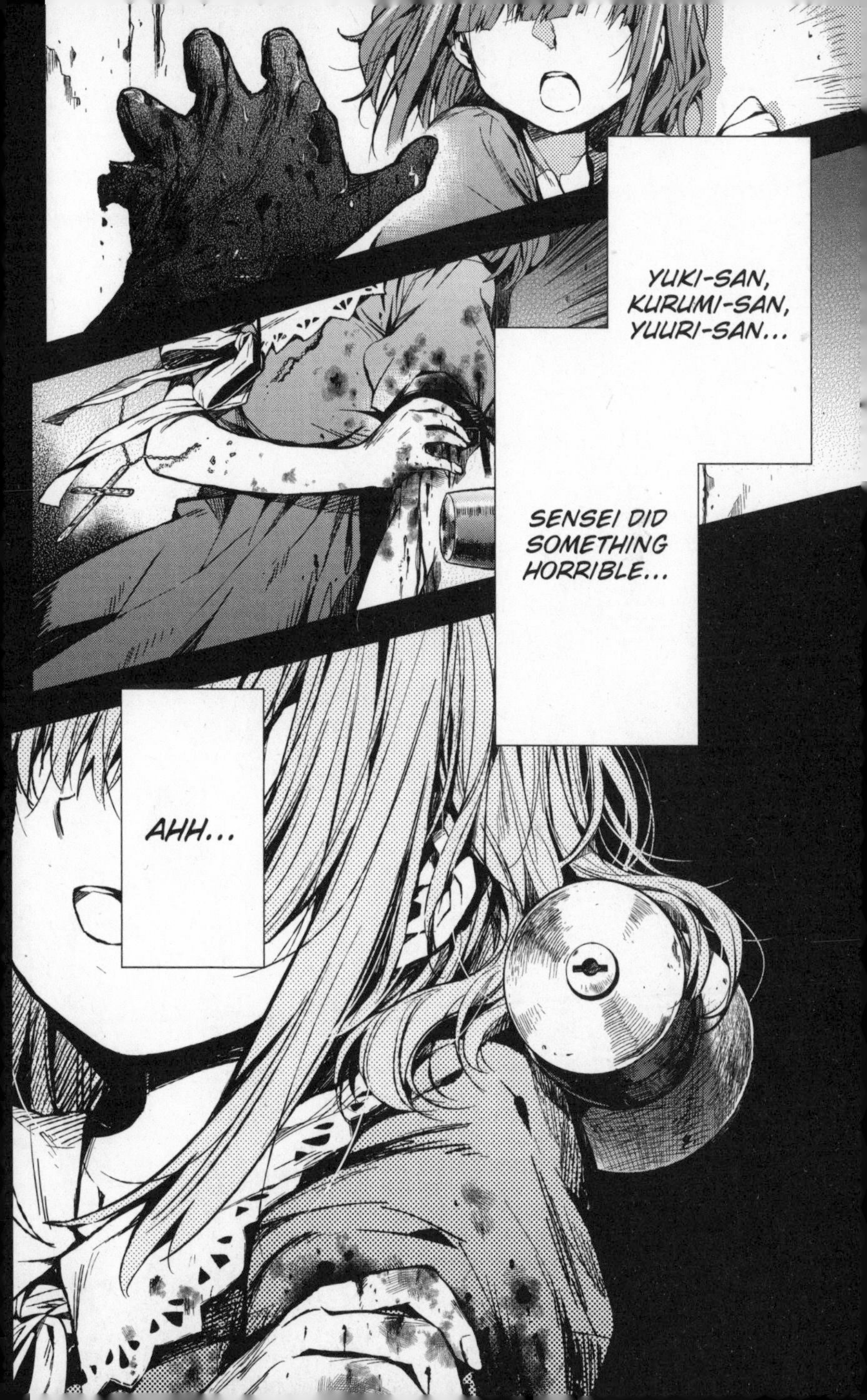
YUKI-SAN, KURUMI-SAN, YUURI-SAN...
SENSEI DID SOMETHING HORRIBLE...
AHH...

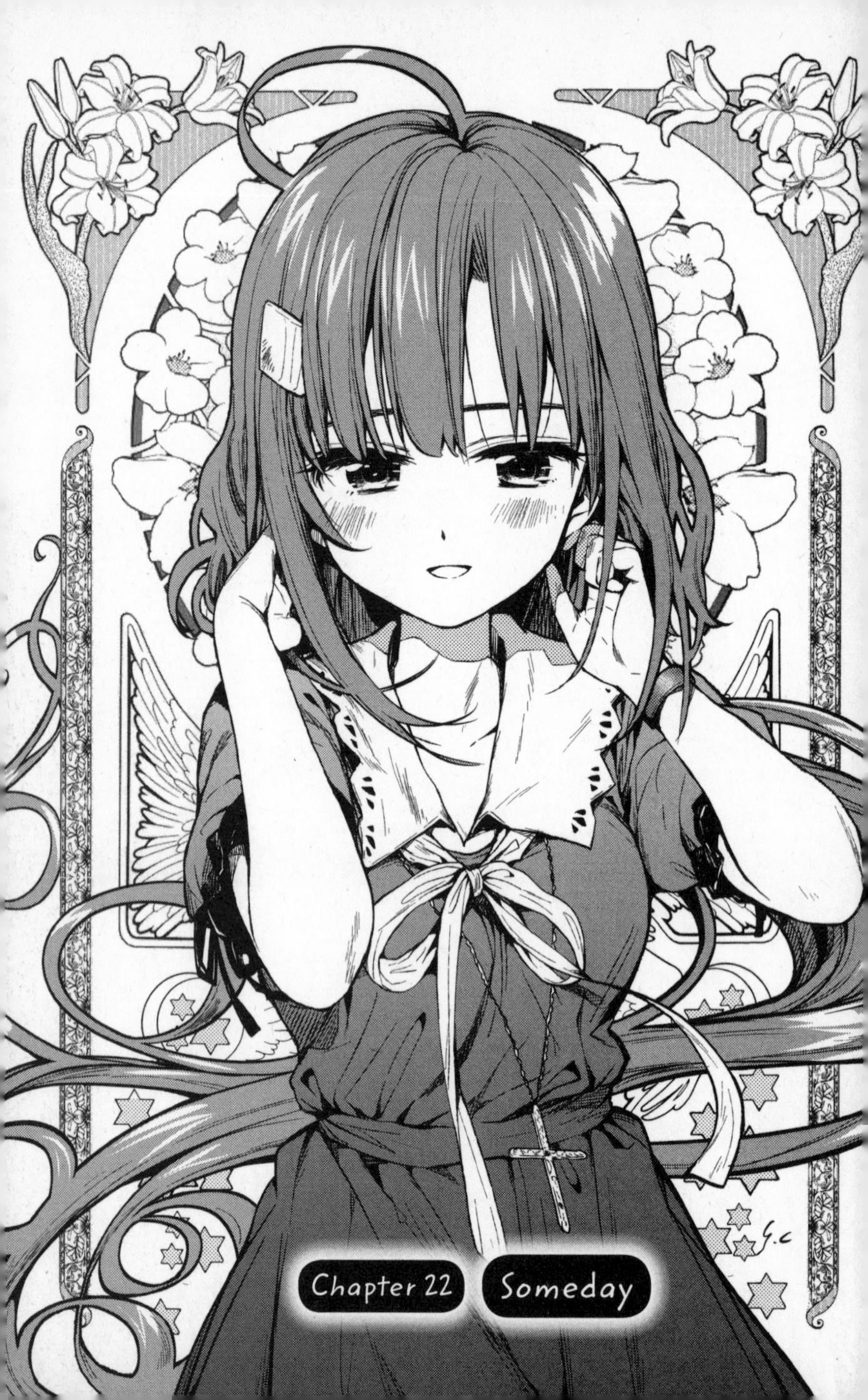
Chapter 22
Someday

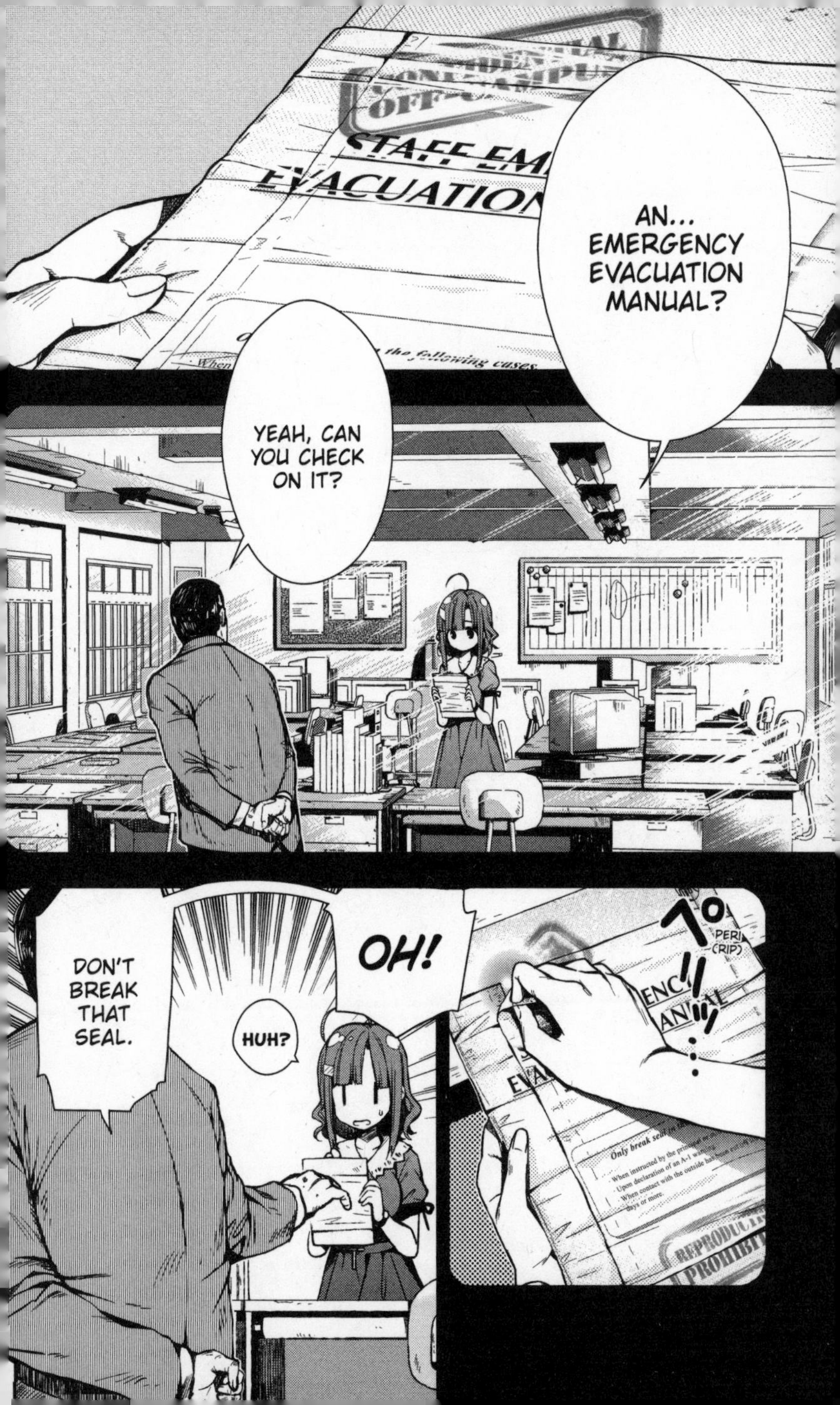

EVACUATION
AN... EMERGENCY EVACUATION MANUAL?
YEAH, CAN YOU CHECK ON IT?
PERI (RIP)
OH!
DON'T BREAK THAT SEAL.
HUH?

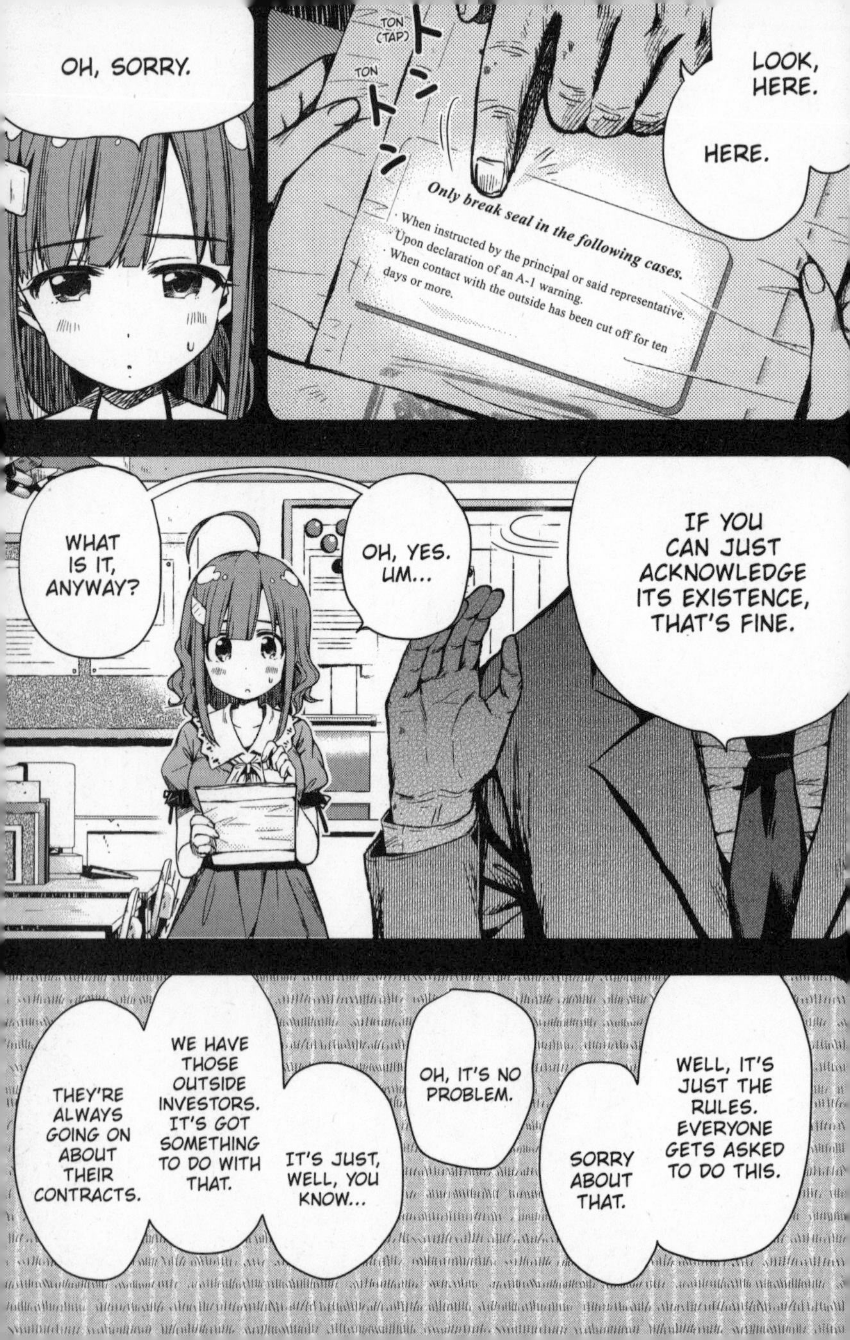
LOOK, HERE.
HERE.
TON (TAP)
TON
Only break seal in the following cases.
· When instructed by the principal or said representative.
· Upon declaration of an A-1 warning.
· When contact with the outside has been cut off for ten days or more.
OH, SORRY.
IF YOU CAN JUST ACKNOWLEDGE ITS EXISTENCE, THAT'S FINE.
OH, YES. UM...
WHAT IS IT, ANYWAY?
WELL, IT'S JUST THE RULES. EVERYONE GETS ASKED TO DO THIS.
SORRY ABOUT THAT.
OH, IT'S NO PROBLEM.
IT'S JUST, WELL, YOU KNOW...
WE HAVE THOSE OUTSIDE INVESTORS. IT'S GOT SOMETHING TO DO WITH THAT.
THEY'RE ALWAYS GOING ON ABOUT THEIR CONTRACTS.

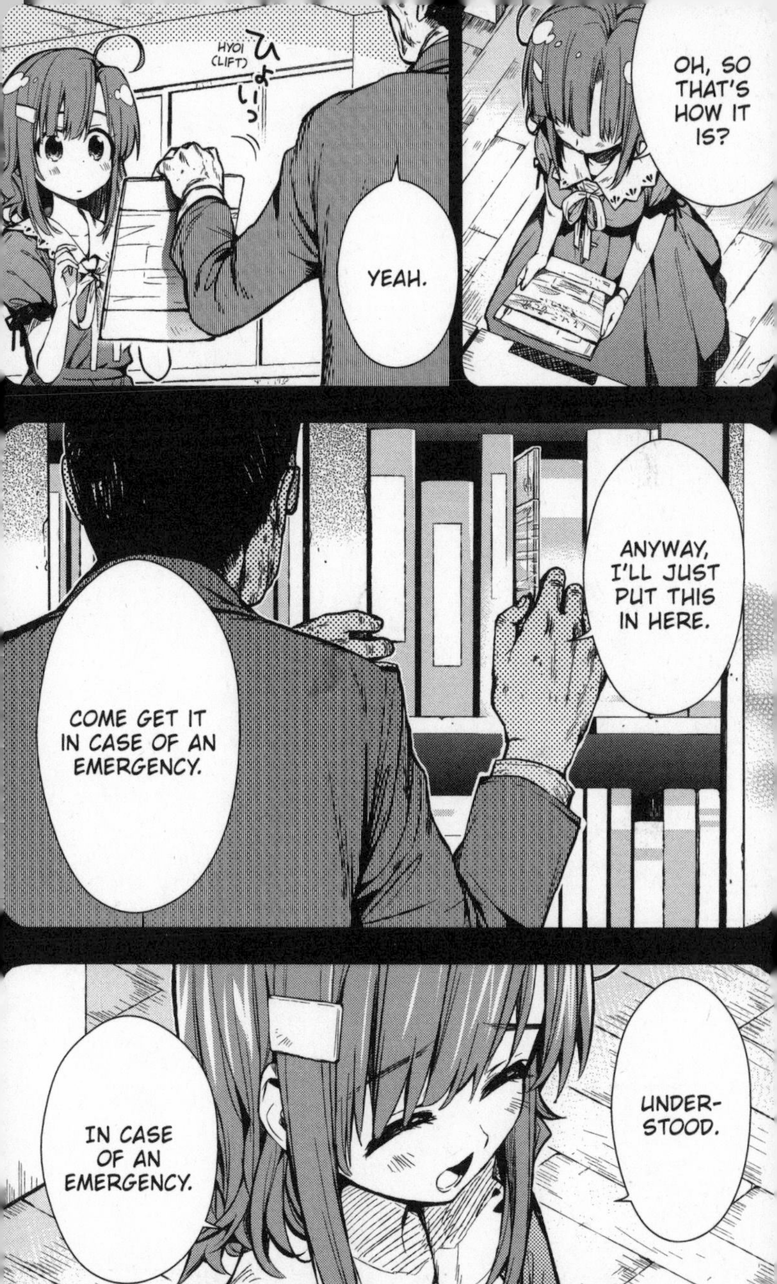
OH, SO THAT'S HOW IT IS?
ひょいっ
HYOI (LIFT)
YEAH.
ANYWAY, I'LL JUST PUT THIS IN HERE.
COME GET IT IN CASE OF AN EMERGENCY.
UNDER-STOOD.
IN CASE OF AN EMERGENCY.

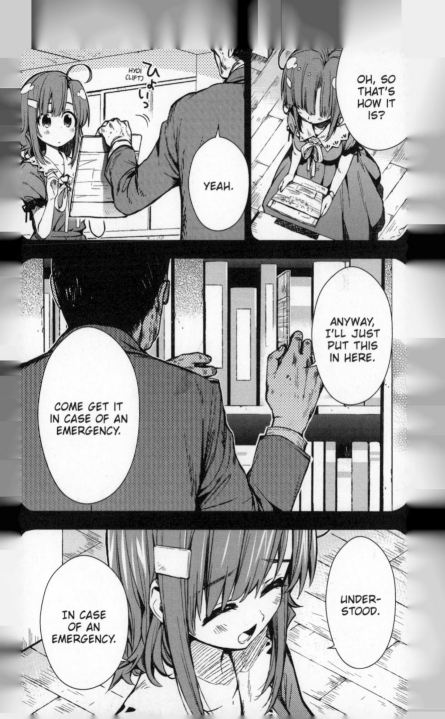

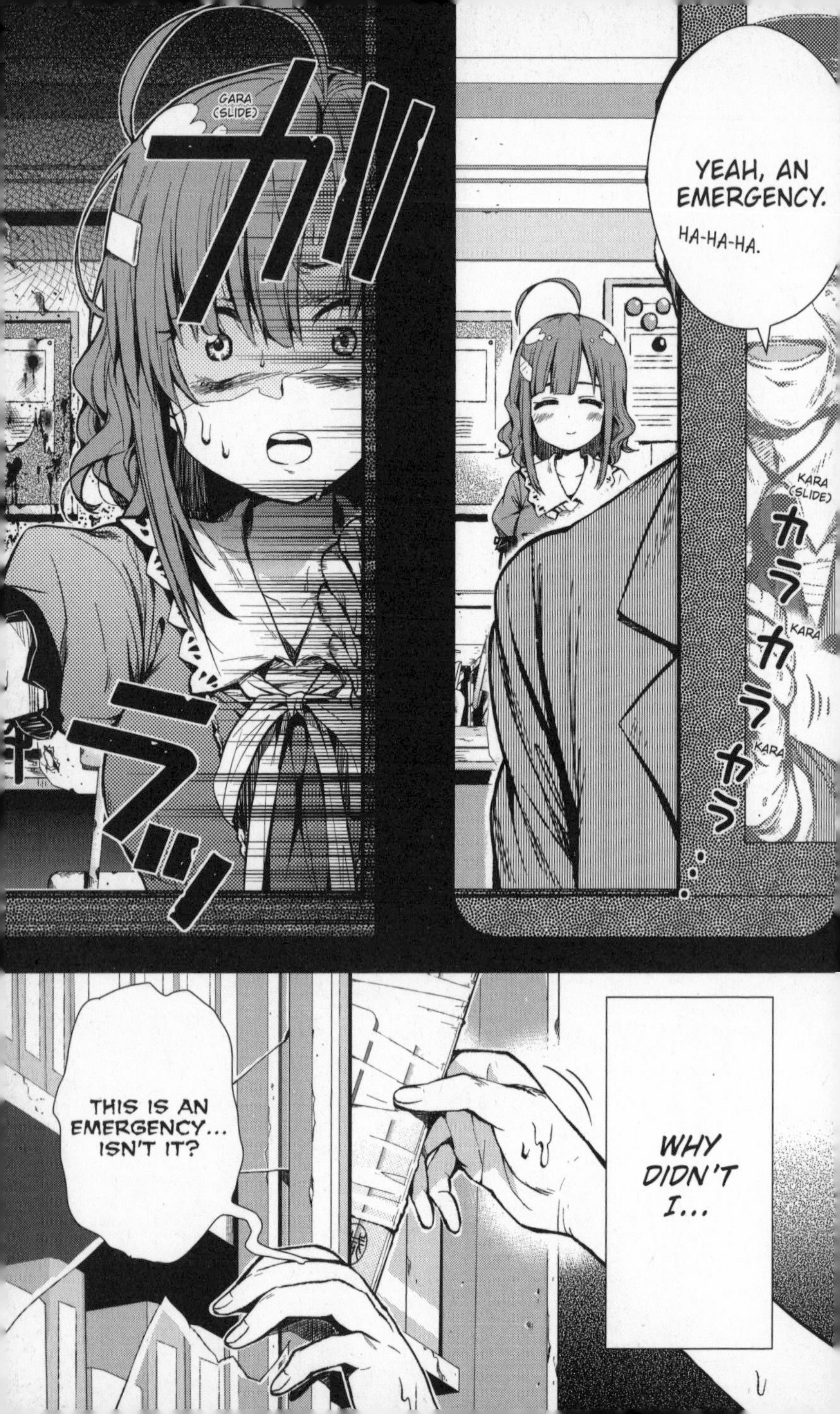
YEAH, AN EMERGENCY.
HA-HA-HA.
KARA (SLIDE)
カラカラカラ
KARA
KARA
GARA (SLIDE)
ガラッ
WHY DIDN'T I...
THIS IS AN EMERGENCY... ISN'T IT?

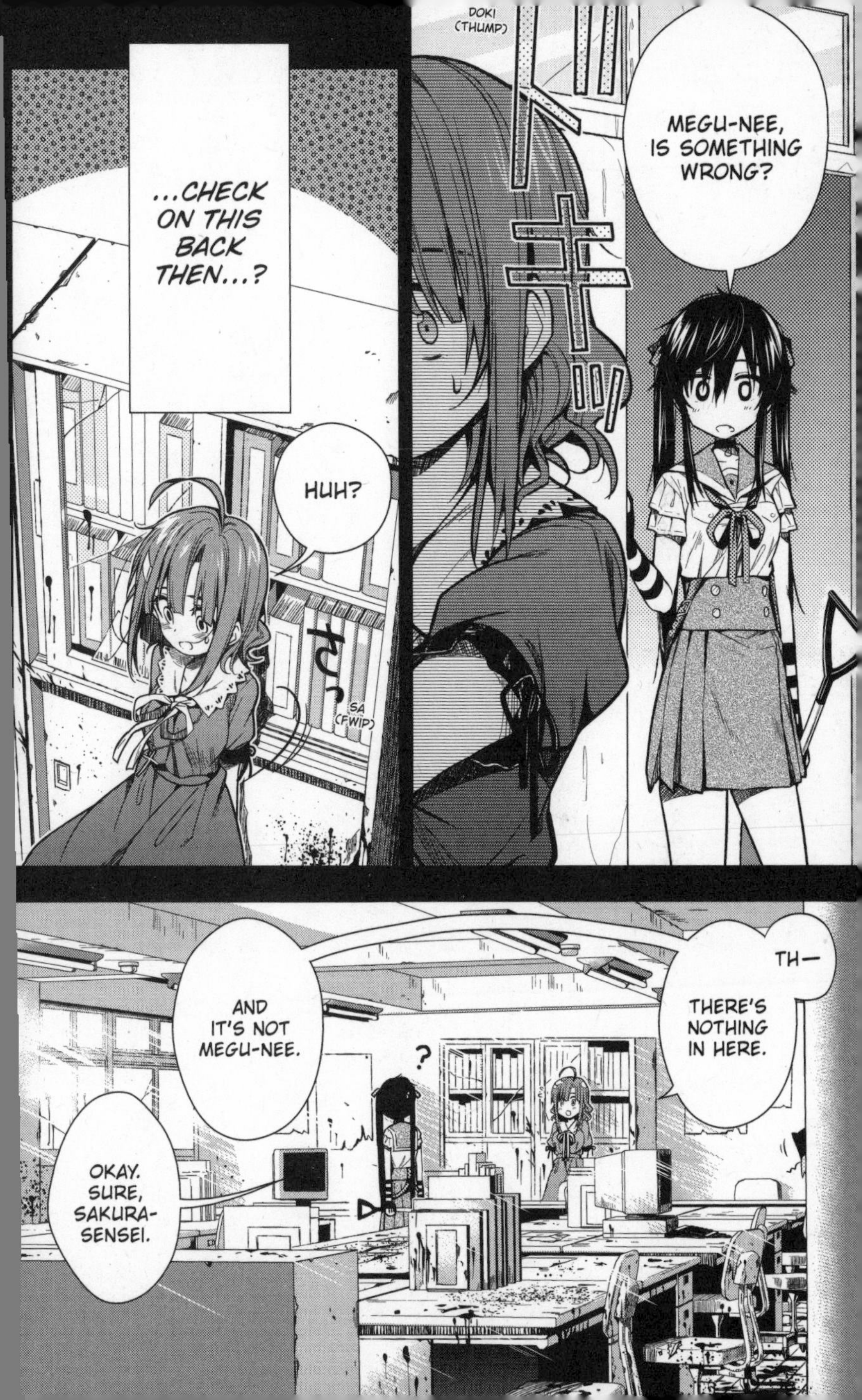
DOKI (THUMP)
MEGU-NEE, IS SOMETHING WRONG?
...CHECK ON THIS BACK THEN...?
HUH?
SA (FWIP)
TH—
THERE'S NOTHING IN HERE.
AND IT'S NOT MEGU-NEE.
OKAY. SURE, SAKURA-SENSEI.

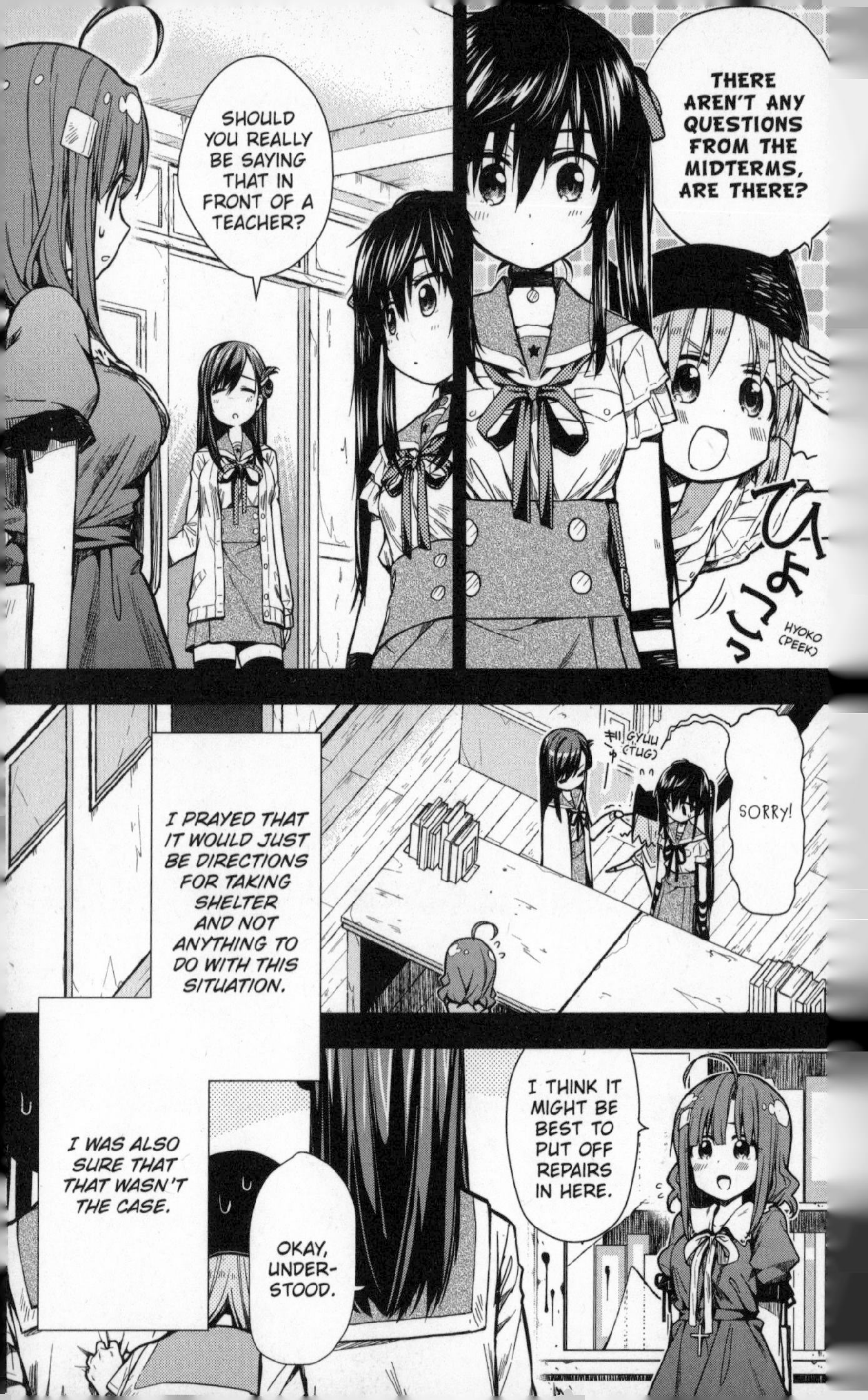
THERE AREN'T ANY QUESTIONS FROM THE MIDTERMS, ARE THERE?
ひょこっ
HYOKO (PEEK)
SHOULD YOU REALLY BE SAYING THAT IN FRONT OF A TEACHER?
SORRY!
GYUU (TUG)
I PRAYED THAT IT WOULD JUST BE DIRECTIONS FOR TAKING SHELTER AND NOT ANYTHING TO DO WITH THIS SITUATION.
I THINK IT MIGHT BE BEST TO PUT OFF REPAIRS IN HERE.
OKAY, UNDERSTOOD.
I WAS ALSO SURE THAT THAT WASN'T THE CASE.

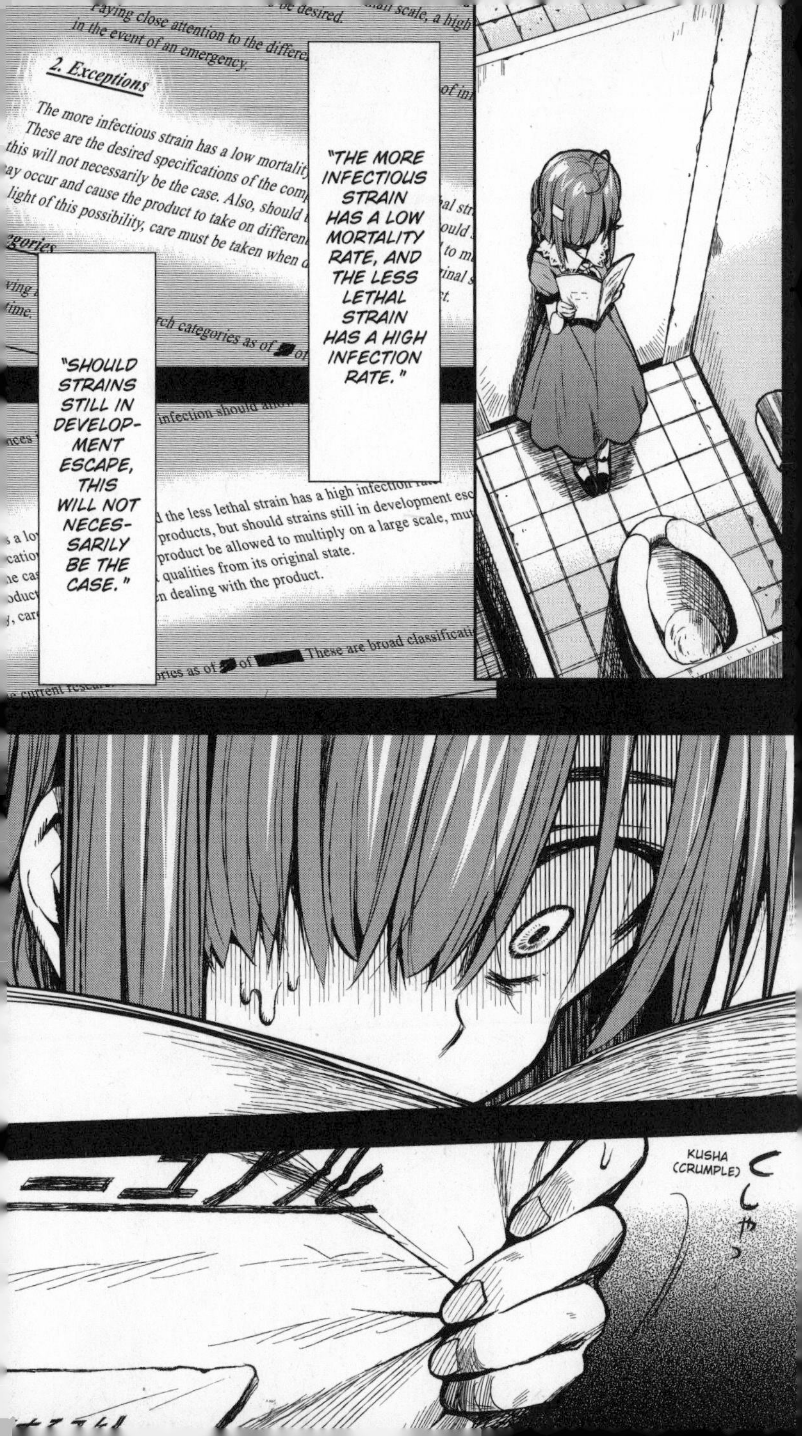
2. Exceptions
"THE MORE INFECTIOUS STRAIN HAS A LOW MORTALITY RATE, AND THE LESS LETHAL STRAIN HAS A HIGH INFECTION RATE."
"SHOULD STRAINS STILL IN DEVELOPMENT ESCAPE, THIS WILL NOT NECESSARILY BE THE CASE."
KUSHA (CRUMPLE)
くしゃっ

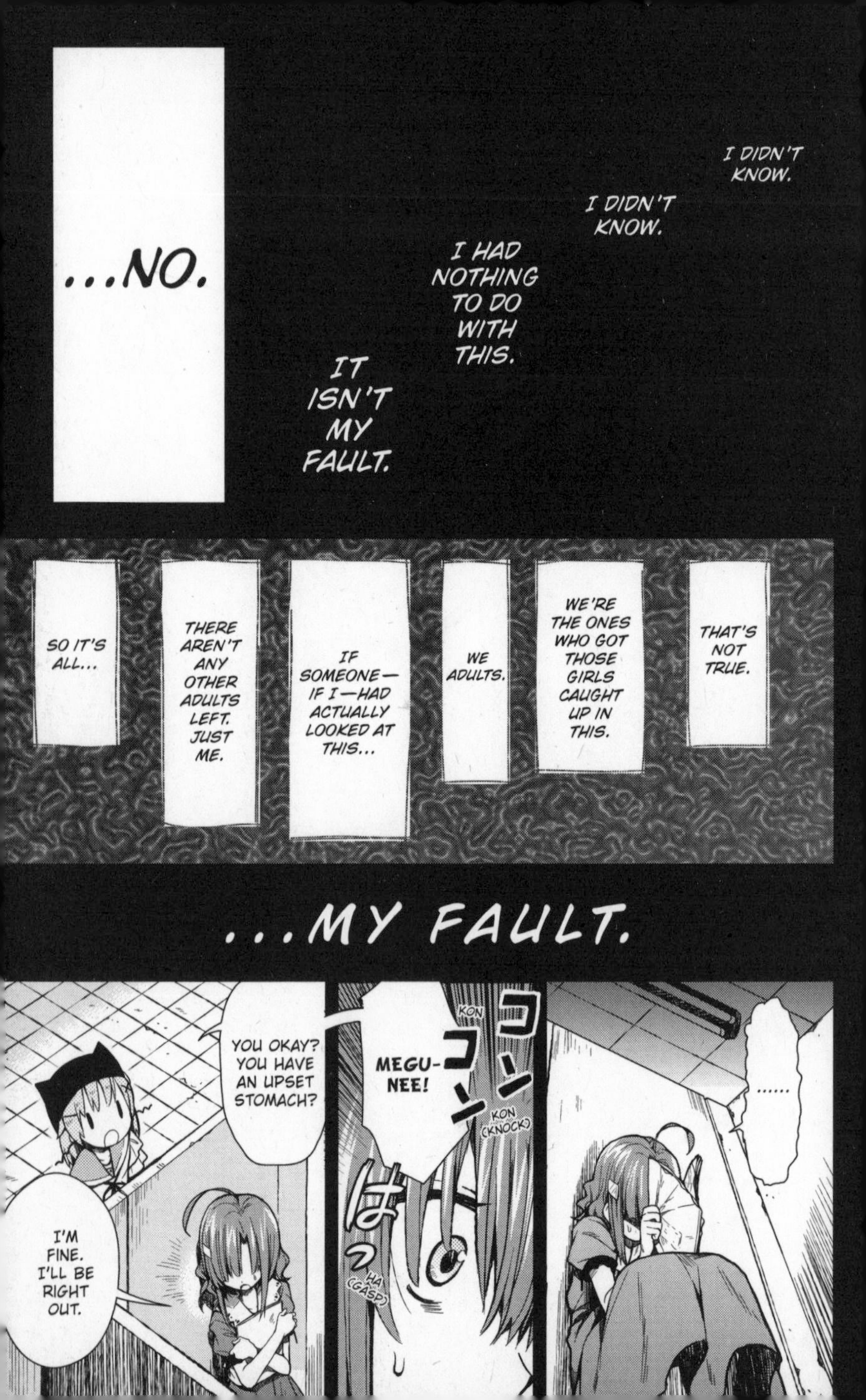
I DIDN'T KNOW.
I DIDN'T KNOW.
I HAD NOTHING TO DO WITH THIS.
IT ISN'T MY FAULT.
...NO.
THAT'S NOT TRUE.
WE'RE THE ONES WHO GOT THOSE GIRLS CAUGHT UP IN THIS.
WE ADULTS.
IF SOMEONE—IF I—HAD ACTUALLY LOOKED AT THIS...
THERE AREN'T ANY OTHER ADULTS LEFT. JUST ME.
SO IT'S ALL...
...MY FAULT.
......
KON
KON (KNOCK)
MEGU-NEE!
HA (GASP)
YOU OKAY? YOU HAVE AN UPSET STOMACH?
I'M FINE. I'LL BE RIGHT OUT.

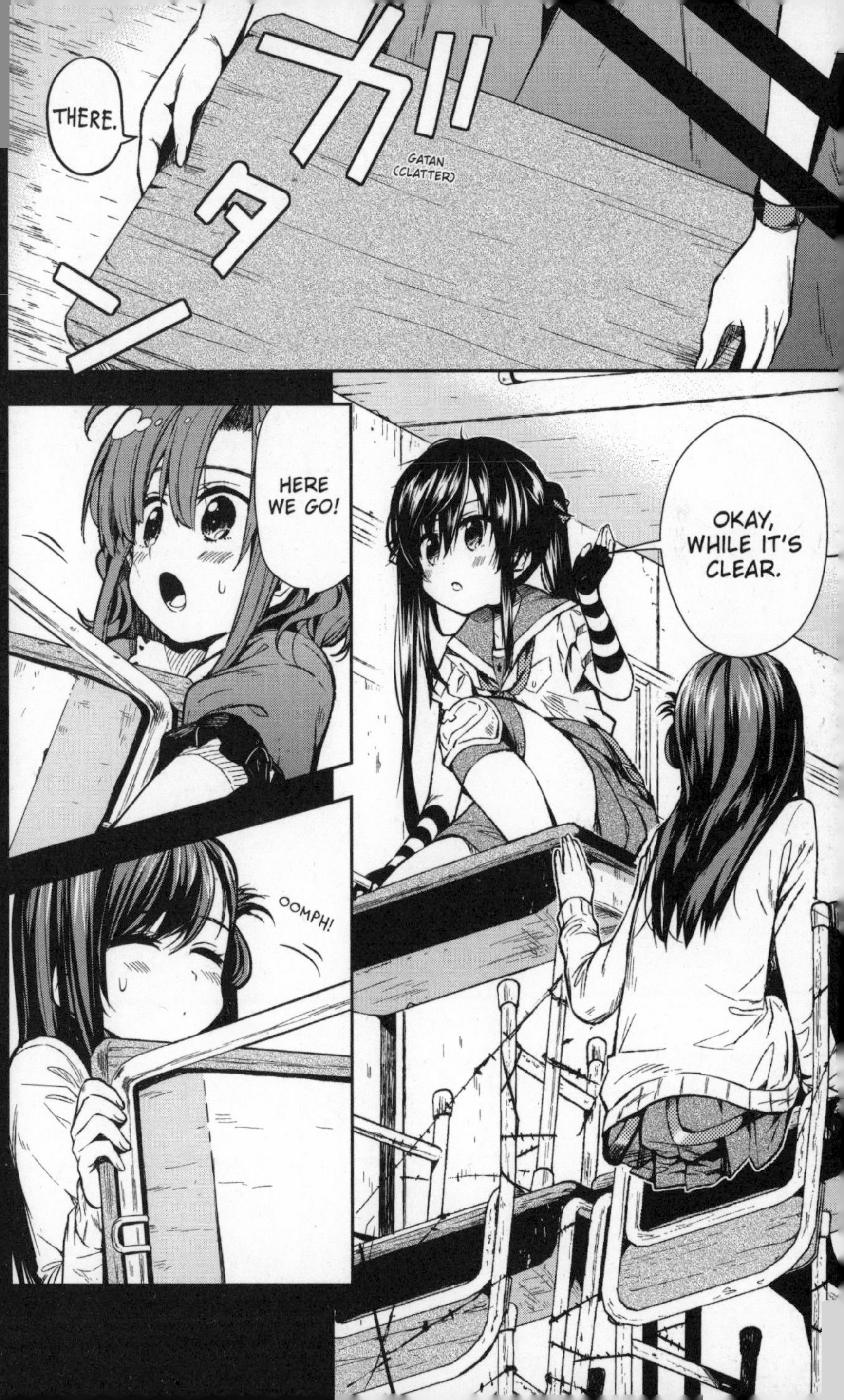
THERE.
ガタン
GATAN (CLATTER)
OKAY, WHILE IT'S CLEAR.
HERE WE GO!
OOMPH!

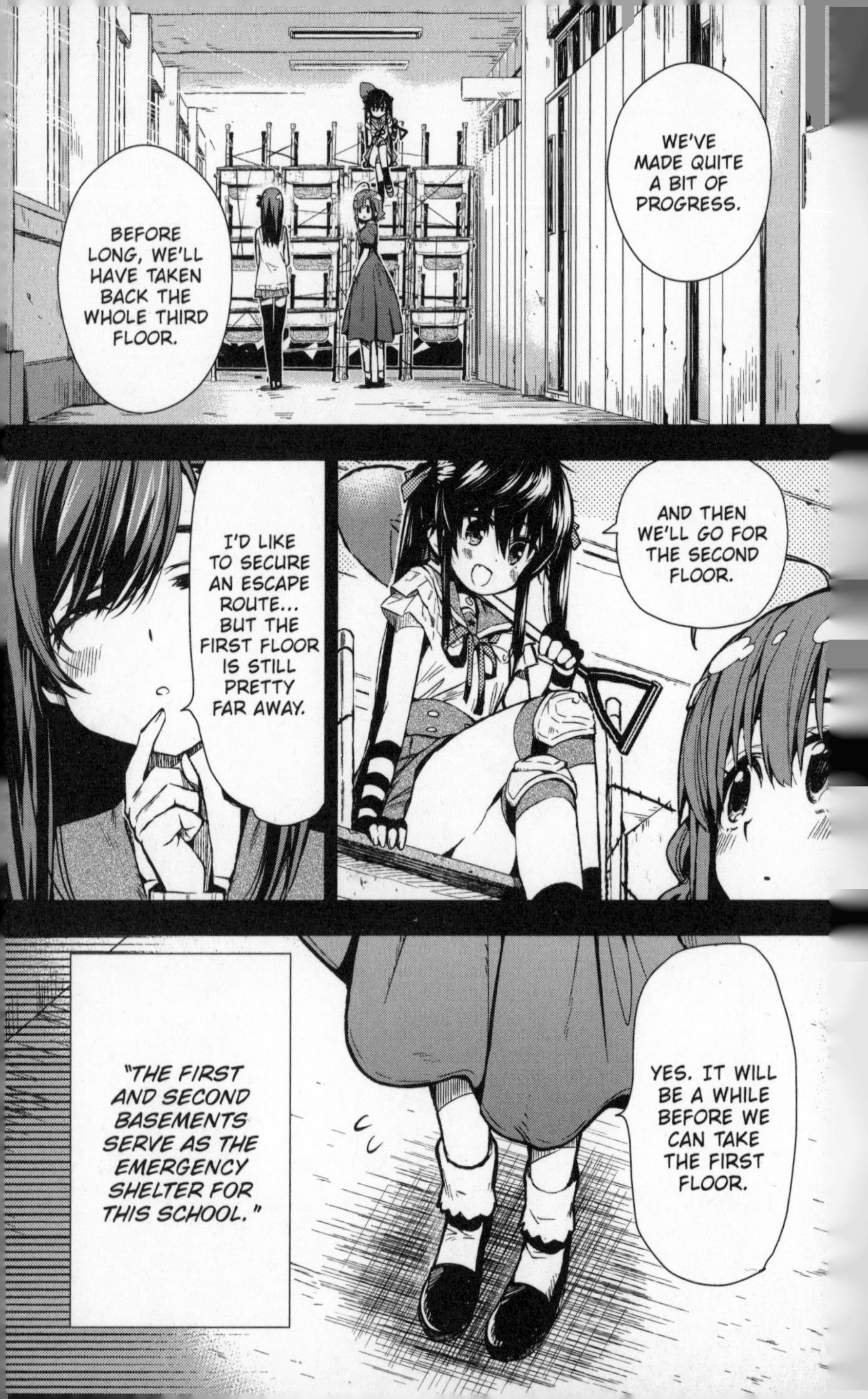
WE'VE MADE QUITE A BIT OF PROGRESS.
BEFORE LONG, WE'LL HAVE TAKEN BACK THE WHOLE THIRD FLOOR.
AND THEN WE'LL GO FOR THE SECOND FLOOR.
I'D LIKE TO SECURE AN ESCAPE ROUTE... BUT THE FIRST FLOOR IS STILL PRETTY FAR AWAY.
YES. IT WILL BE A WHILE BEFORE WE CAN TAKE THE FIRST FLOOR.
"THE FIRST AND SECOND BASEMENTS SERVE AS THE EMERGENCY SHELTER FOR THIS SCHOOL."

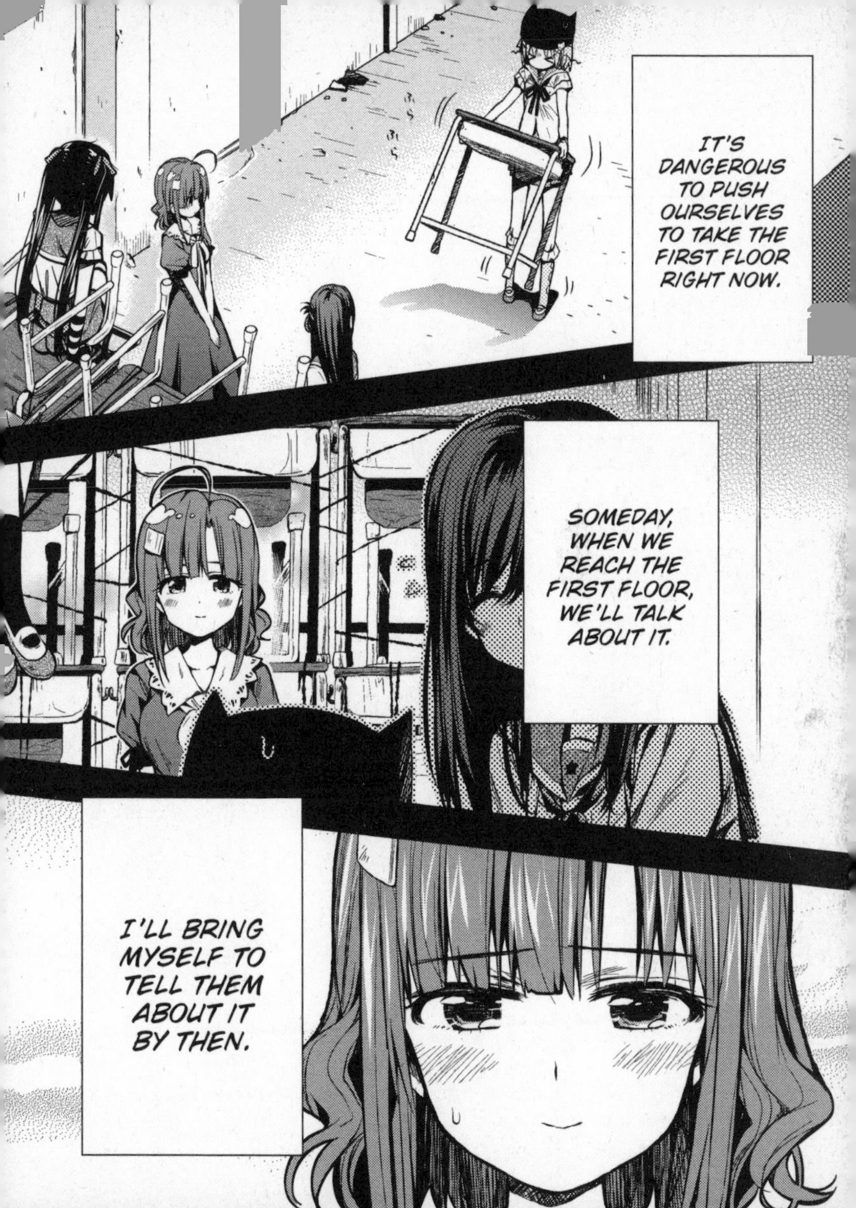
IT'S DANGEROUS TO PUSH OURSELVES TO TAKE THE FIRST FLOOR RIGHT NOW.
SOMEDAY, WHEN WE REACH THE FIRST FLOOR, WE'LL TALK ABOUT IT.
I'LL BRING MYSELF TO TELL THEM ABOUT IT BY THEN.

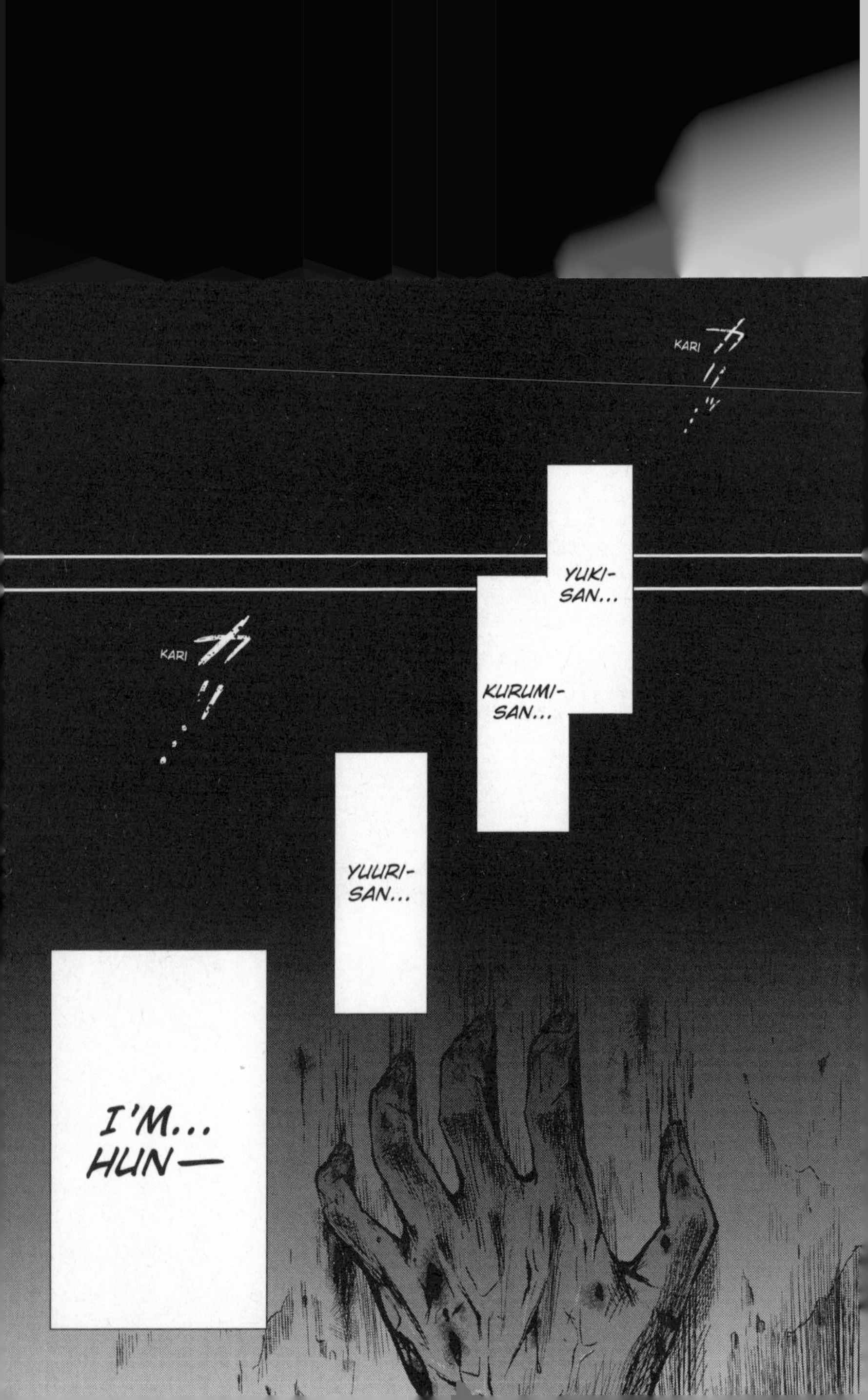
KARI
YUKI-SAN...
KURUMI-SAN...
KARI
YUURI-SAN...
I'M... HUN—

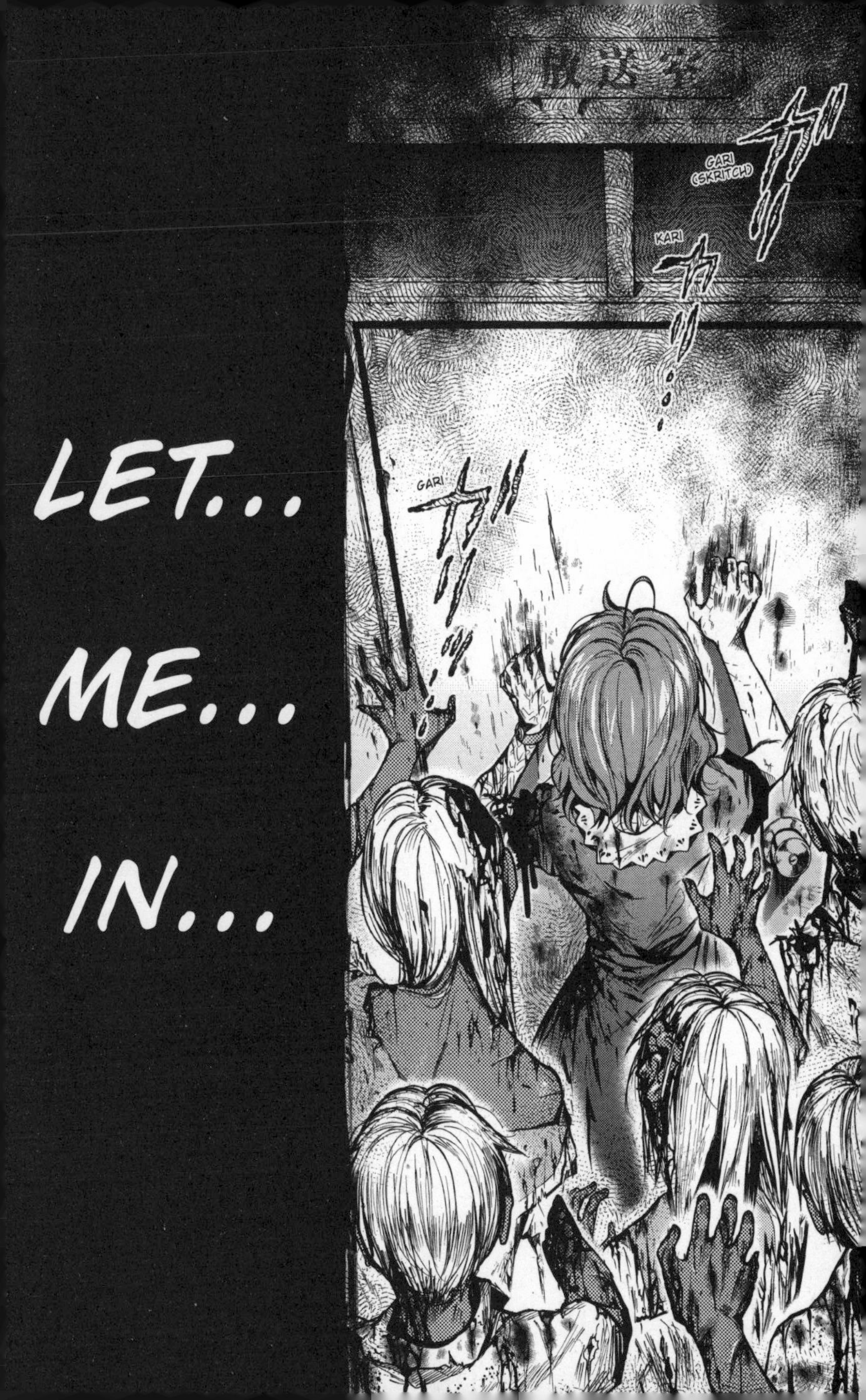
放送室
GARI (SKRITCH)
KARI
GARI
LET...
ME...
IN...

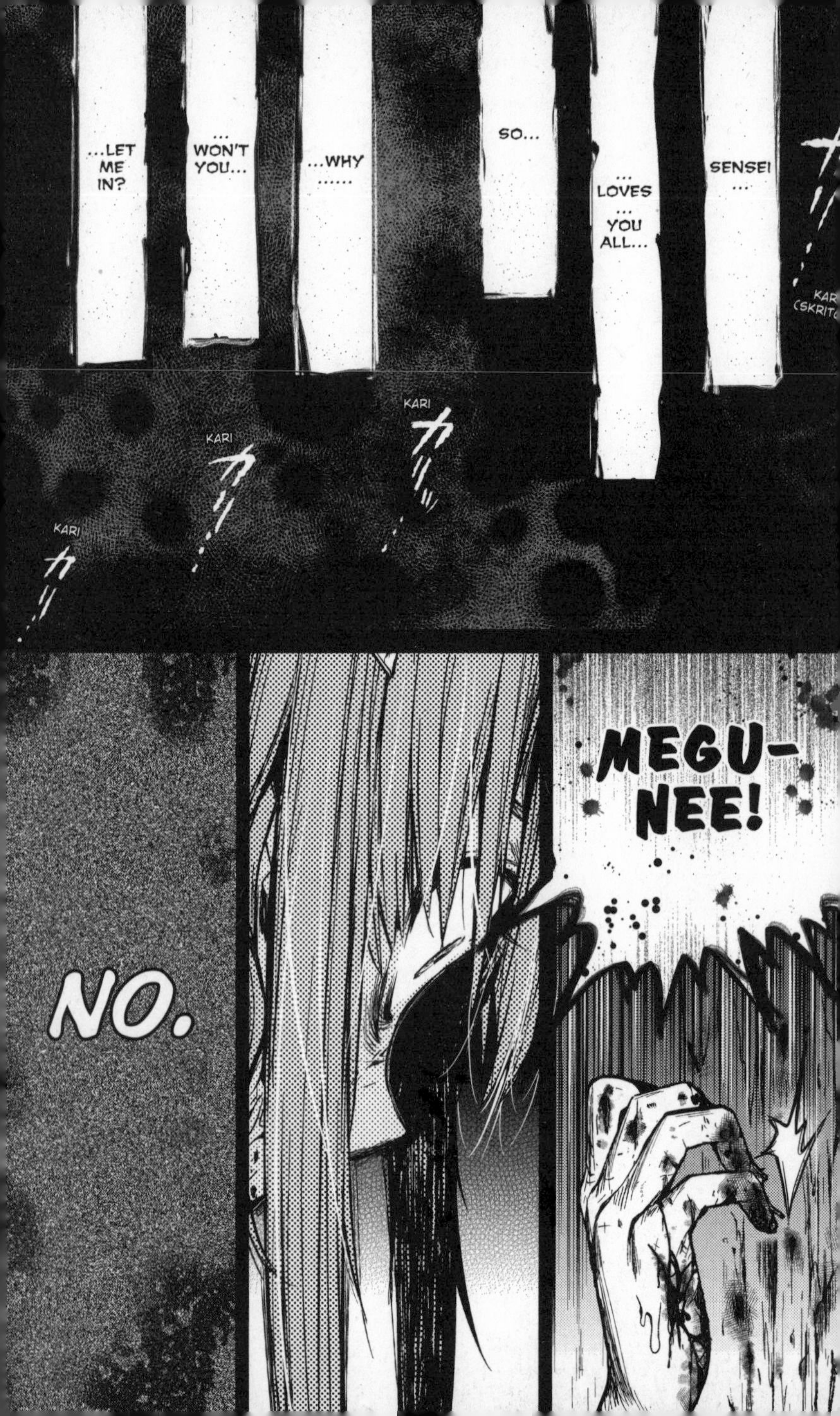

KARI
SENSEI ...
... LOVES ... YOU ALL...
SO...
...WHY ......
... WON'T YOU...
...LET ME IN?
KARI
KARI
KARI
MEGU-NEE!
NO.

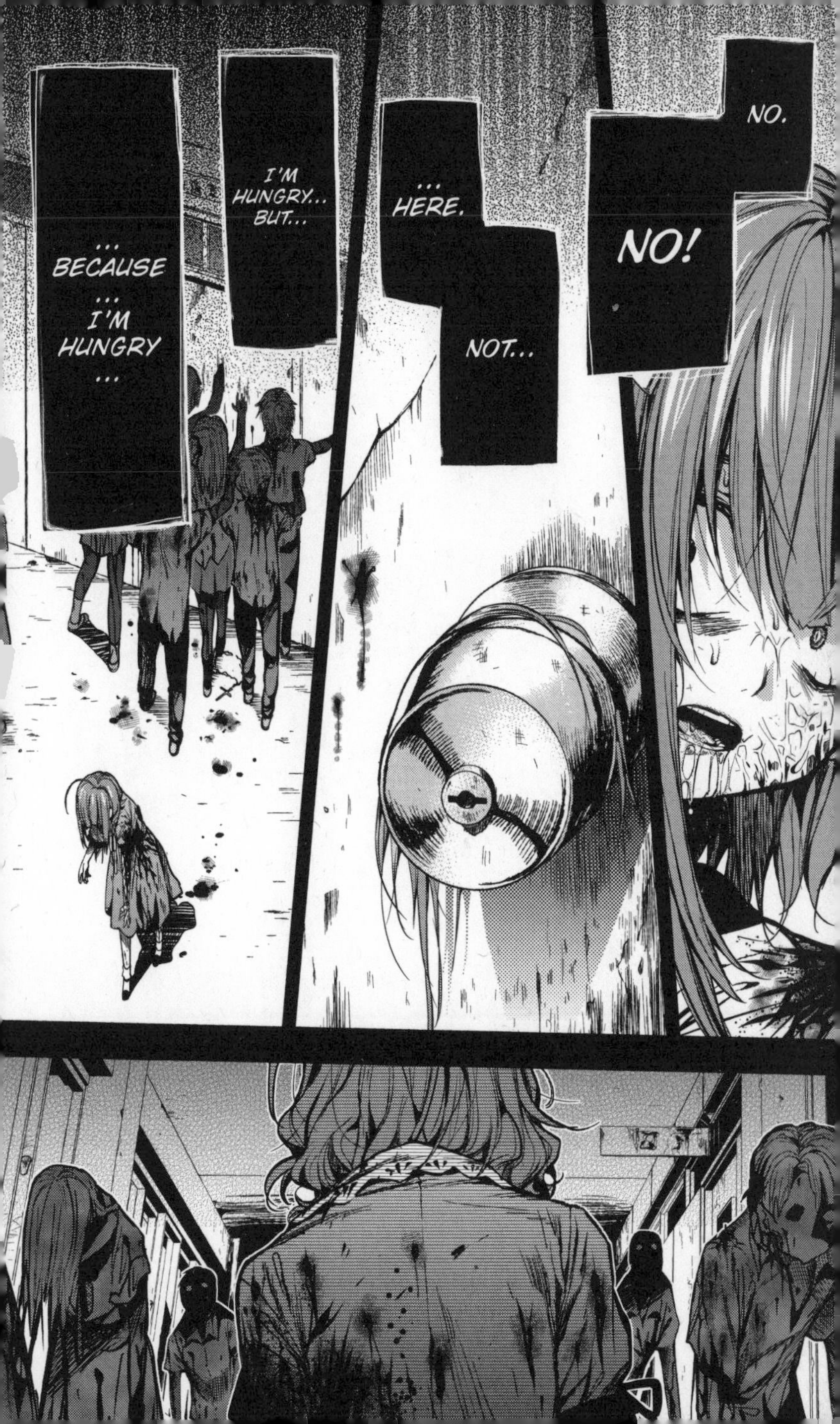
NO.
NO!
NOT...
... HERE.
I'M HUNGRY... BUT...
... BECAUSE ... I'M HUNGRY ...

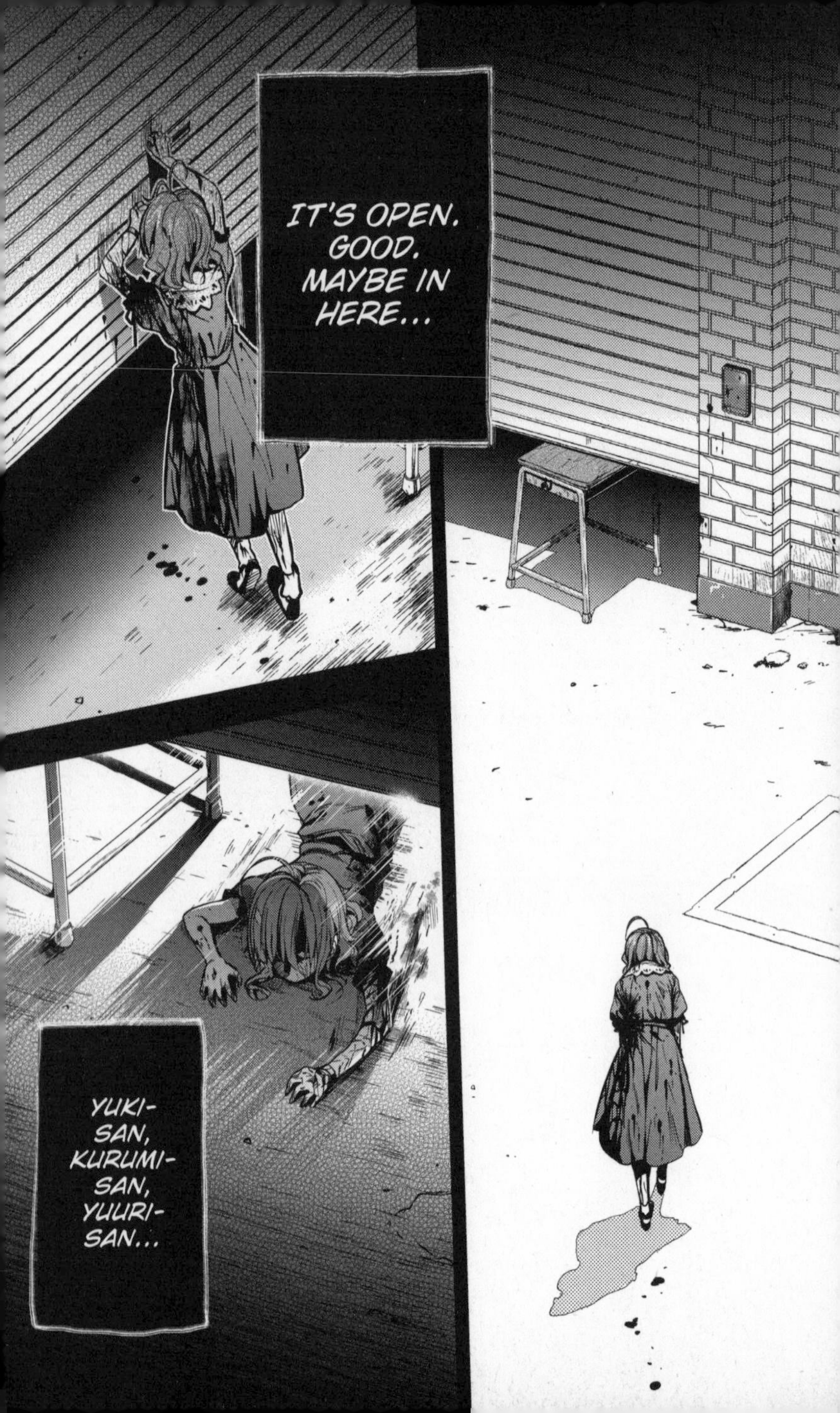
IT'S OPEN. GOOD. MAYBE IN HERE...
YUKI-SAN, KURUMI-SAN, YUURI-SAN...

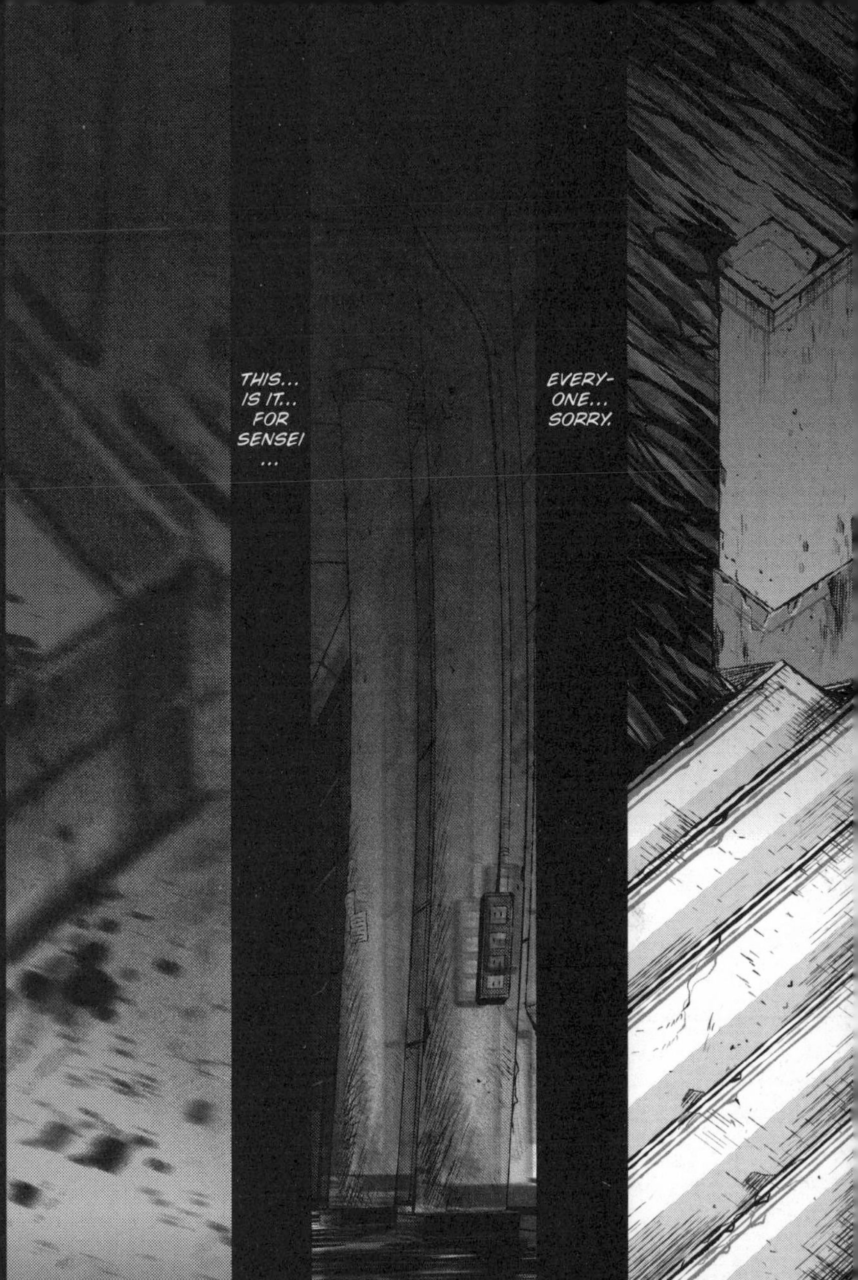
EVERY-ONE... SORRY.
THIS... IS IT... FOR SENSEI ...

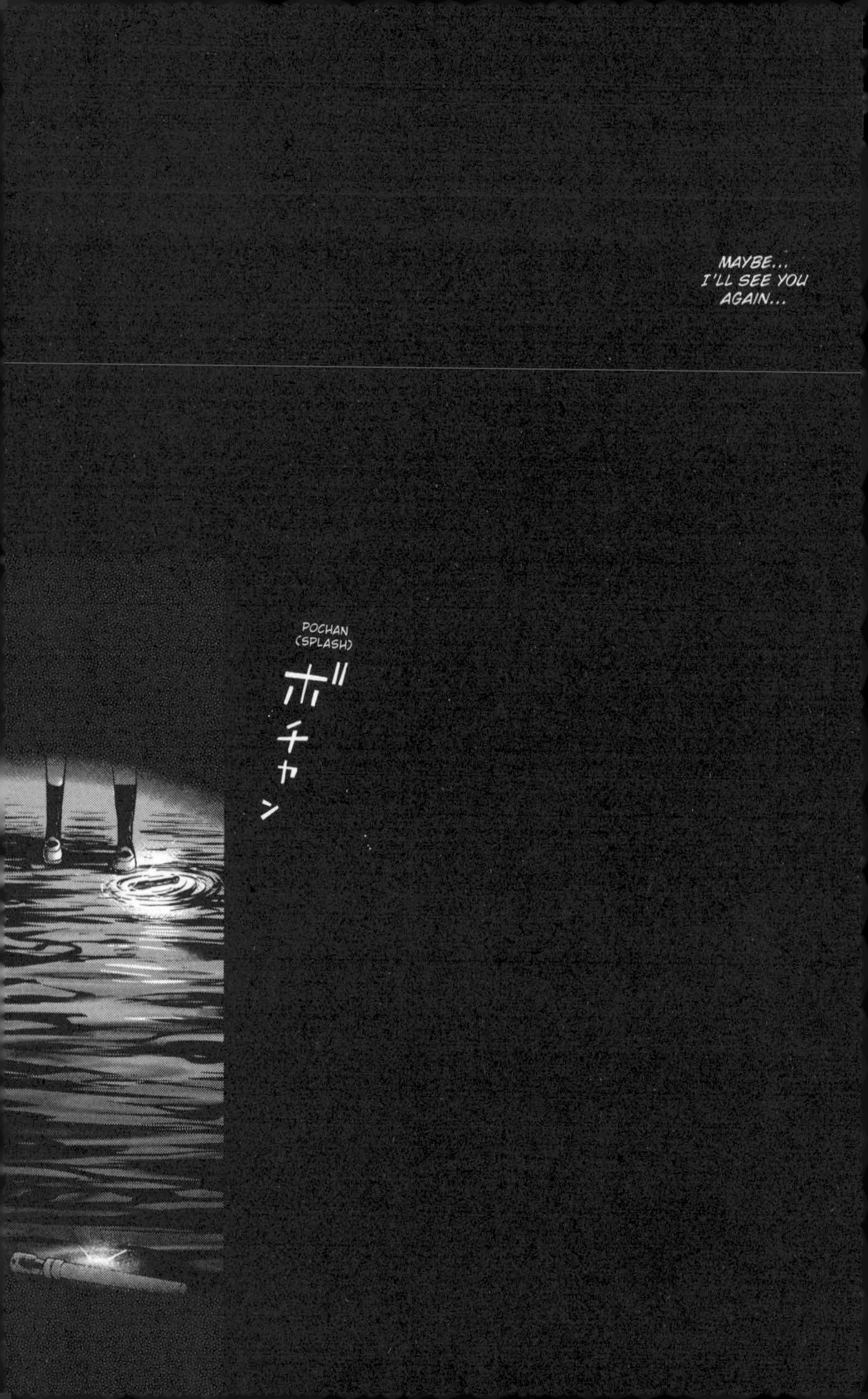
MAYBE... I'LL SEE YOU AGAIN...
POCHAN (SPLASH)
ボチャン

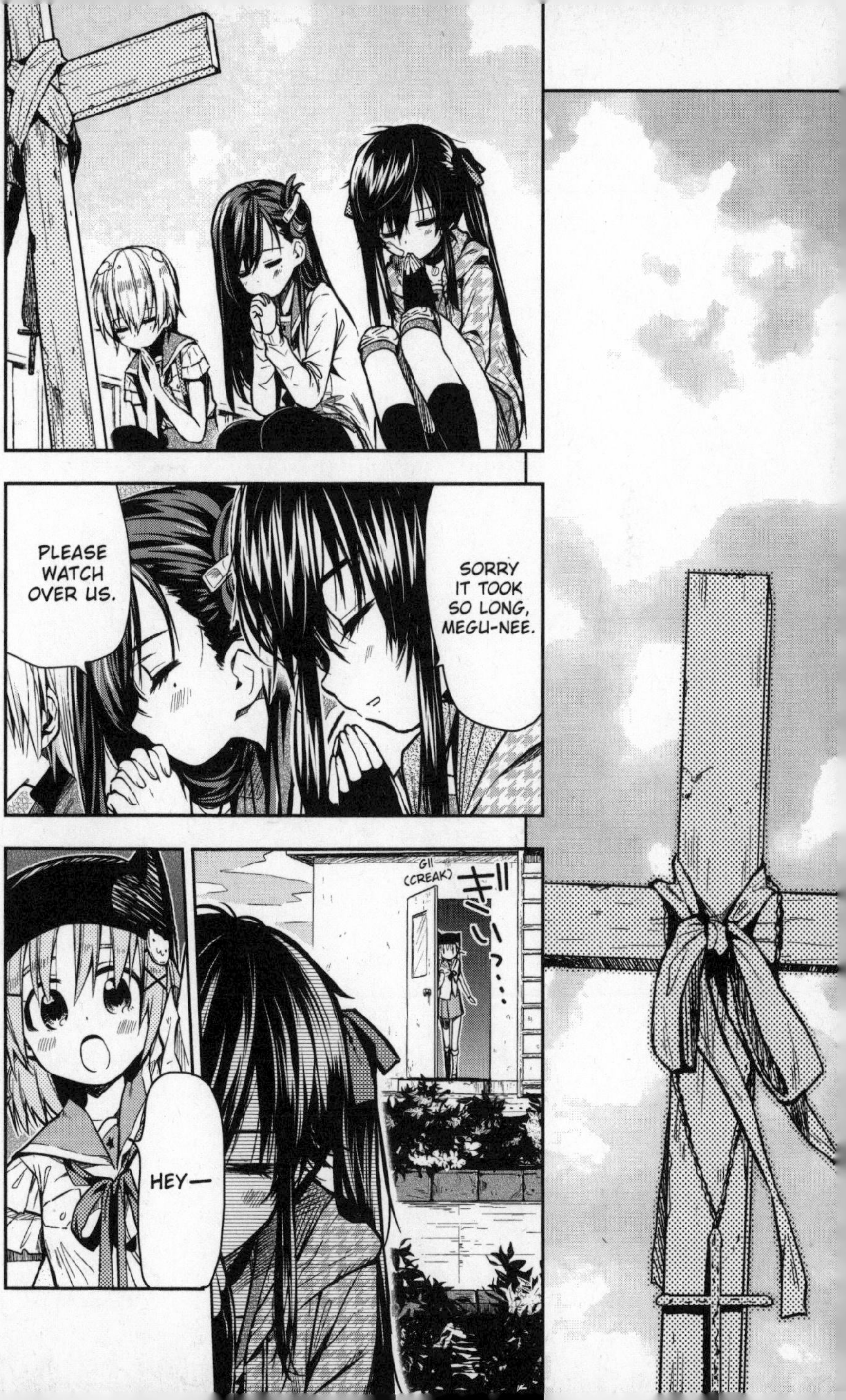
SORRY IT TOOK SO LONG, MEGU-NEE.
PLEASE WATCH OVER US.
GII (CREAK)
HEY—

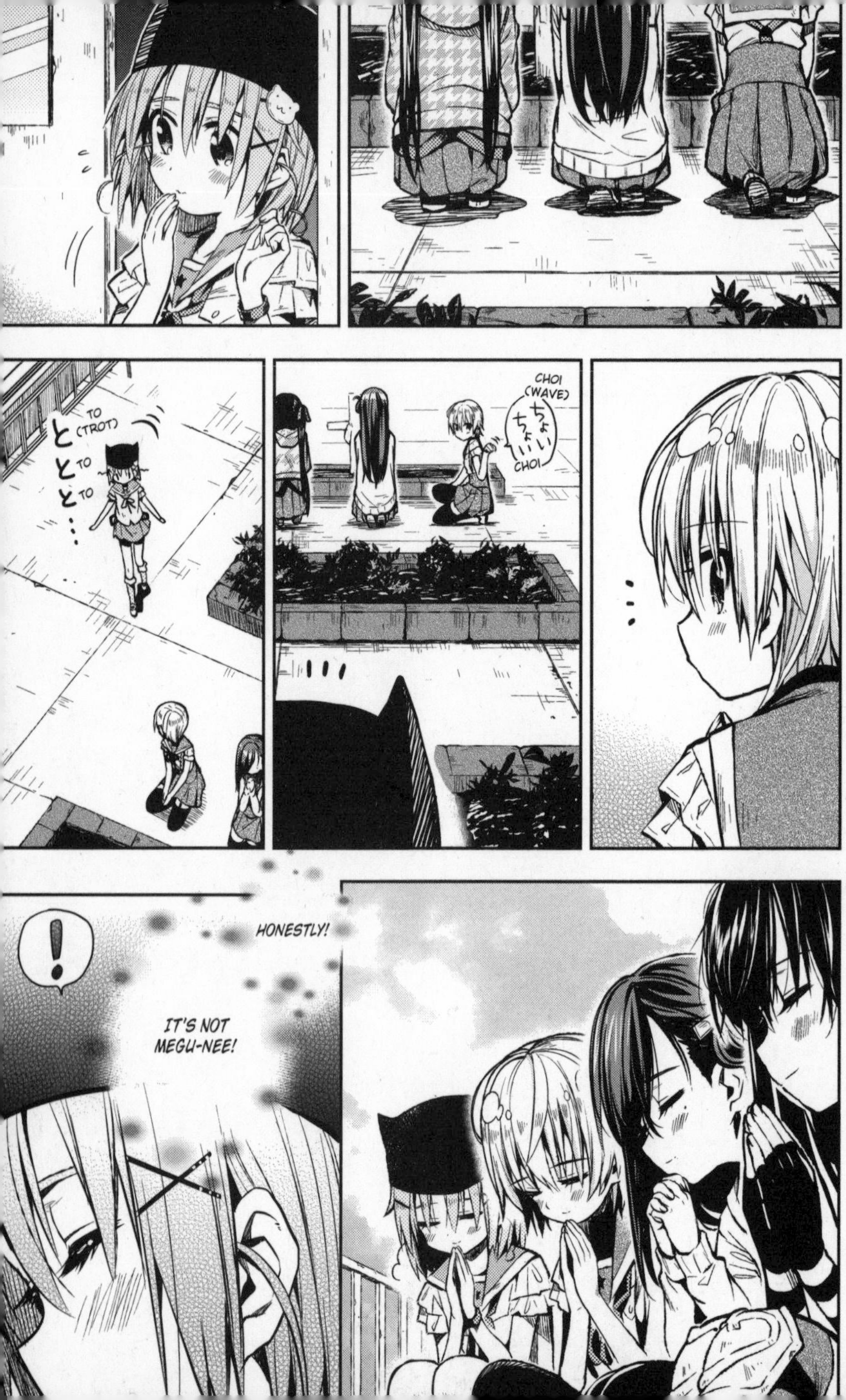
...
CHOI (WAVE)
ちょいちょい
CHOI
!!!
とととと…
TO (TROT)
TO
TO
!
HONESTLY!
IT'S NOT MEGU-NEE!

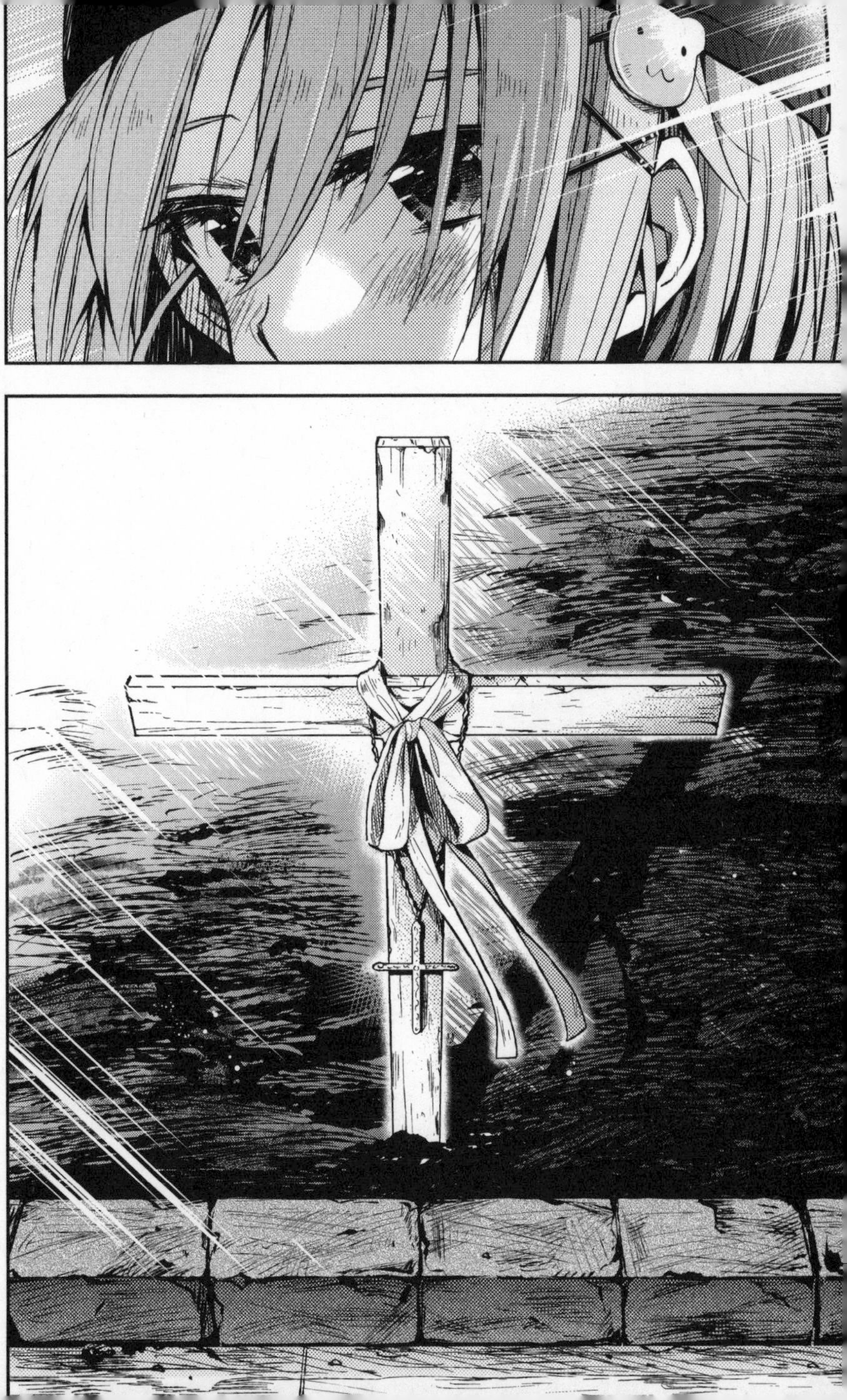

STATE EMERGENCY
EVACUATION MANUAL

... ... wing cases.

When instructed by the principal or said ....
.... occurrence of state manuals.
....
....

Text 15-10286 Last Revision 10/1/

SCHOOL-LIVE!

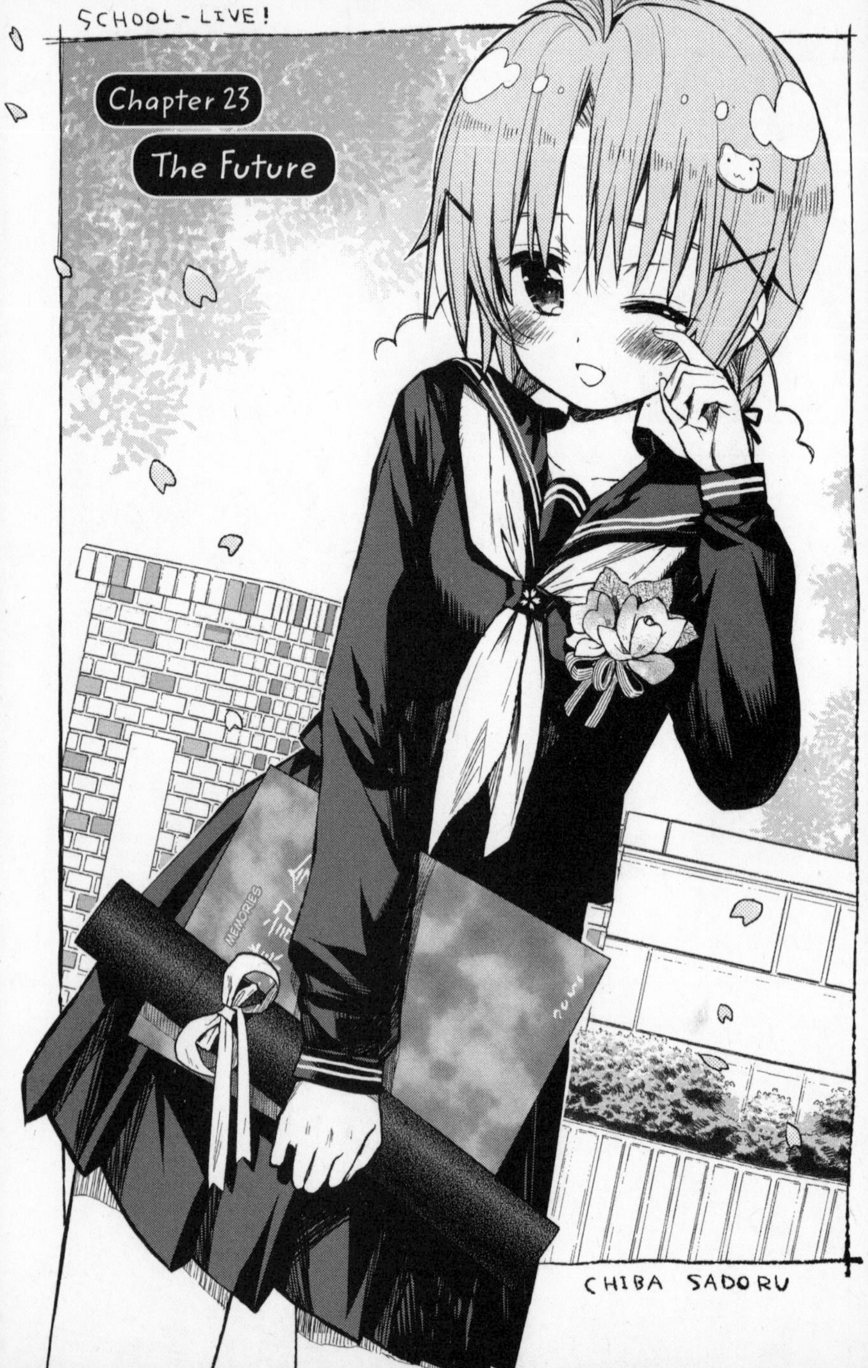
SCHOOL-LIVE!
Chapter 23
The Future
MEMORIES
CHIBA SADORU

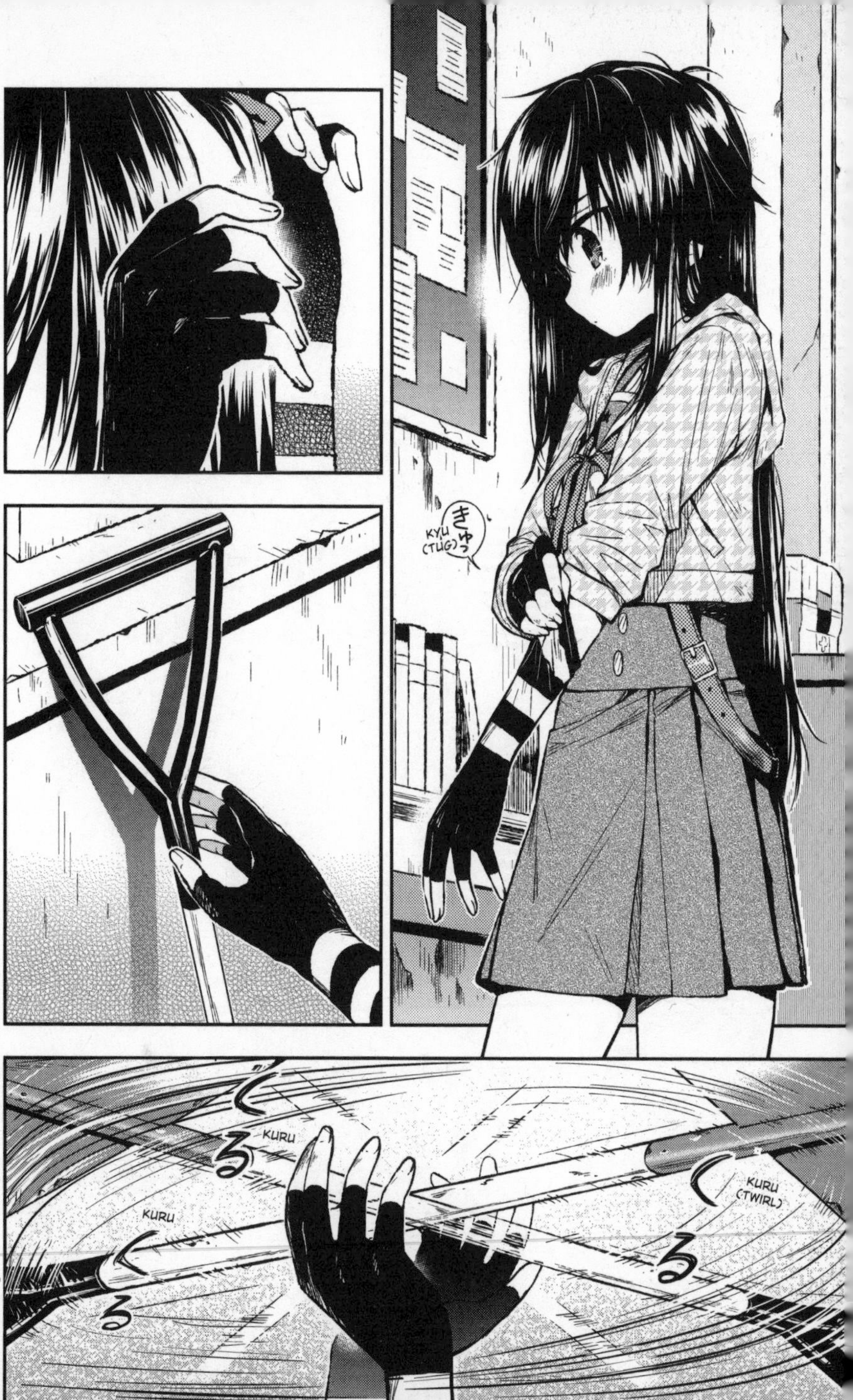
きゅっ
KYU (TUG)
くる
KURU (TWIRL)
くる
KURU
くる
KURU

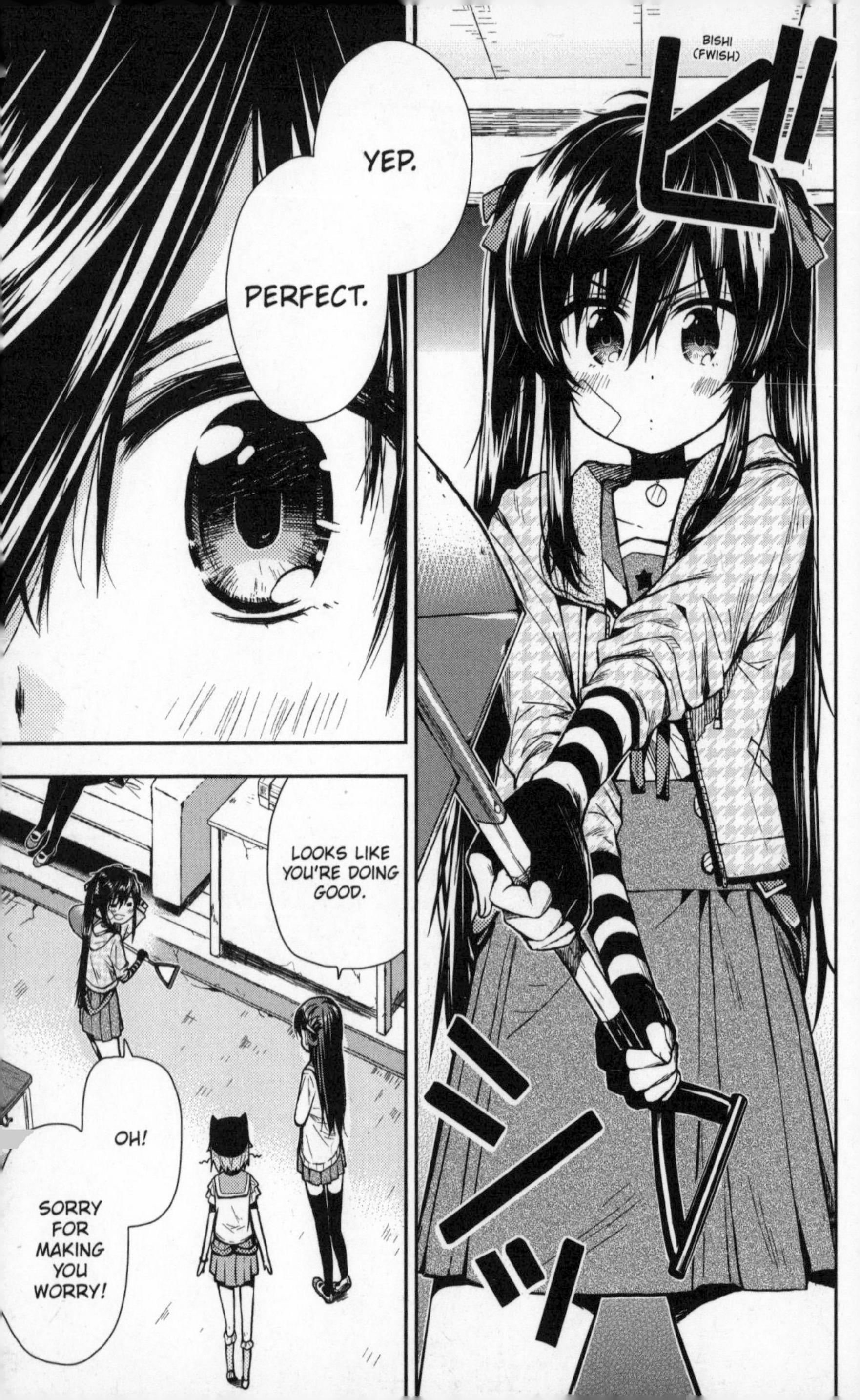
BISHI
(FWISH)
YEP.
PERFECT.
LOOKS LIKE YOU'RE DOING GOOD.
OH!
SORRY FOR MAKING YOU WORRY!

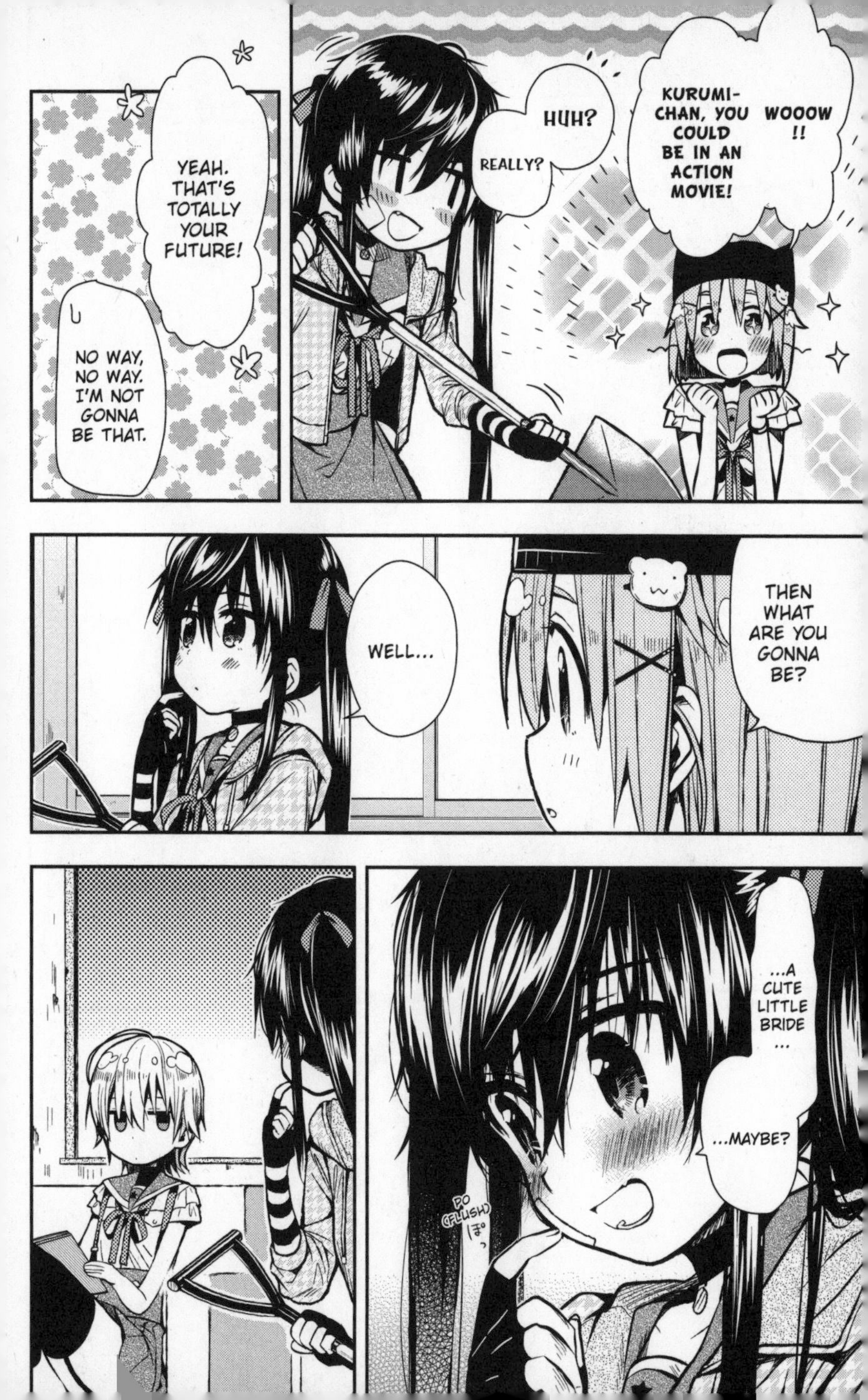
WOOOW!!
KURUMI-CHAN, YOU COULD BE IN AN ACTION MOVIE!
HUH?
REALLY?
YEAH. THAT'S TOTALLY YOUR FUTURE!
NO WAY, NO WAY. I'M NOT GONNA BE THAT.
THEN WHAT ARE YOU GONNA BE?
WELL...
...A CUTE LITTLE BRIDE ...
...MAYBE?
PO (FLUSH) ぽっ

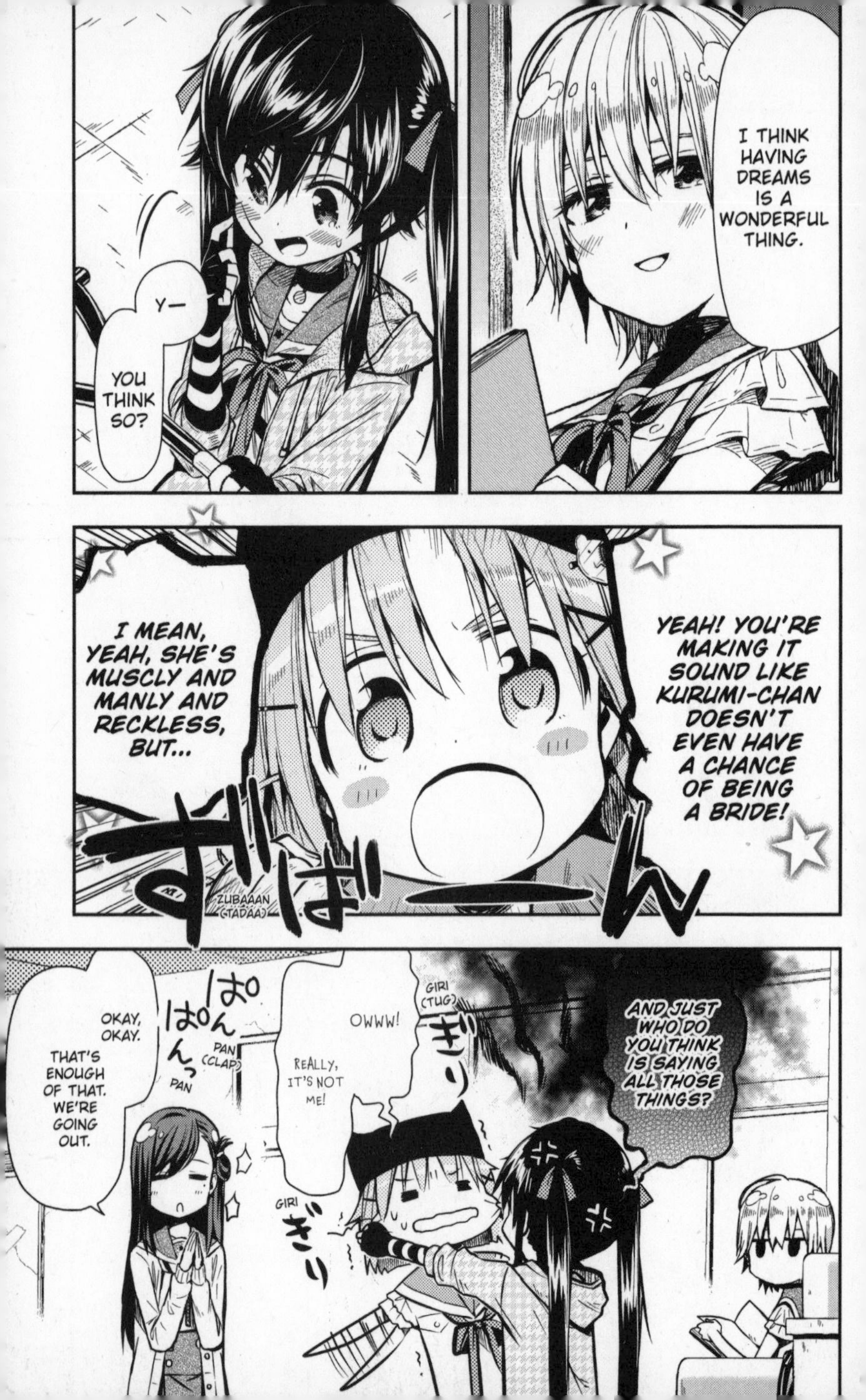
I THINK HAVING DREAMS IS A WONDERFUL THING.
Y—
YOU THINK SO?
YEAH! YOU'RE MAKING IT SOUND LIKE KURUMI-CHAN DOESN'T EVEN HAVE A CHANCE OF BEING A BRIDE!
I MEAN, YEAH, SHE'S MUSCLY AND MANLY AND RECKLESS, BUT...
ずばーん
ZUBAAAN (TADAA)
AND JUST WHO DO YOU THINK IS SAYING ALL THOSE THINGS?
ぎり
GIRI (TUG)
OWWW!
REALLY, IT'S NOT ME!
ぎり
GIRI
ぱんぱんっ
PAN (CLAP)
PAN
OKAY, OKAY.
THAT'S ENOUGH OF THAT. WE'RE GOING OUT.

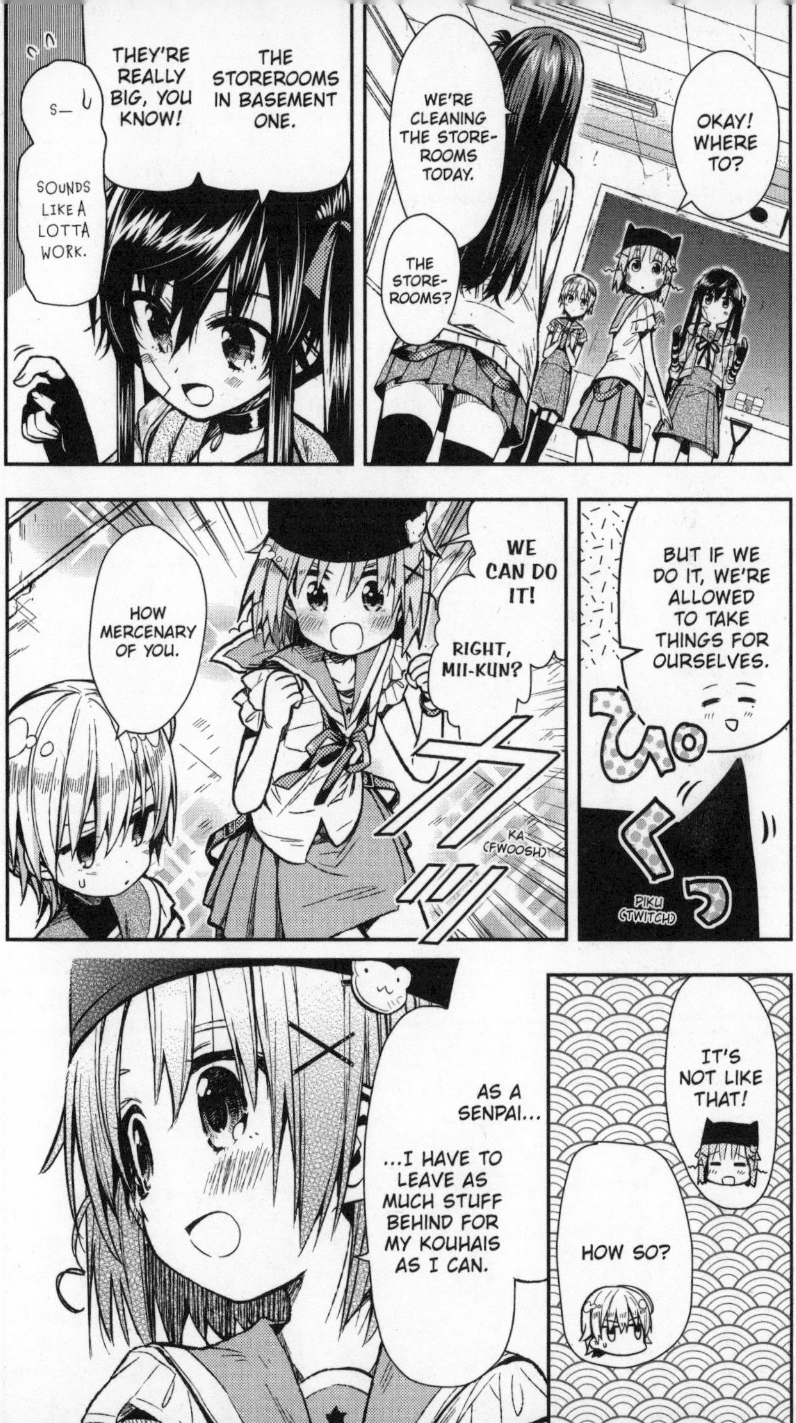
OKAY! WHERE TO?
WE'RE CLEANING THE STOREROOMS TODAY.
THE STOREROOMS?
THE STOREROOMS IN BASEMENT ONE.
THEY'RE REALLY BIG, YOU KNOW!
S—
SOUNDS LIKE A LOTTA WORK.
BUT IF WE DO IT, WE'RE ALLOWED TO TAKE THINGS FOR OURSELVES.
PIKU (TWITCH)
WE CAN DO IT!
RIGHT, MII-KUN?
KA (FWOOSH)
HOW MERCENARY OF YOU.
IT'S NOT LIKE THAT!
HOW SO?
AS A SENPAI...
...I HAVE TO LEAVE AS MUCH STUFF BEHIND FOR MY KOUHAIS AS I CAN.

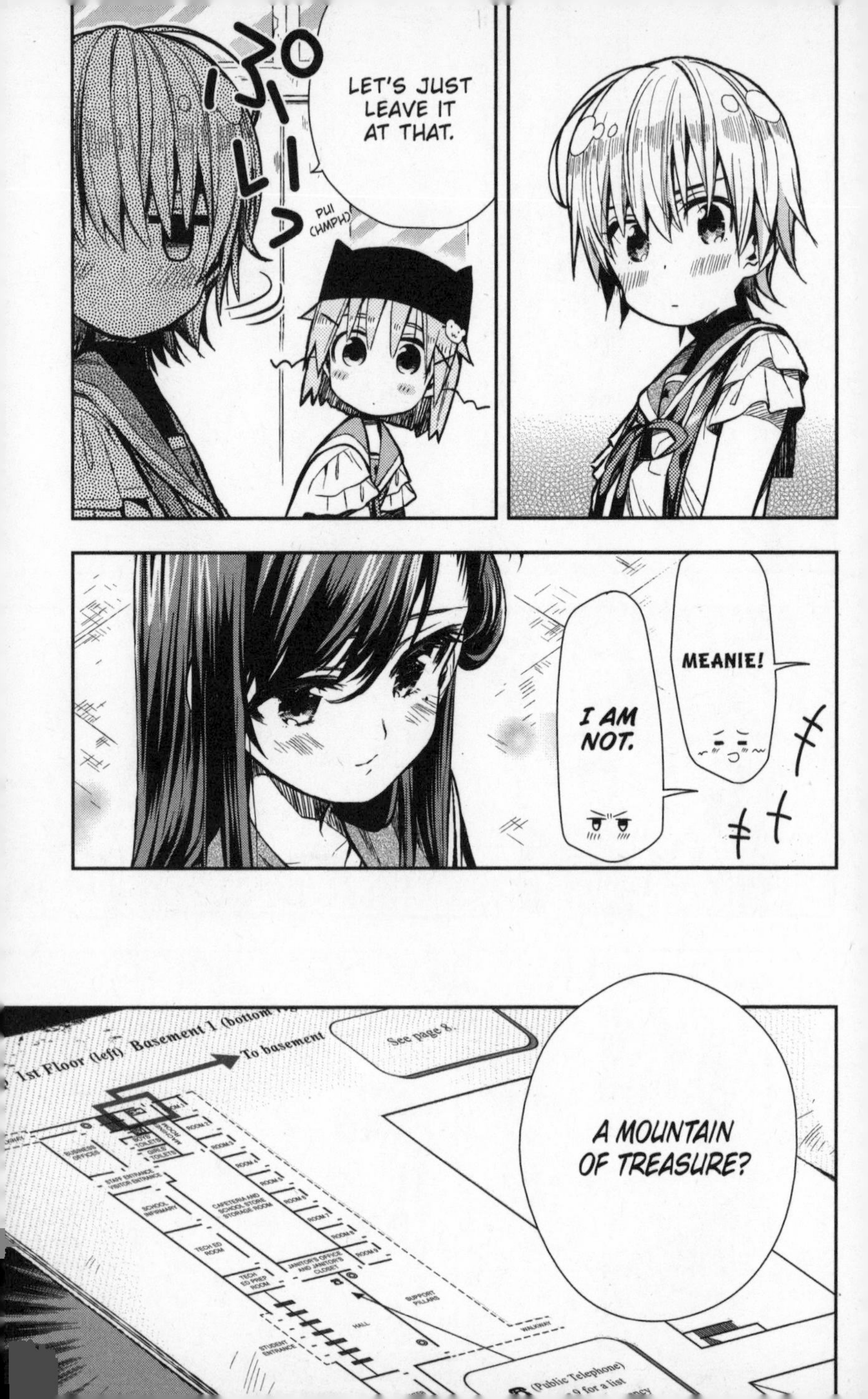

LET'S JUST LEAVE IT AT THAT.
PUI (HMPH)
MEANIE!
I AM NOT.
A MOUNTAIN OF TREASURE?
1st Floor (left)
To basement
See page 8.
BUSINESS OFFICES
STAFF ENTRANCE VISITOR ENTRANCE
SCHOOL INFIRMARY
CAFETERIA AND SCHOOL STORE STORAGE ROOM
TECH ED ROOM
TECH ED PREP ROOM
JANITOR'S OFFICE AND JANITOR'S CLOSET
SUPPORT PILLARS
HALL
WALKWAY
STUDENT ENTRANCE
(Public Telephone)

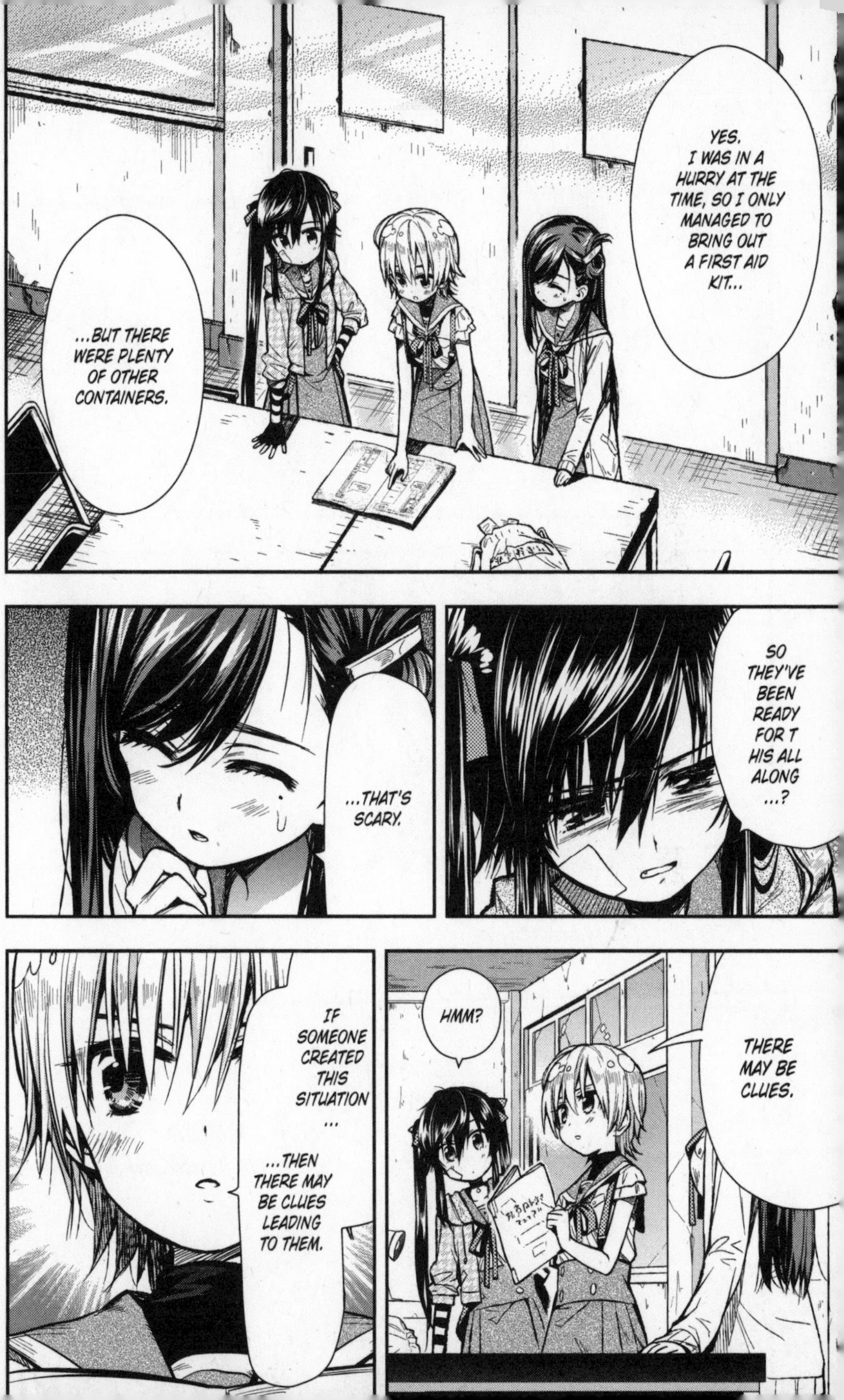
YES. I WAS IN A HURRY AT THE TIME, SO I ONLY MANAGED TO BRING OUT A FIRST AID KIT...
...BUT THERE WERE PLENTY OF OTHER CONTAINERS.
SO THEY'VE BEEN READY FOR T HIS ALL ALONG ...?
...THAT'S SCARY.
THERE MAY BE CLUES.
HMM?
IF SOMEONE CREATED THIS SITUATION ...
...THEN THERE MAY BE CLUES LEADING TO THEM.

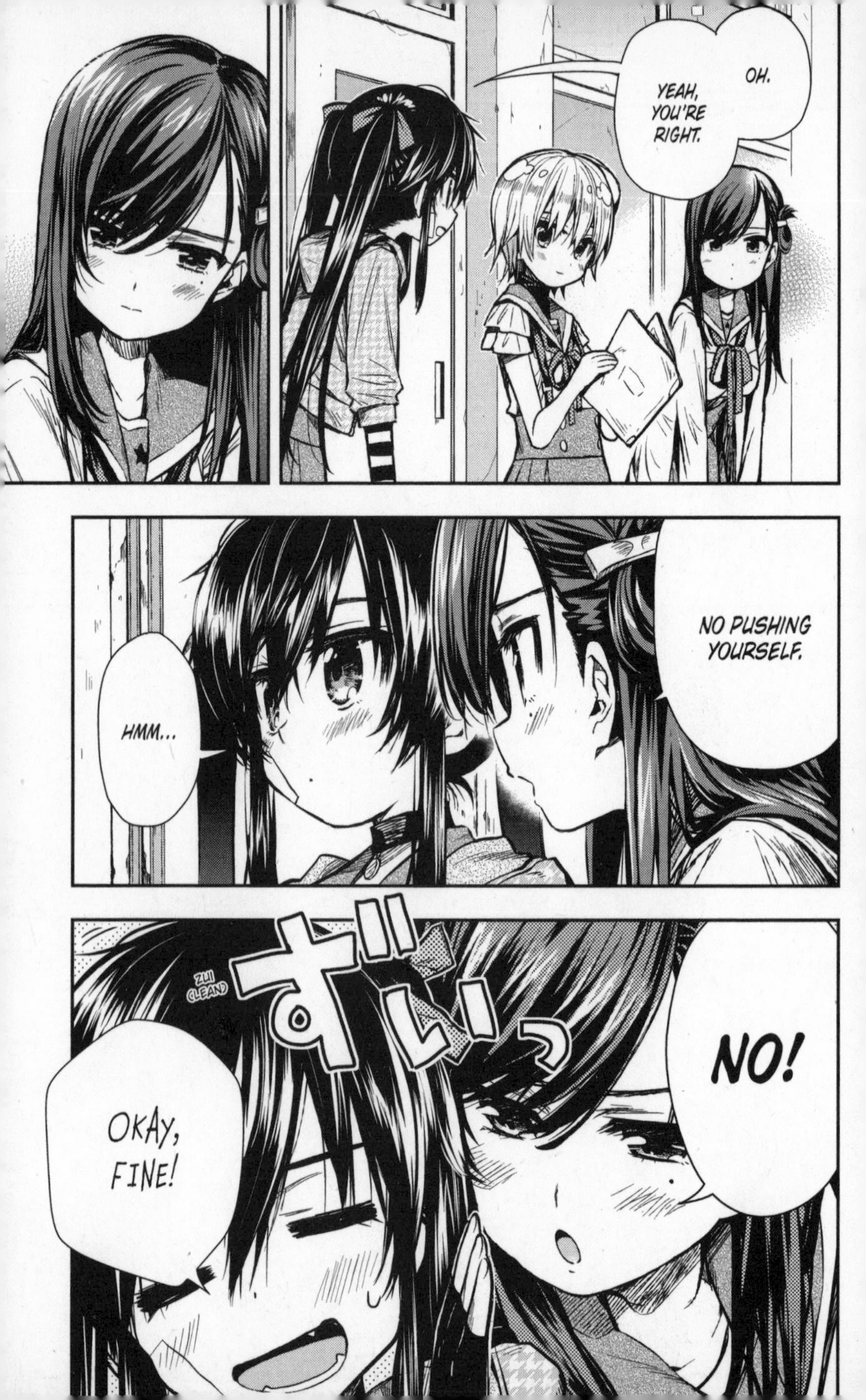
OH.
YEAH, YOU'RE RIGHT.
NO PUSHING YOURSELF.
HMM...
NO!
ずいっ
ZUI (LEAN)
OKAY, FINE!

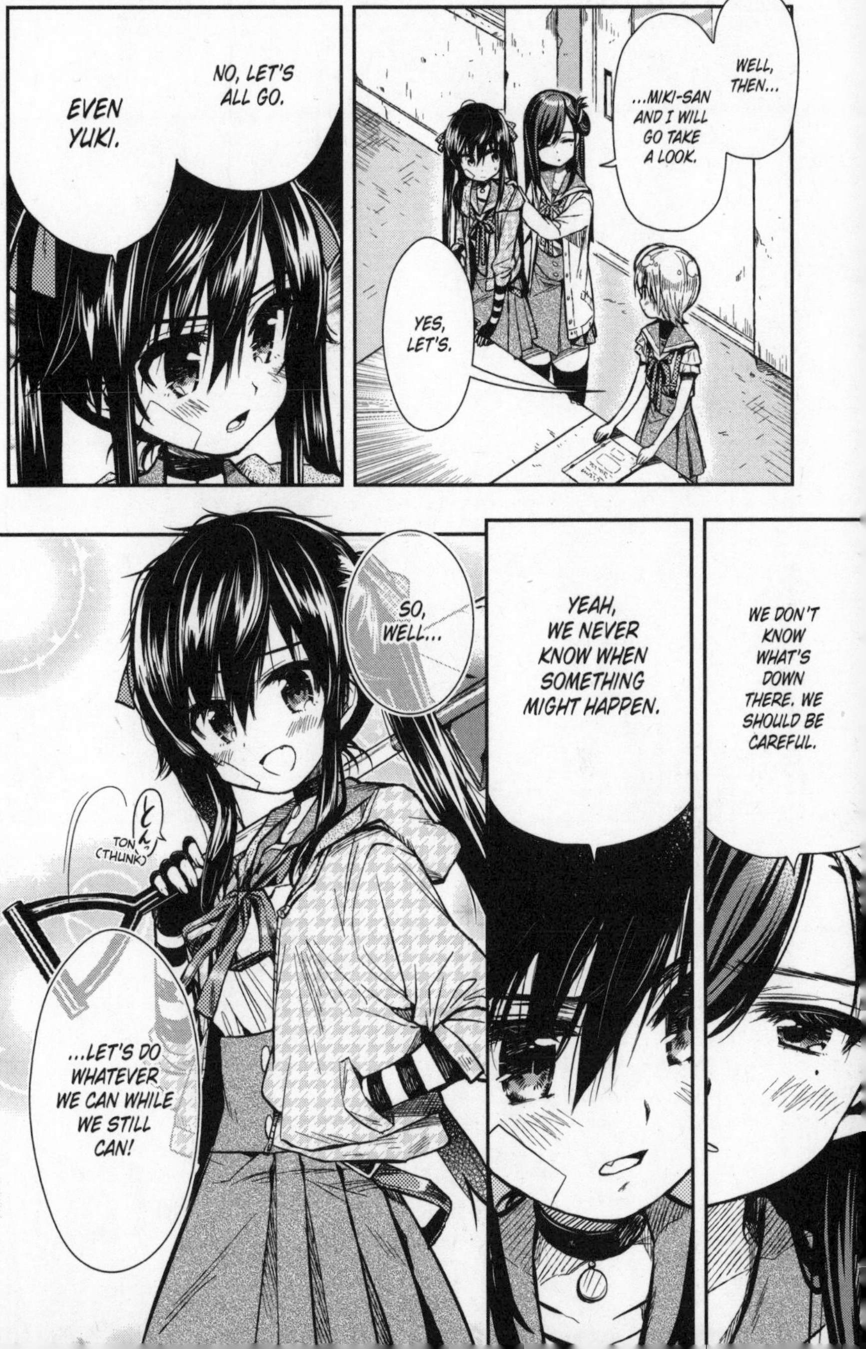
WELL, THEN...
...MIKI-SAN AND I WILL GO TAKE A LOOK.
YES, LET'S.
NO, LET'S ALL GO.
EVEN YUKI.
WE DON'T KNOW WHAT'S DOWN THERE. WE SHOULD BE CAREFUL.
YEAH, WE NEVER KNOW WHEN SOMETHING MIGHT HAPPEN.
SO, WELL...
とんっ
TON (THUNK)
...LET'S DO WHATEVER WE CAN WHILE WE STILL CAN!

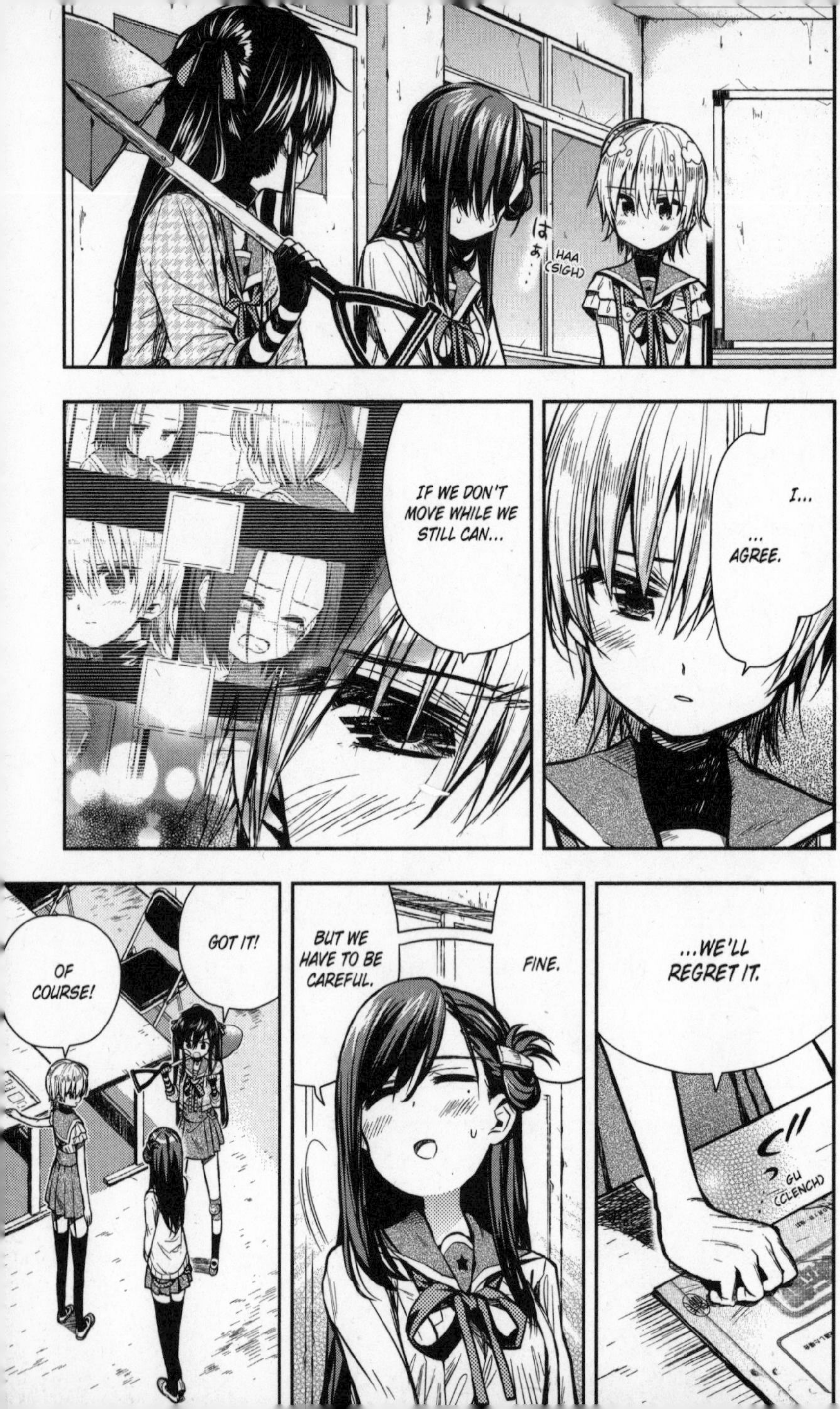
はぁ…
HAA (SIGH)
I...
... AGREE.
IF WE DON'T MOVE WHILE WE STILL CAN...
...WE'LL REGRET IT.
ぐっ
GU (CLENCH)
FINE.
BUT WE HAVE TO BE CAREFUL.
GOT IT!
OF COURSE!

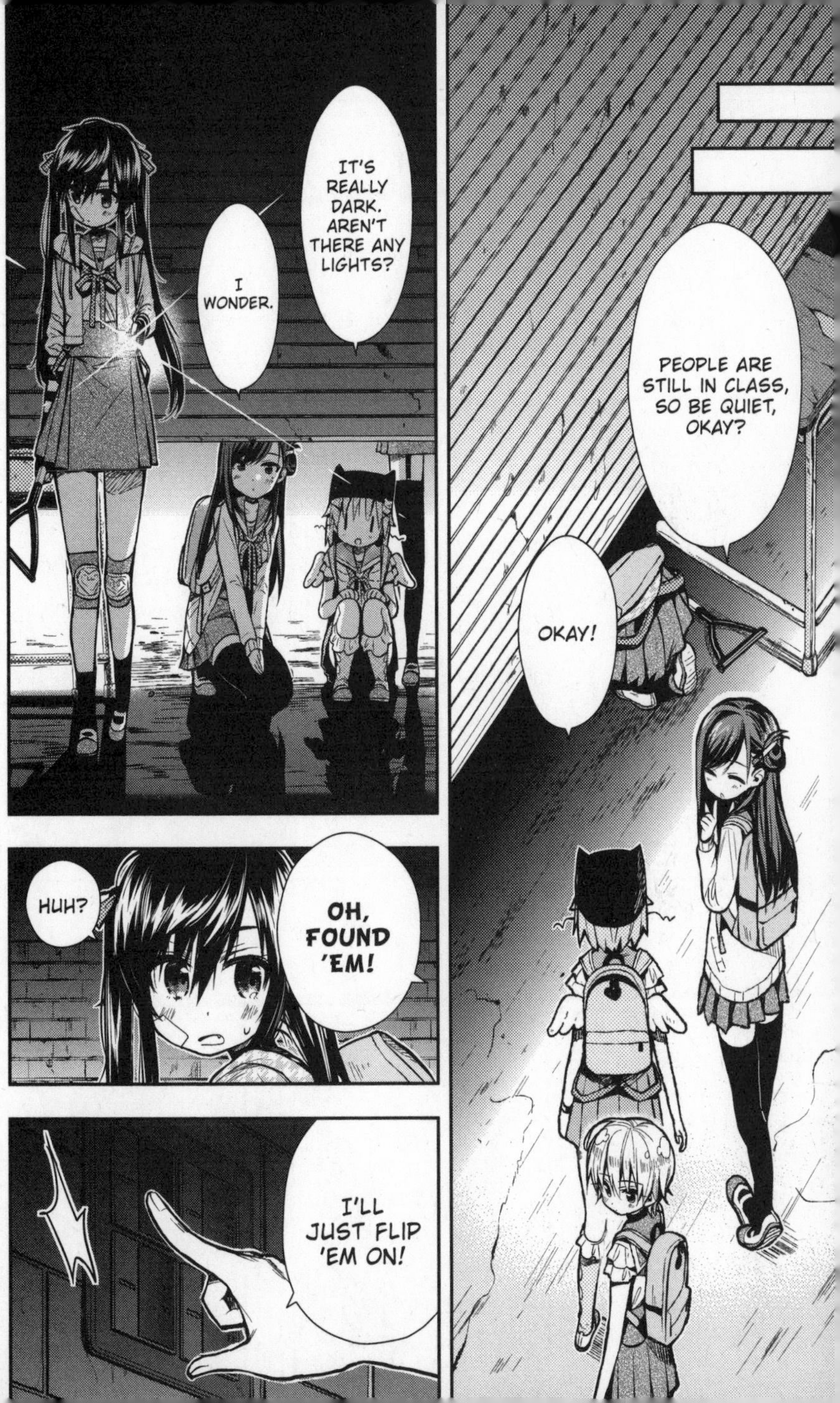
PEOPLE ARE STILL IN CLASS, SO BE QUIET, OKAY?
OKAY!
IT'S REALLY DARK. AREN'T THERE ANY LIGHTS?
I WONDER.
OH, FOUND 'EM!
HUH?
I'LL JUST FLIP 'EM ON!

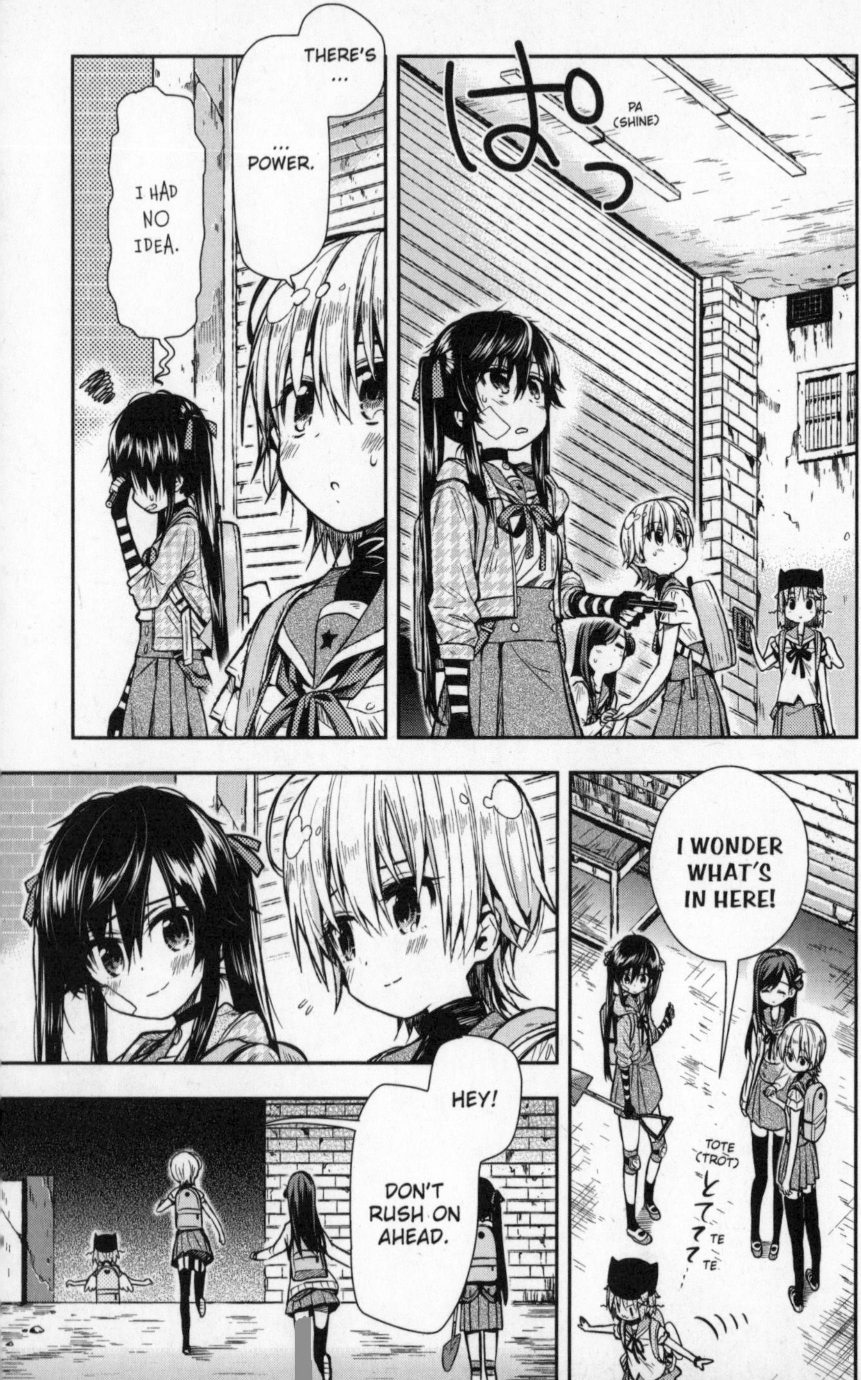
ぱっ
PA (SHINE)
THERE'S ...
... POWER.
I HAD NO IDEA.
I WONDER WHAT'S IN HERE!
TOTE (TROT)
とててて
TE TE
HEY!
DON'T RUSH ON AHEAD.

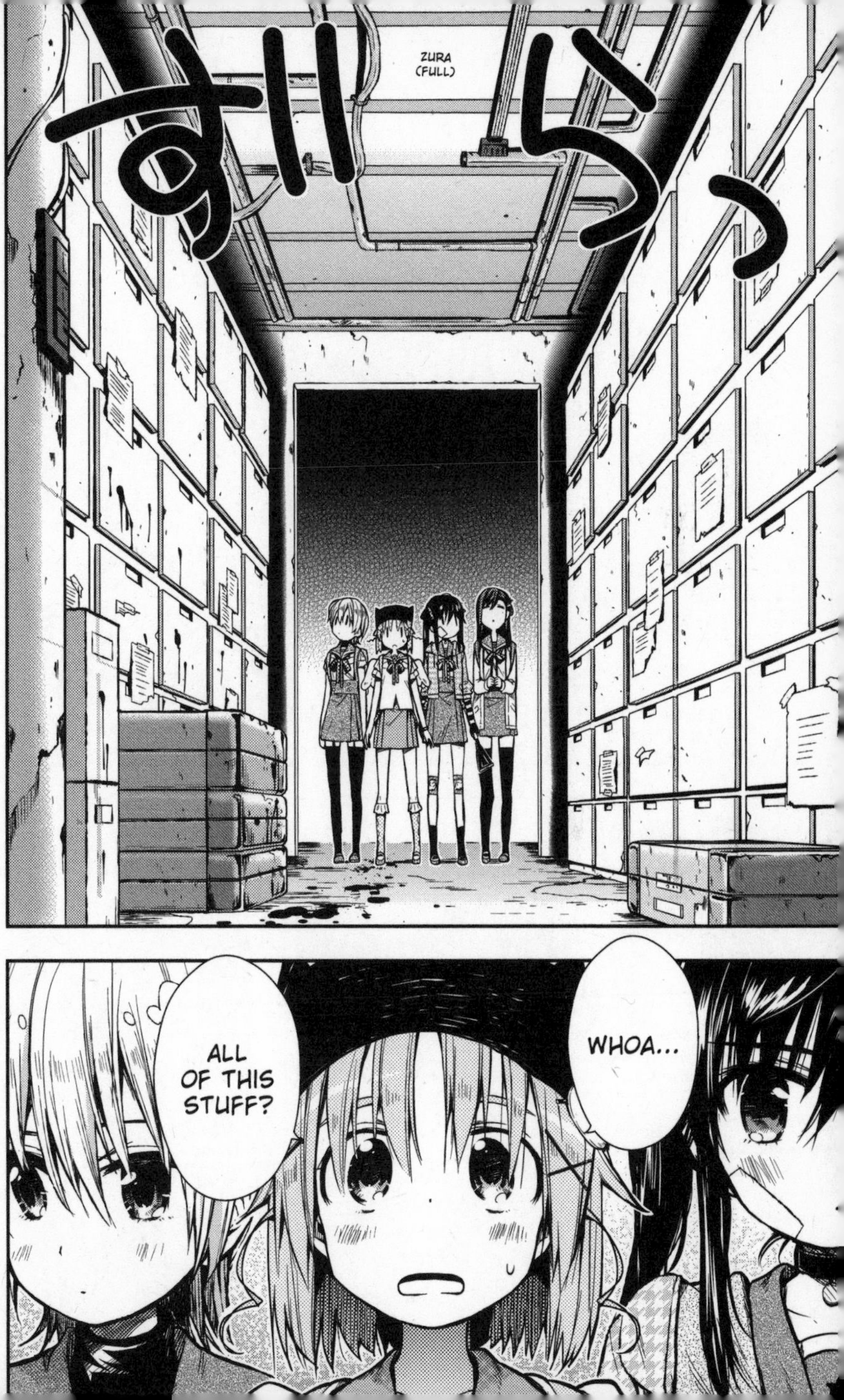
ずらっ
ZURA (FULL)
WHOA...
ALL OF THIS STUFF?

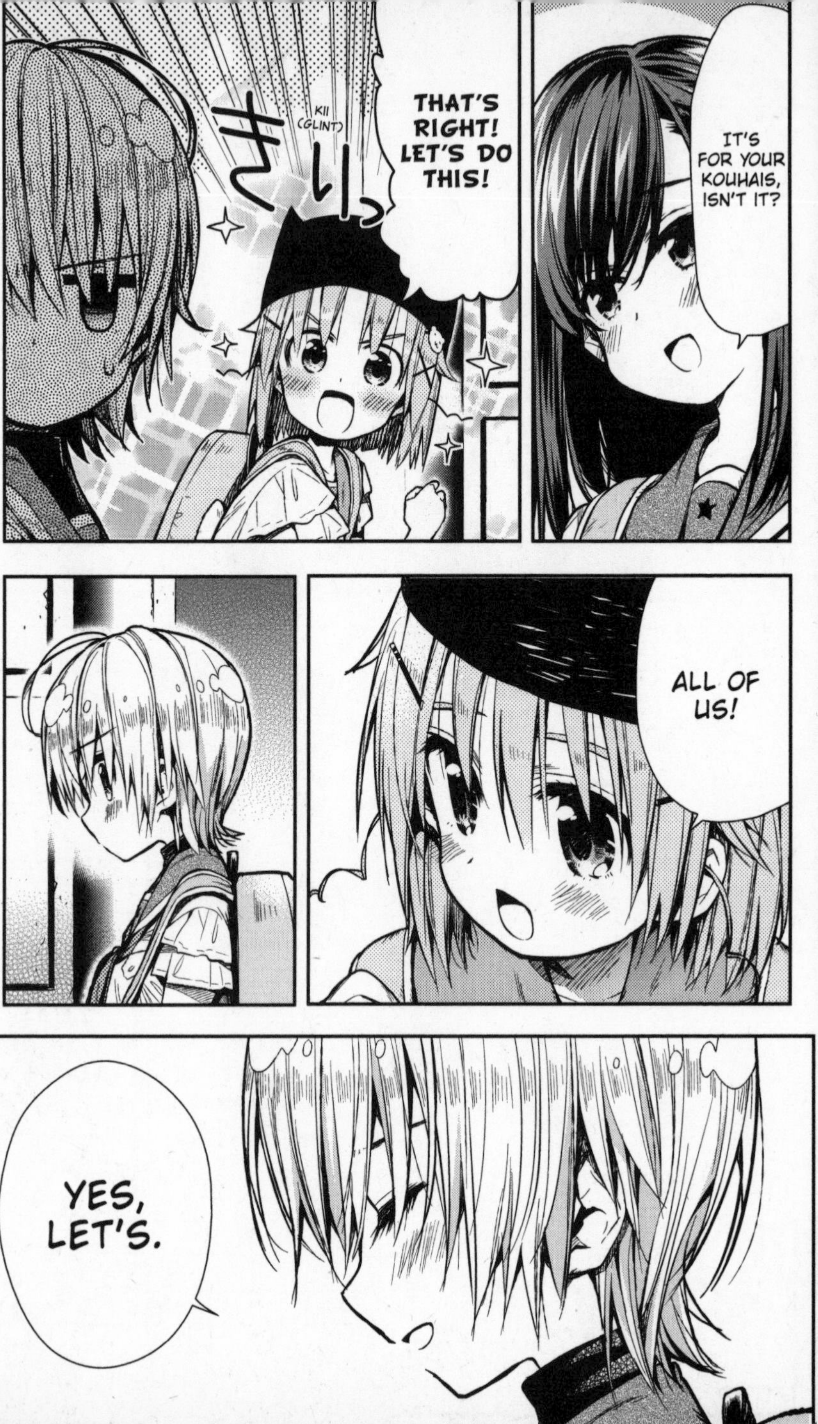
IT'S FOR YOUR KOUHAIS, ISN'T IT?
THAT'S RIGHT! LET'S DO THIS!
きいっ
KII (GLINT)
ALL OF US!
YES, LET'S.

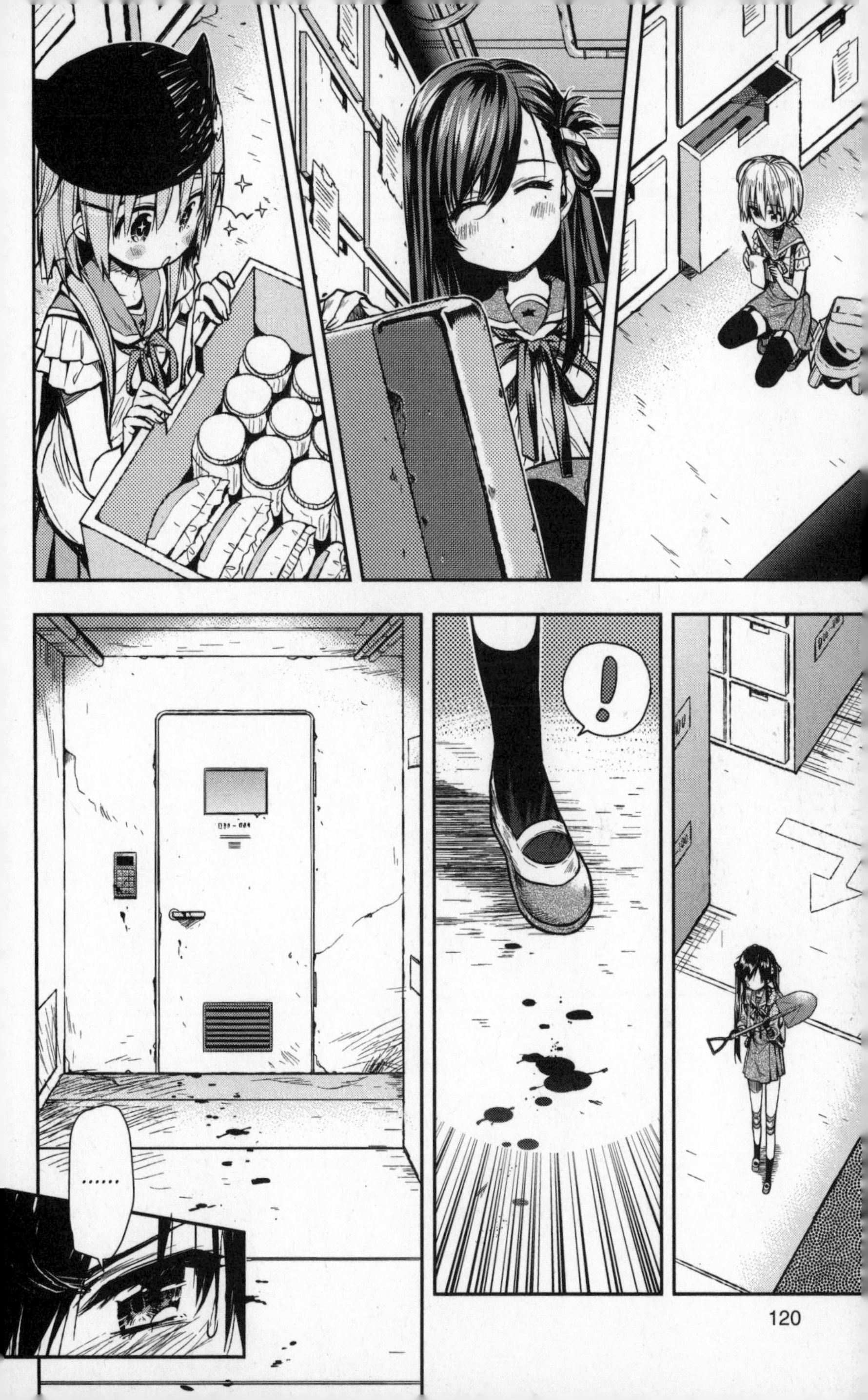
!
……

ギ
(GI)
(CREAK)

DID YOU FIND SOMETHING OVER THERE?

OH, NAH.

THERE'S NOTHING HERE.

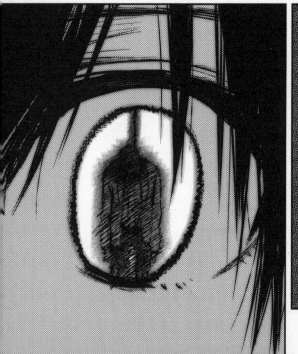

!

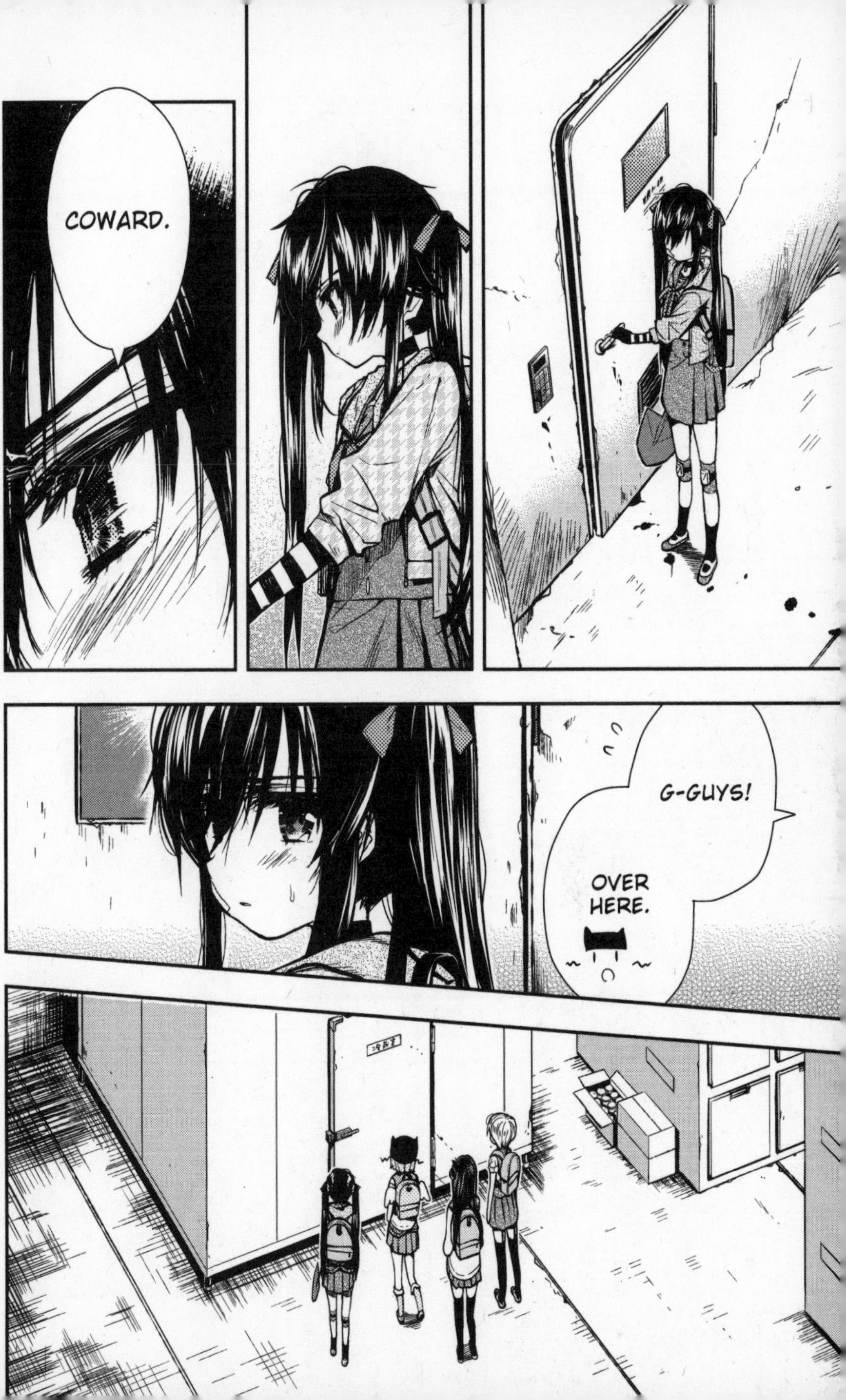
COWARD.
G-GUYS!
OVER HERE.

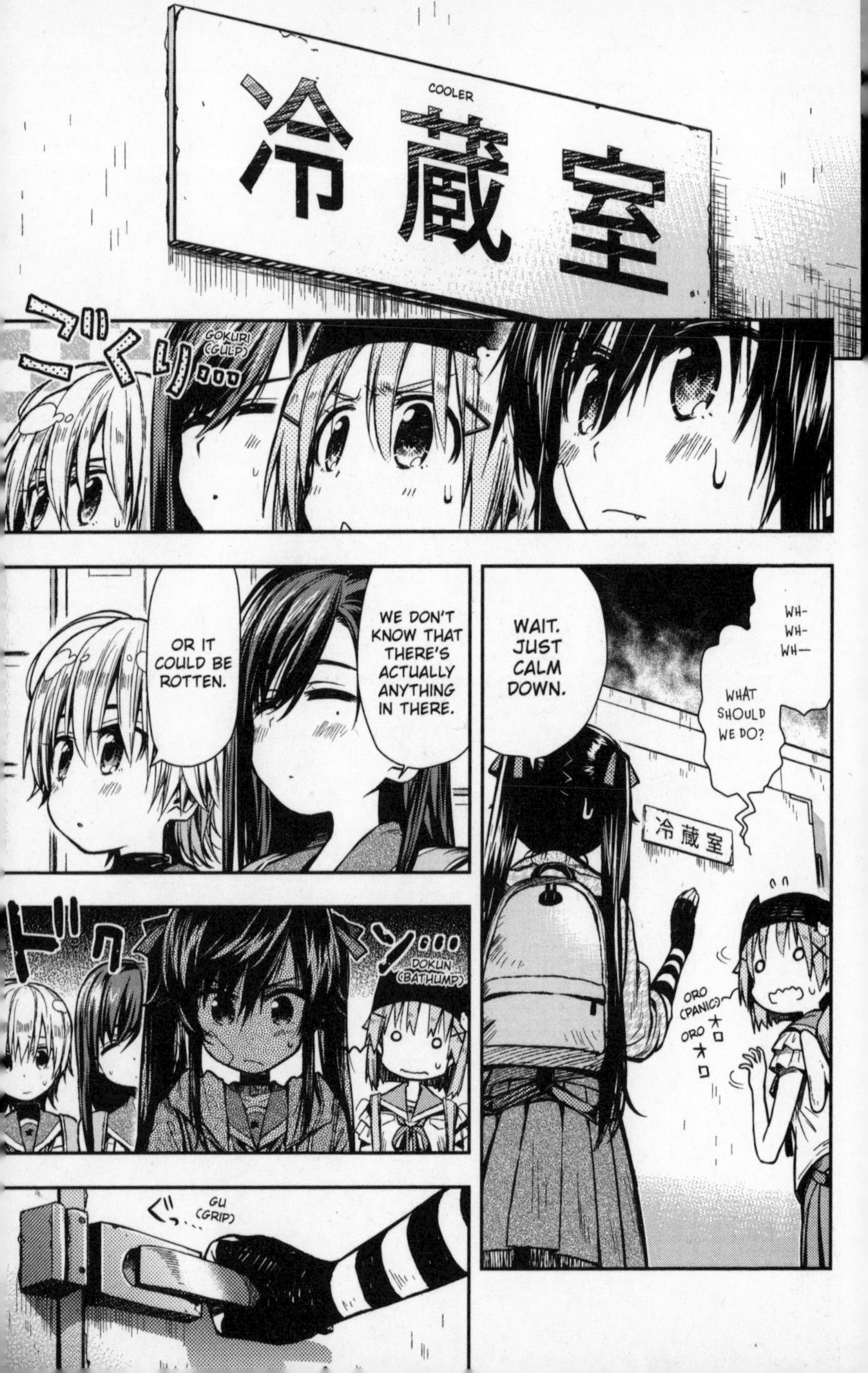
冷蔵室
COOLER
ゴクリ…
GOKURI (GULP)
WH- WH- WH—
WHAT SHOULD WE DO?
WAIT. JUST CALM DOWN.
冷蔵室
ORO (PANIC) ORO
オロオロ
WE DON'T KNOW THAT THERE'S ACTUALLY ANYTHING IN THERE.
OR IT COULD BE ROTTEN.
ドクン…
DOKUN (BATHUMP)
ぐっ…
GU (GRIP)

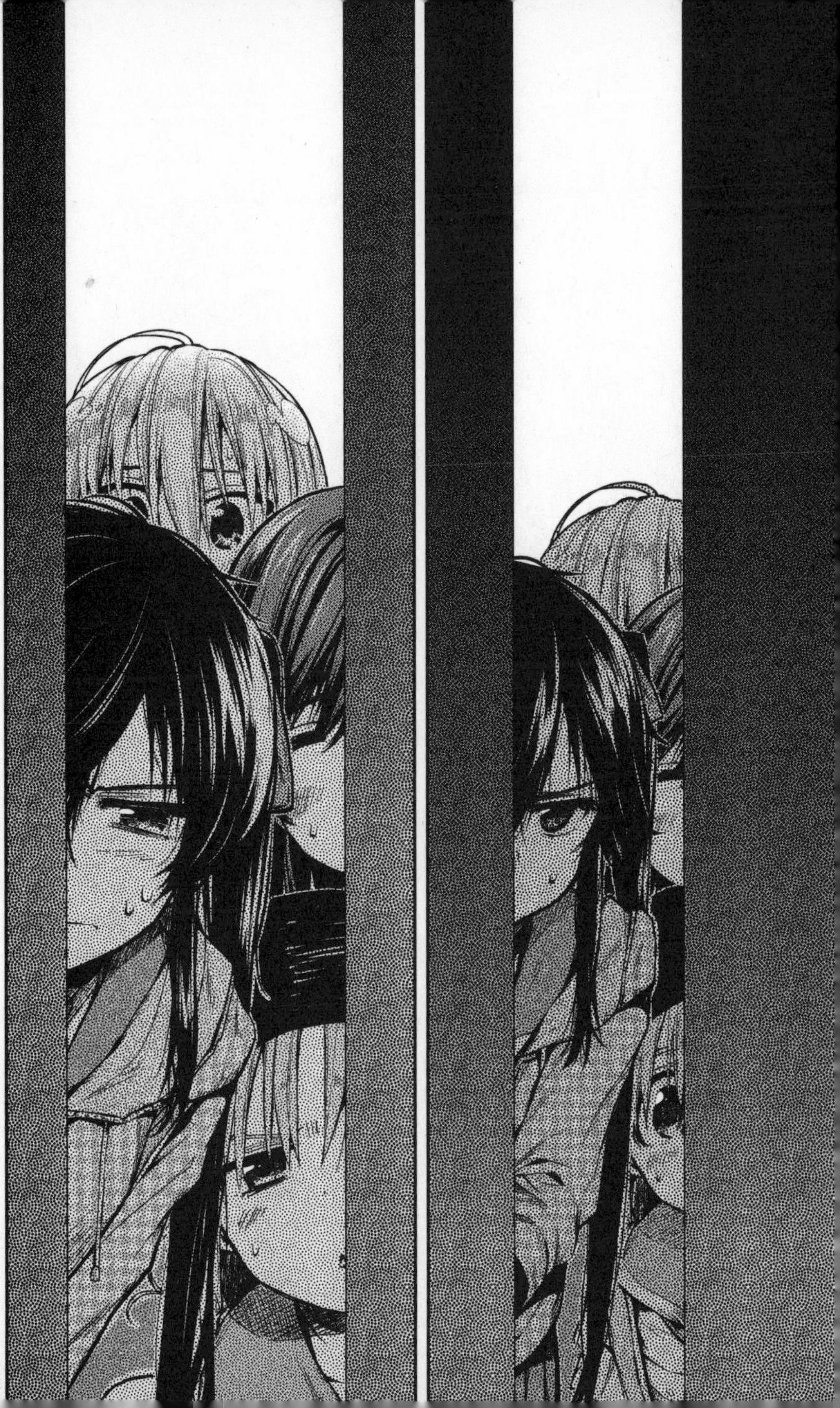

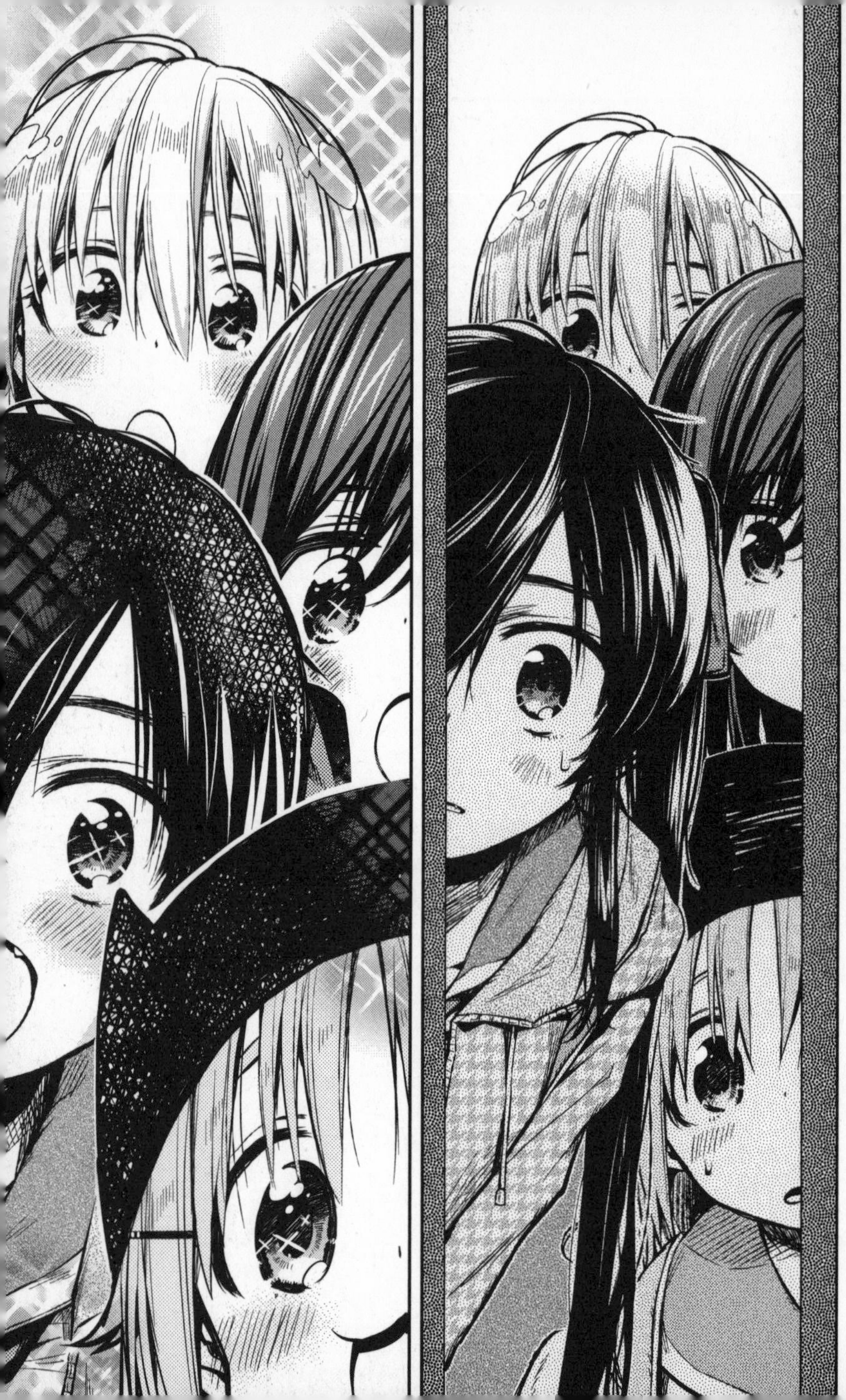

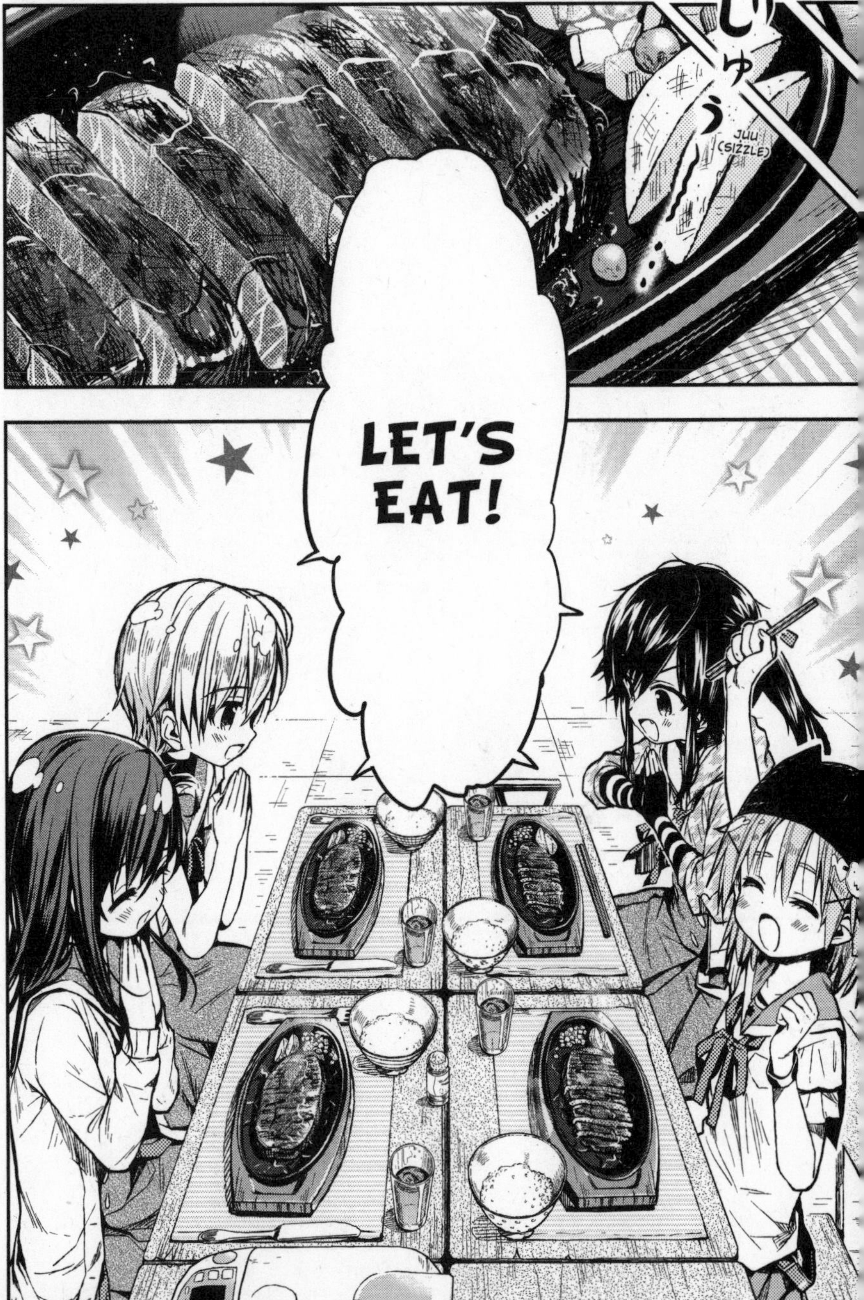
じゅう
JUU (SIZZLE)
LET'S EAT!

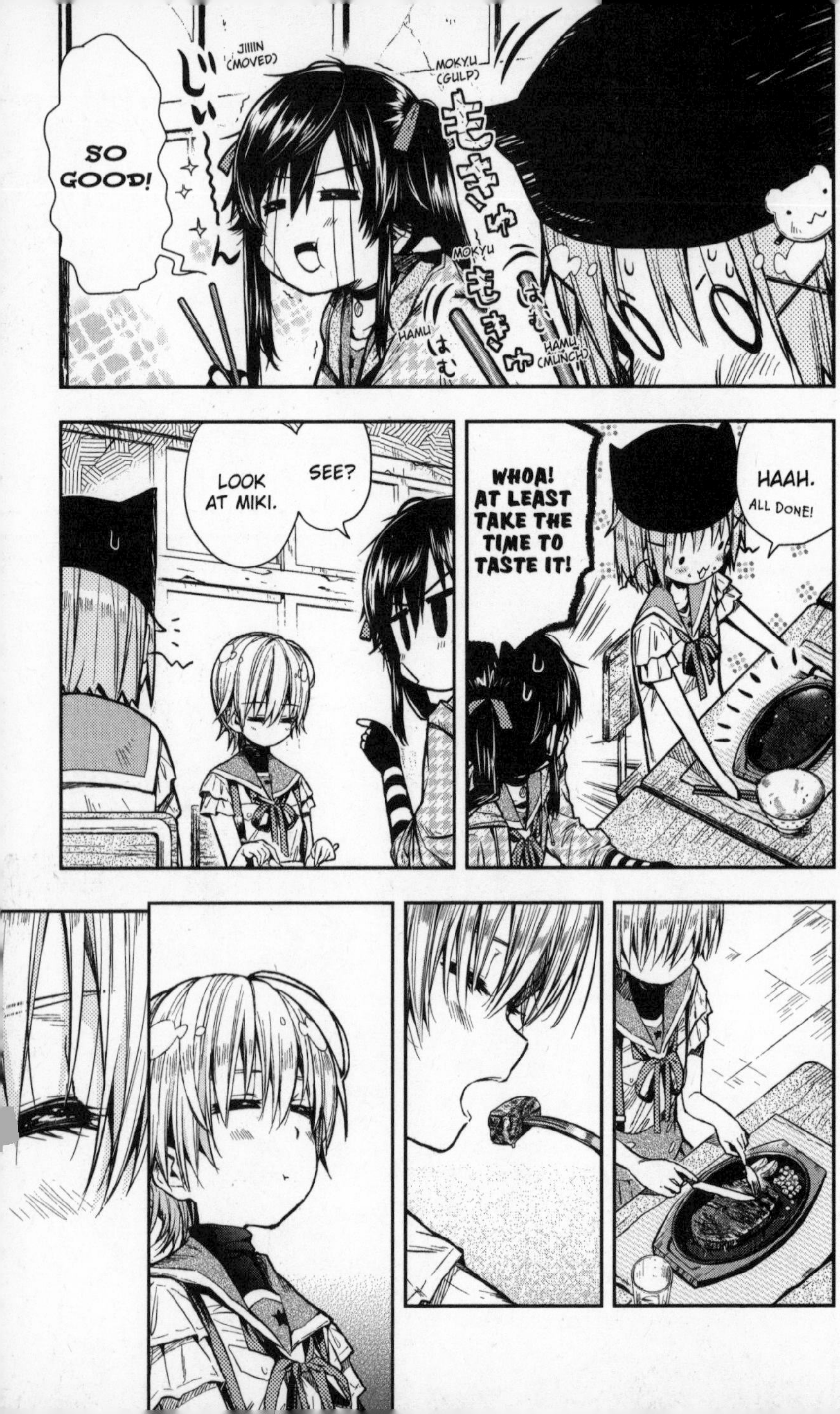
MOKYU (GULP)
もきゅ
MOKYU
もきゅ
HAMU (MUNCH)
はむ
HAMU
はむ
JIIIN (MOVED)
じぃ～ん
SO GOOD!
HAAH. ALL DONE!
WHOA! AT LEAST TAKE THE TIME TO TASTE IT!
SEE?
LOOK AT MIKI.

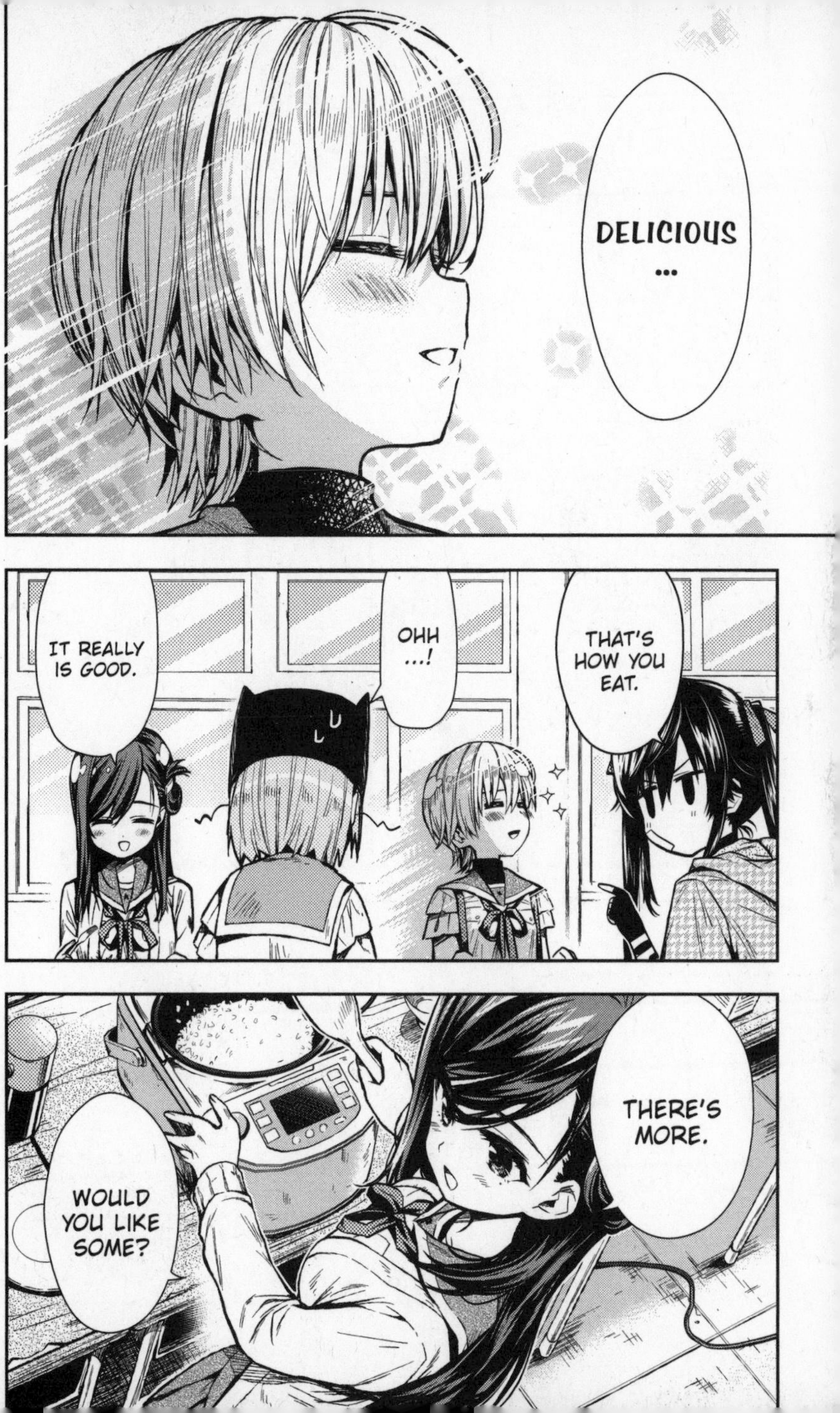
DELICIOUS
...
THAT'S HOW YOU EAT.
OHH ...!
IT REALLY IS GOOD.
THERE'S MORE.
WOULD YOU LIKE SOME?

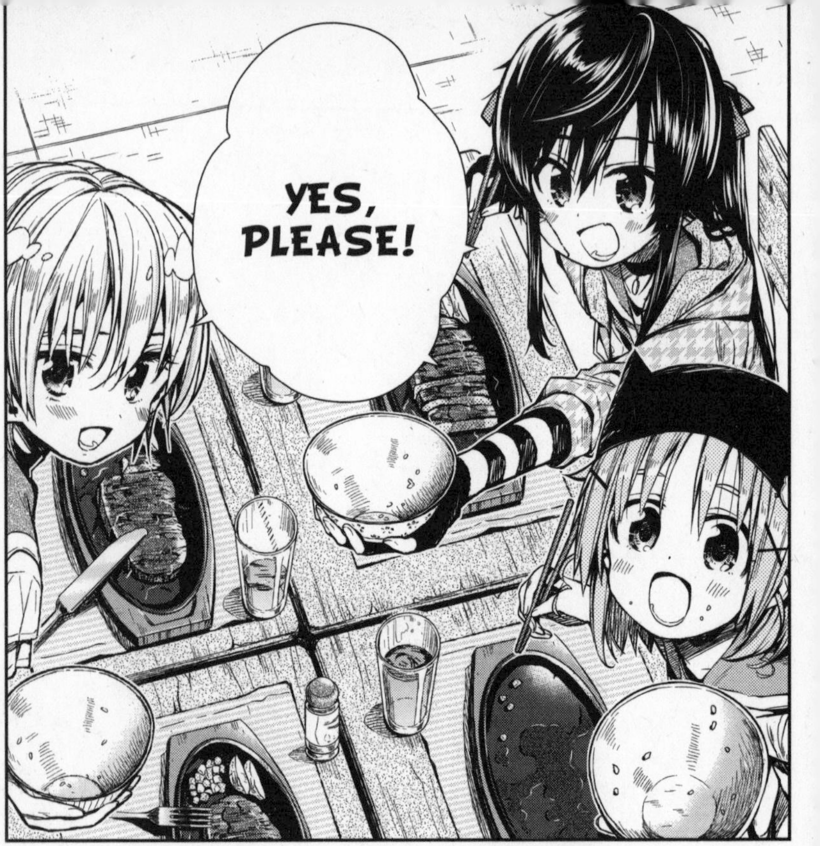
YES, PLEASE!

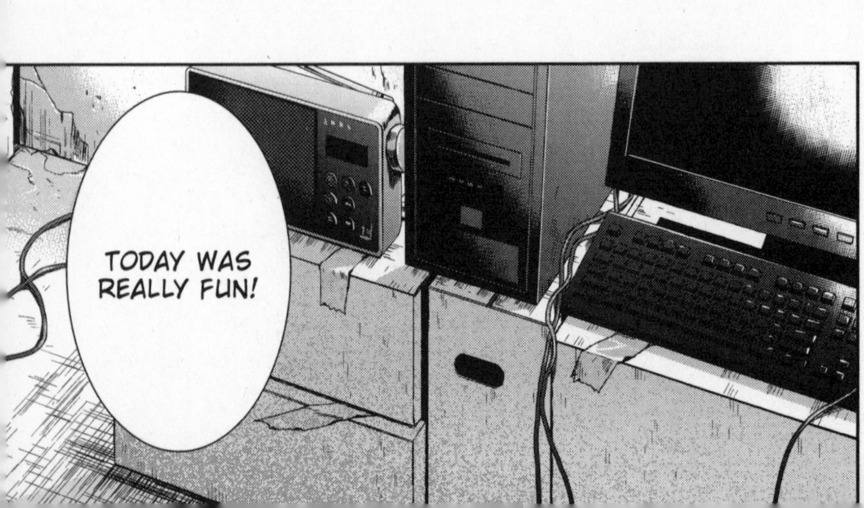
TODAY WAS REALLY FUN!

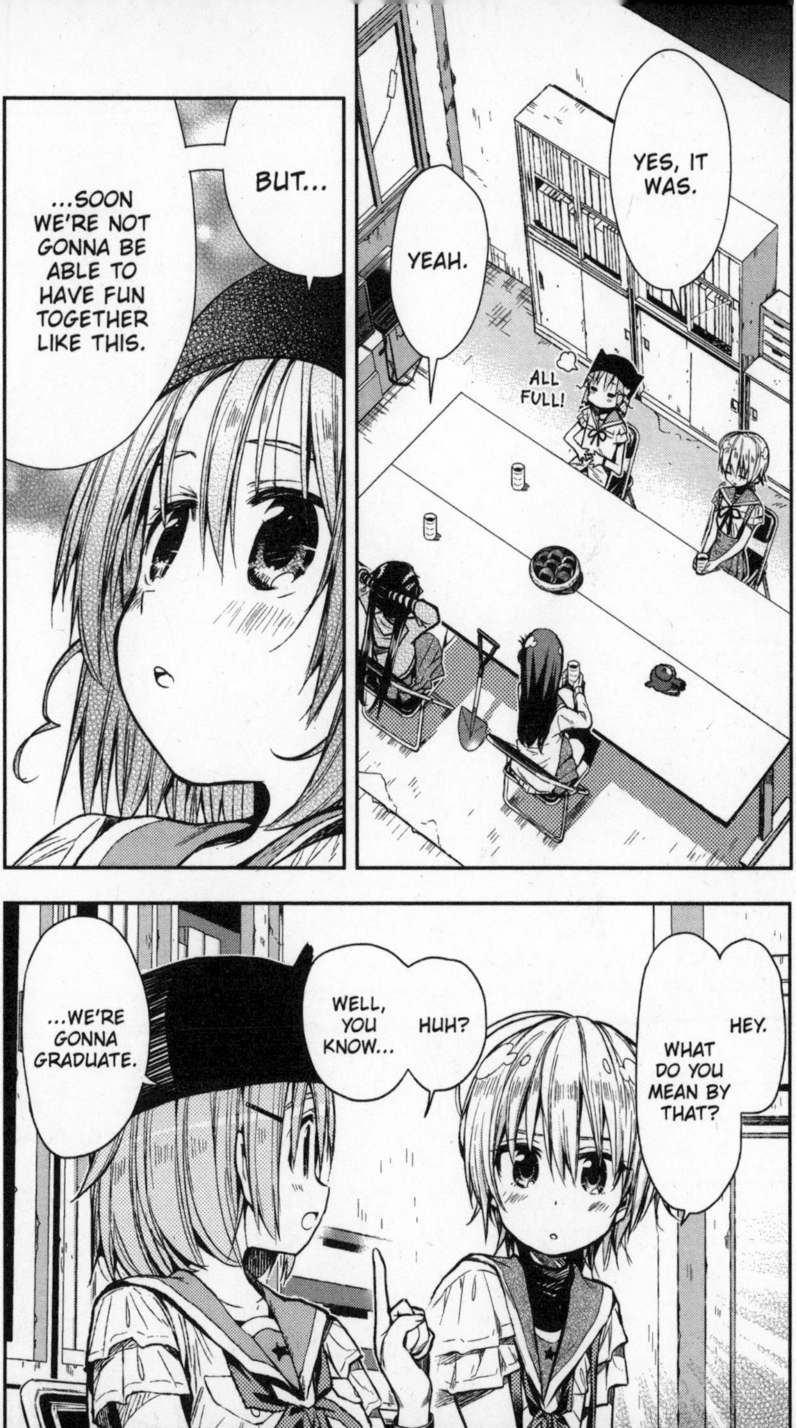
YES, IT WAS.
YEAH.
ALL FULL!
BUT...
...SOON WE'RE NOT GONNA BE ABLE TO HAVE FUN TOGETHER LIKE THIS.
HEY.
WHAT DO YOU MEAN BY THAT?
HUH?
WELL, YOU KNOW...
...WE'RE GONNA GRADUATE.

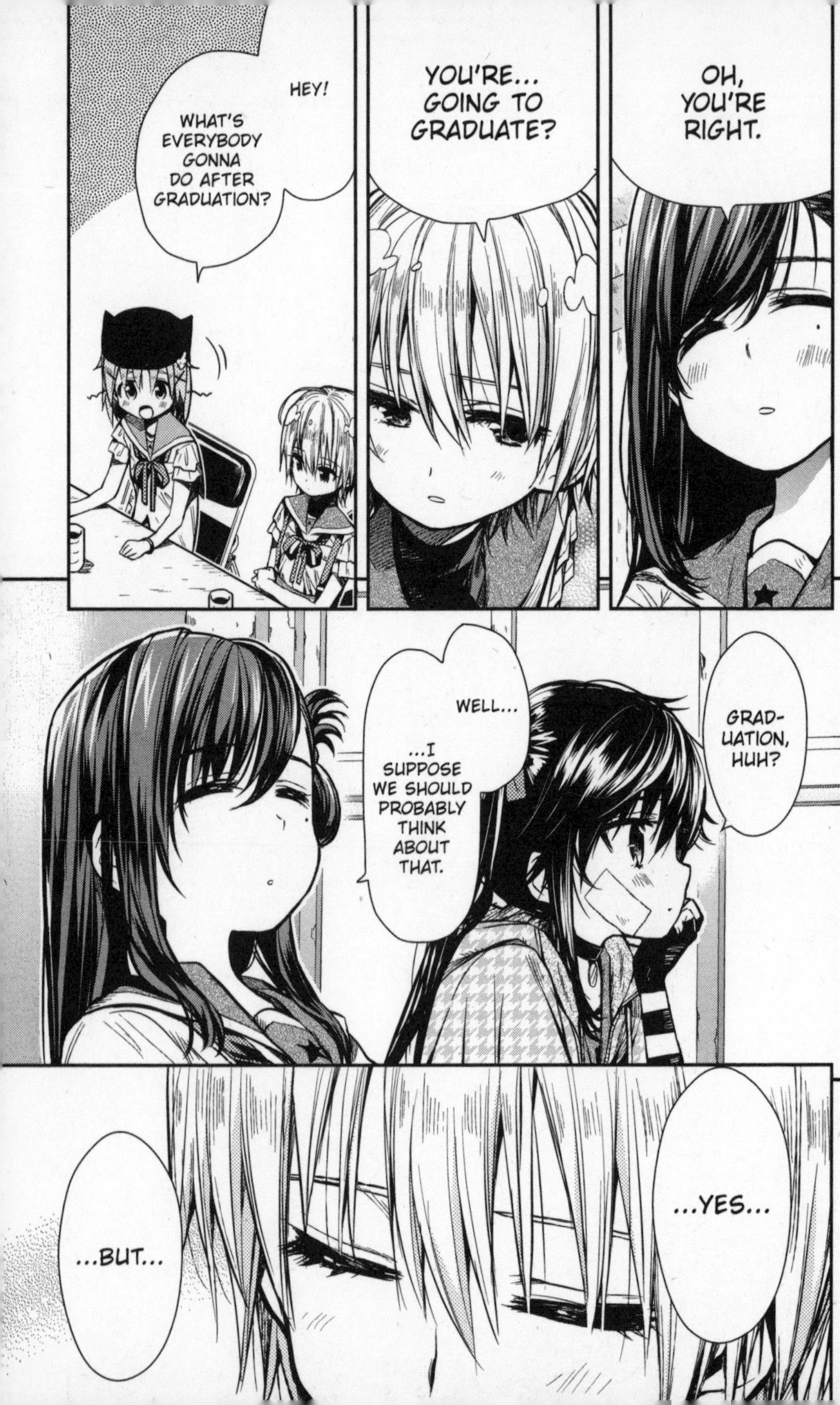
OH, YOU'RE RIGHT.
YOU'RE... GOING TO GRADUATE?
HEY!
WHAT'S EVERYBODY GONNA DO AFTER GRADUATION?
GRAD-UATION, HUH?
WELL...
...I SUPPOSE WE SHOULD PROBABLY THINK ABOUT THAT.
...YES...
...BUT...

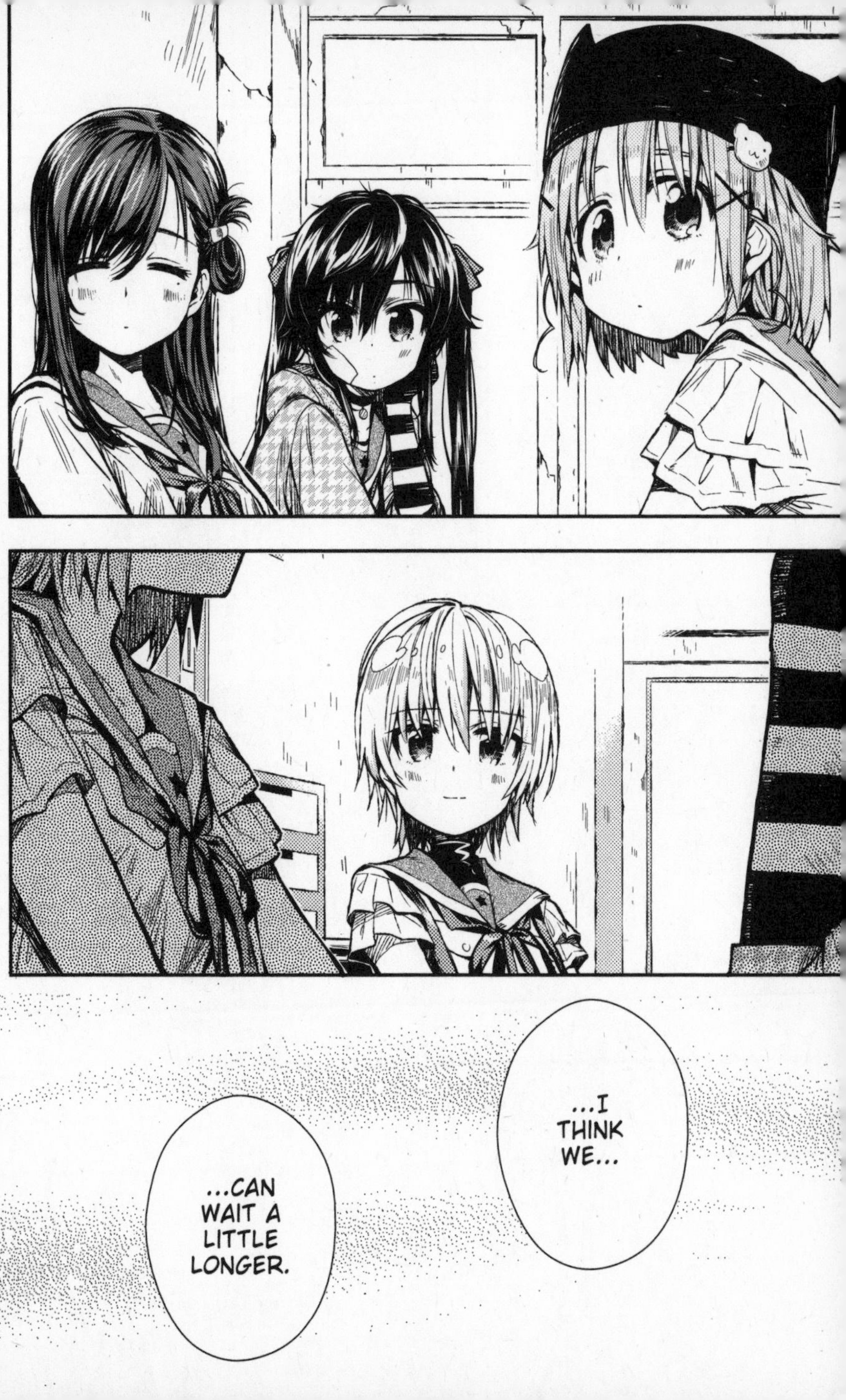
...I THINK WE...
...CAN WAIT A LITTLE LONGER.

SCHOOL-LIVE!

LABEL: FIELD DISCOVERIES

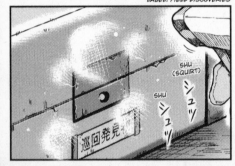

SHU
(SQUIRT)

SHU
シュッ

シュッ

巡回発見

SHUKOO
(THUNK)

シュコー……

シュコー……

SHUKOO

GACHA
(KACHAK)

ガッチャ…

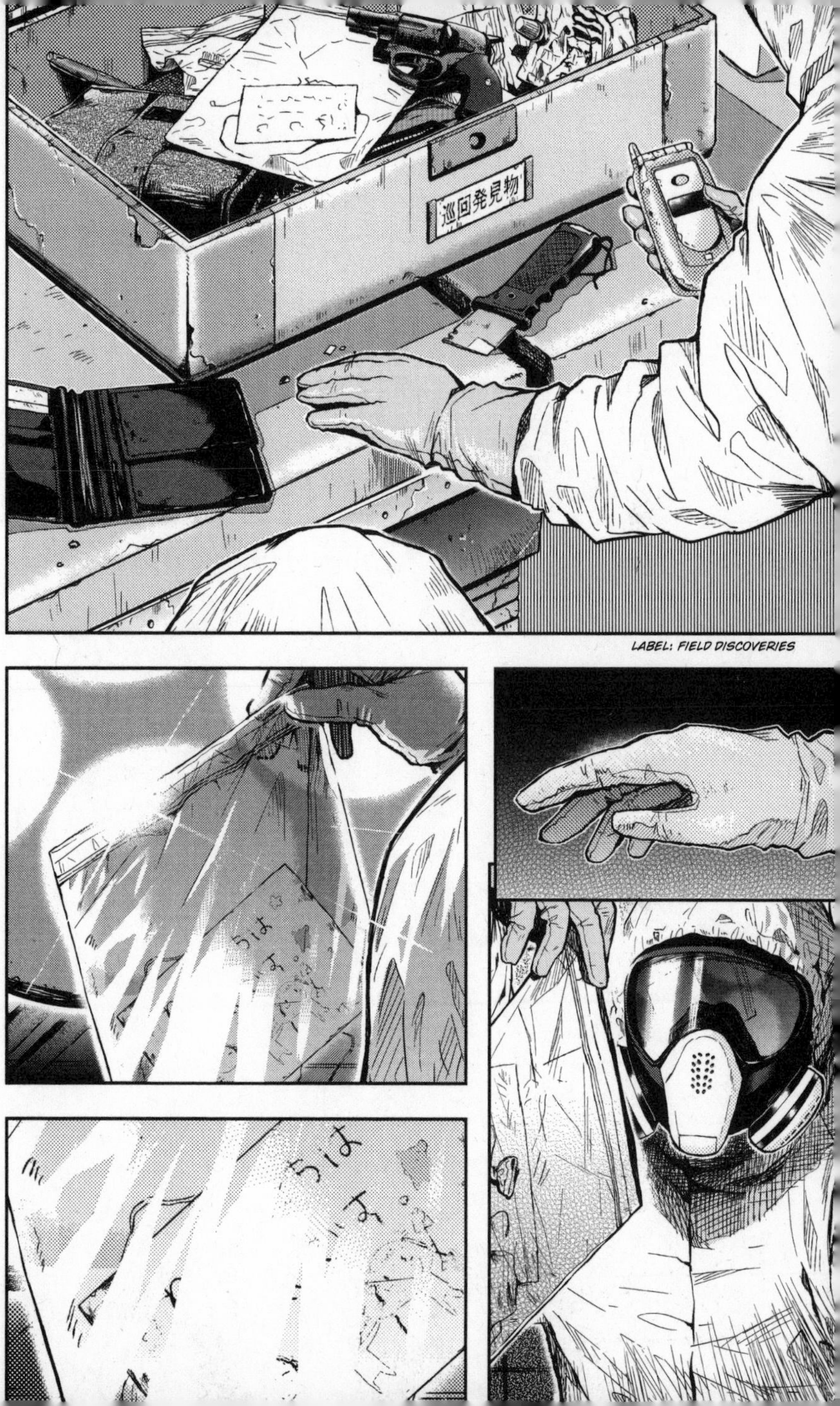
巡回発見物
LABEL: FIELD DISCOVERIES

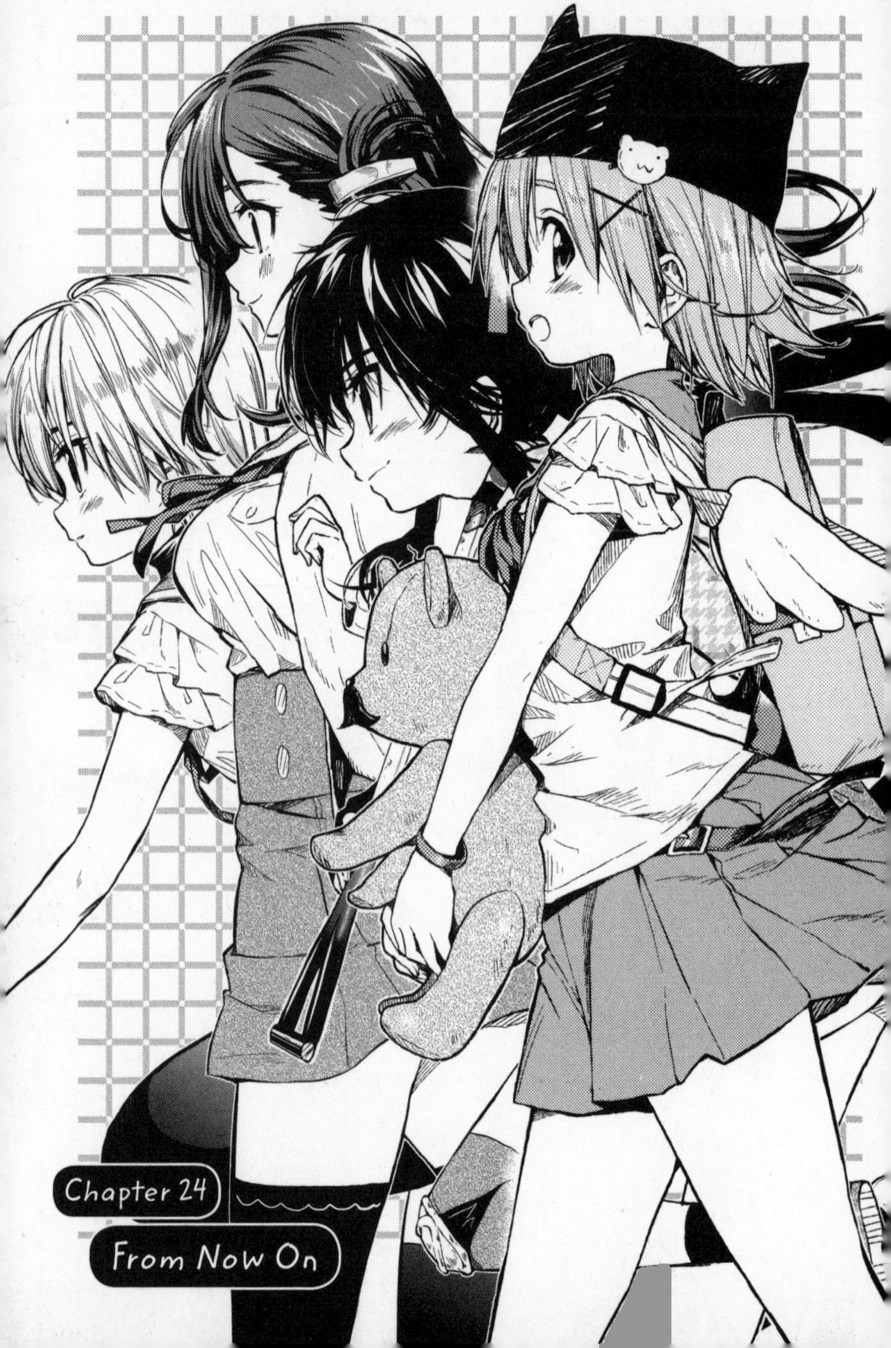
Chapter 24
From Now On

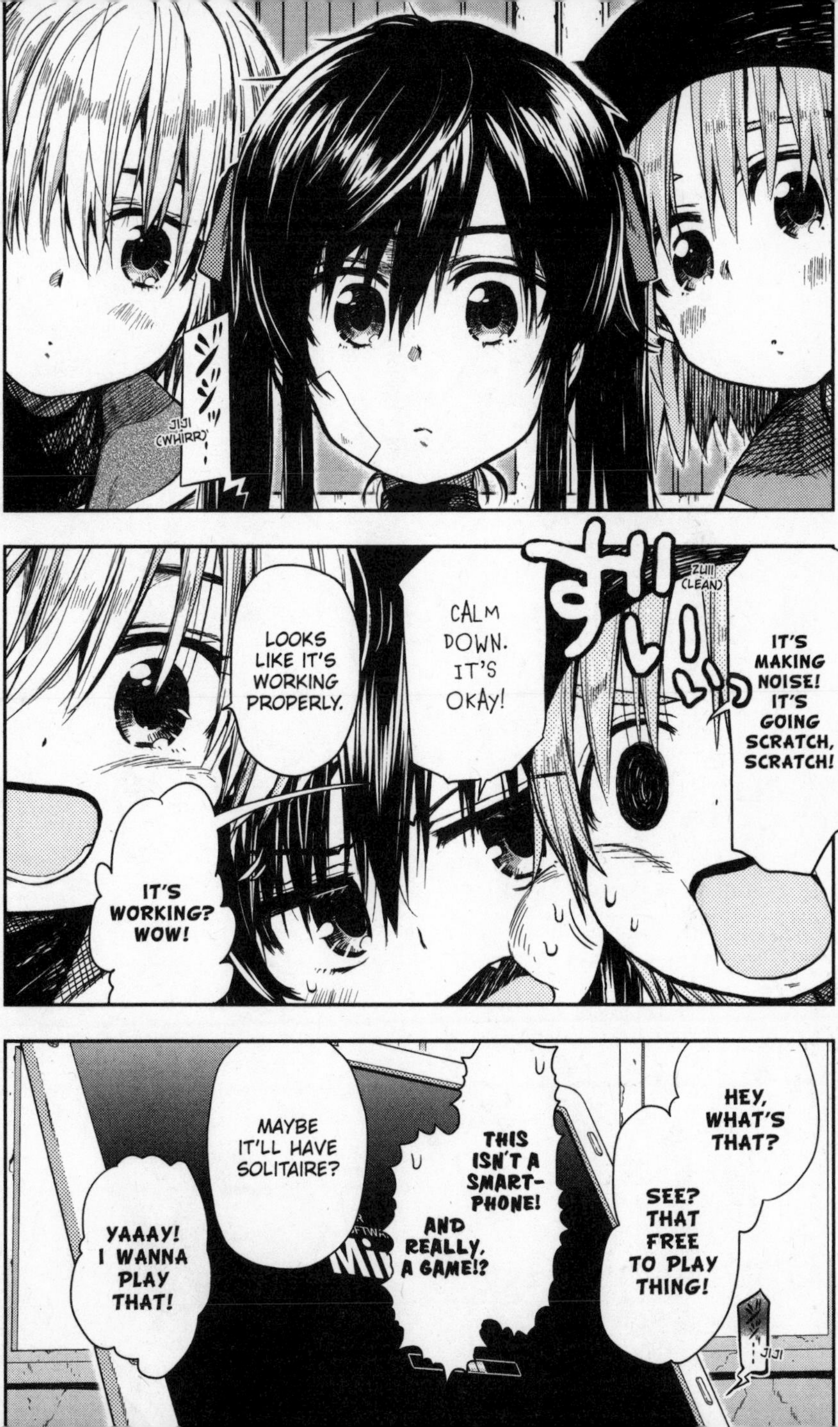
JIJI (WHIRR)
ZUIII (CLEAN)
IT'S MAKING NOISE! IT'S GOING SCRATCH, SCRATCH!
CALM DOWN. IT'S OKAY!
LOOKS LIKE IT'S WORKING PROPERLY.
IT'S WORKING? WOW!
HEY, WHAT'S THAT?
SEE? THAT FREE TO PLAY THING!
JIJI
THIS ISN'T A SMARTPHONE!
AND REALLY, A GAME!?
MAYBE IT'LL HAVE SOLITAIRE?
YAAAY! I WANNA PLAY THAT!

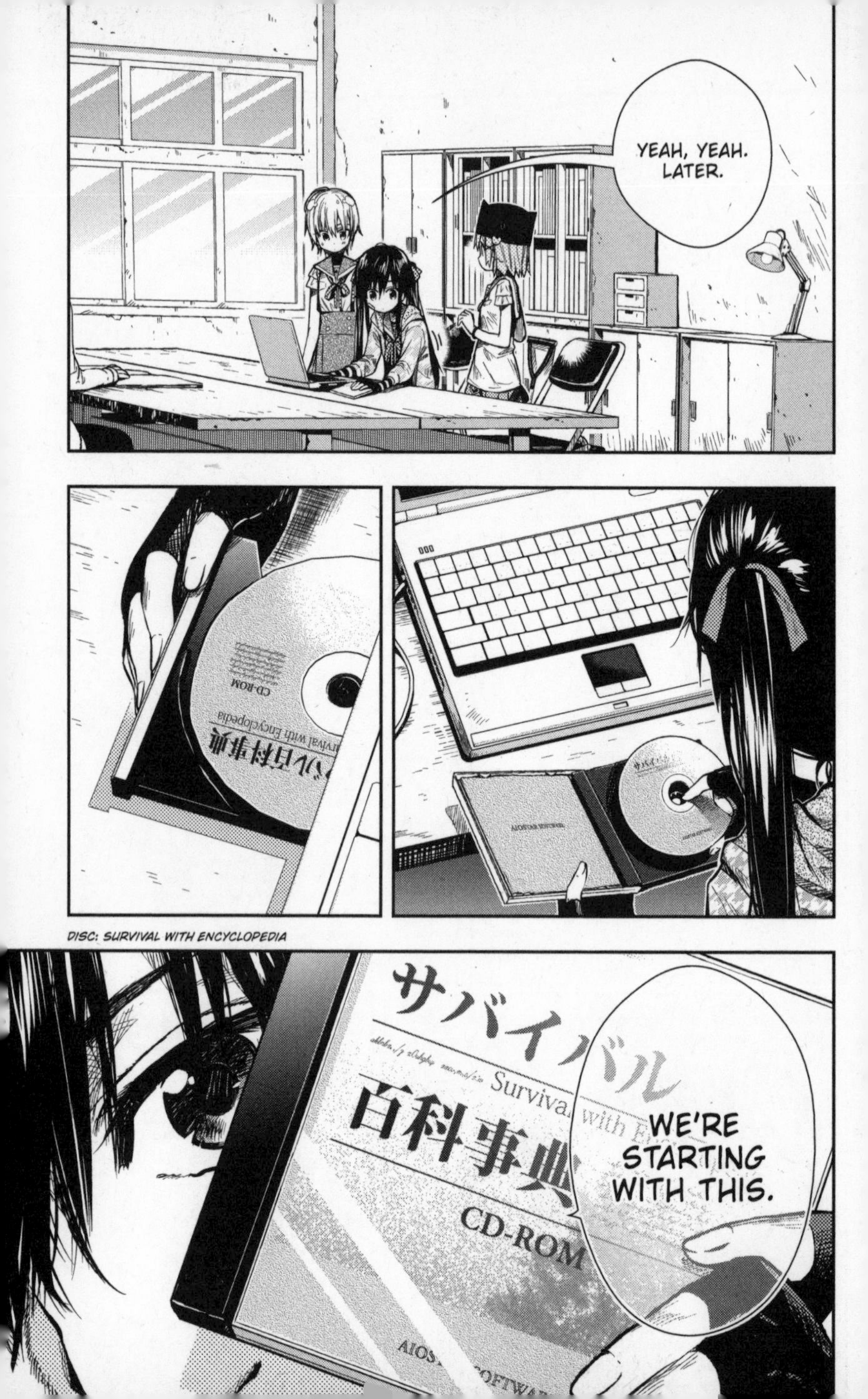
YEAH, YEAH. LATER.
CD-ROM
Survival with Encyclopedia
DISC: SURVIVAL WITH ENCYCLOPEDIA
サバイバル
百科事典
CD-ROM
WE'RE STARTING WITH THIS.

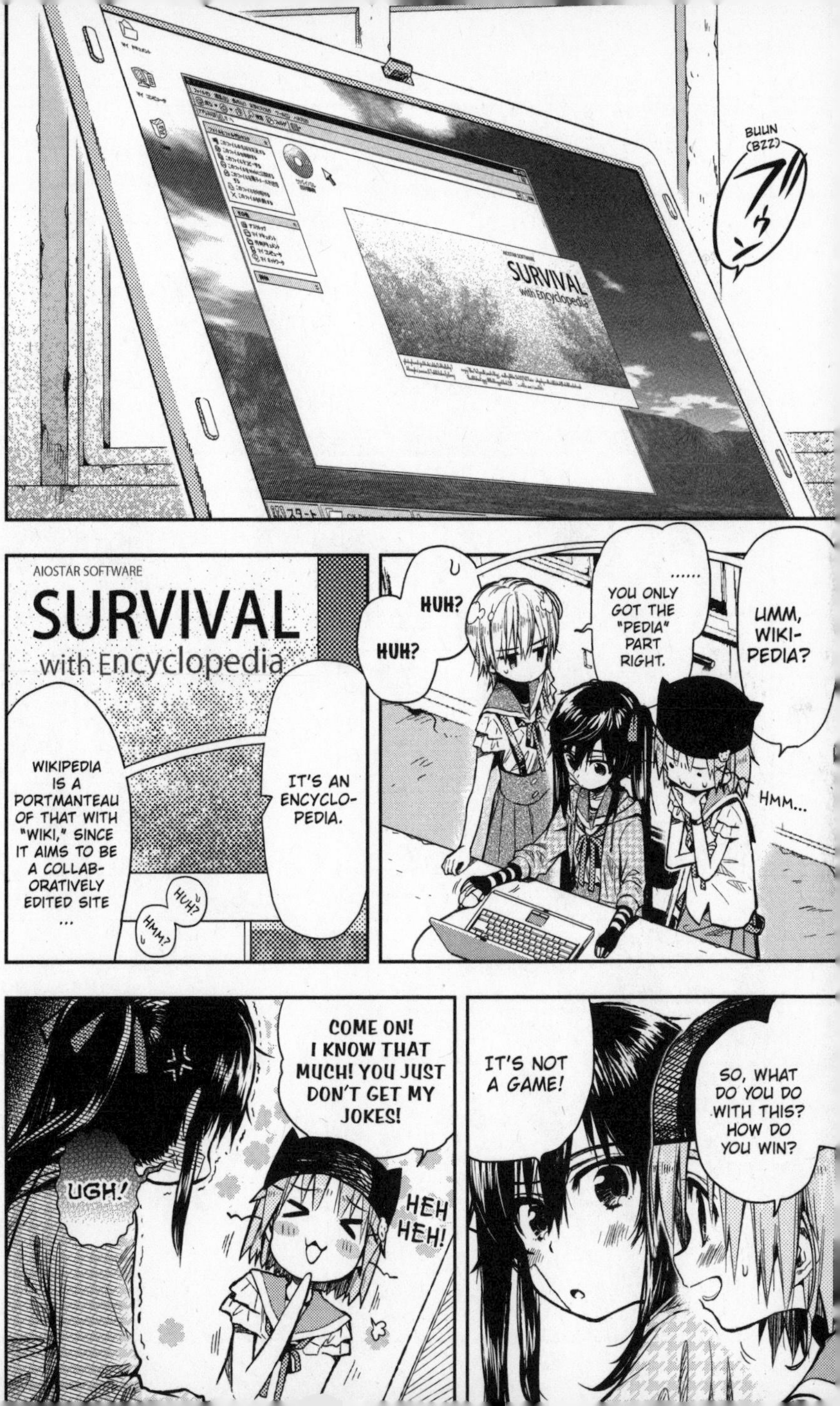
BUUN (BZZ)
AIOSTAR SOFTWARE
SURVIVAL
with Encyclopedia
UMM, WIKI-PEDIA?
...... YOU ONLY GOT THE "PEDIA" PART RIGHT.
HUH?
HUH?
HMM...
AIOSTAR SOFTWARE
SURVIVAL
with Encyclopedia
IT'S AN ENCYCLO-PEDIA.
WIKIPEDIA IS A PORTMANTEAU OF THAT WITH "WIKI," SINCE IT AIMS TO BE A COLLAB-ORATIVELY EDITED SITE ...
HUH?
HMM?
SO, WHAT DO YOU DO WITH THIS? HOW DO YOU WIN?
IT'S NOT A GAME!
COME ON! I KNOW THAT MUCH! YOU JUST DON'T GET MY JOKES!
HEH HEH!
UGH!

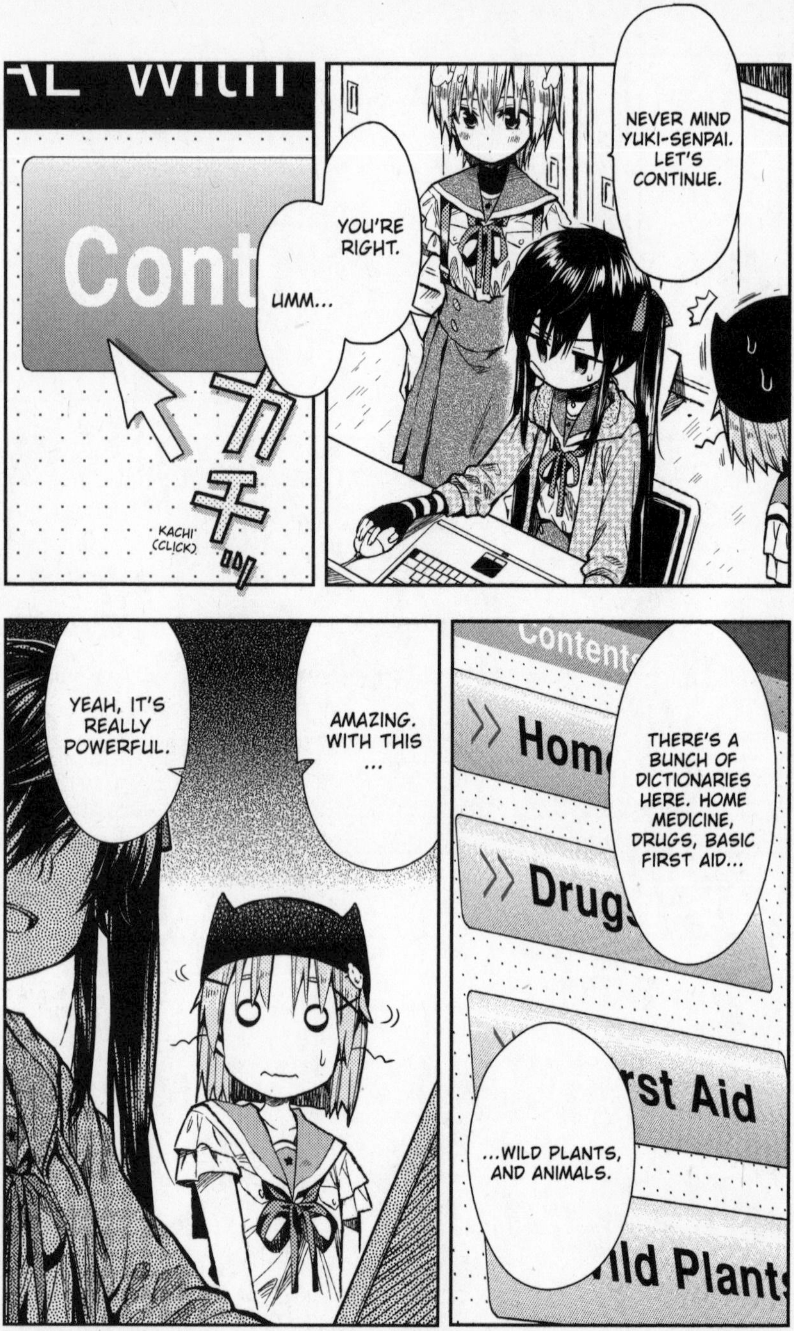
NEVER MIND YUKI-SENPAI. LET'S CONTINUE.
YOU'RE RIGHT.
UMM...
KACHI' (CLICK)
THERE'S A BUNCH OF DICTIONARIES HERE. HOME MEDICINE, DRUGS, BASIC FIRST AID...
...WILD PLANTS, AND ANIMALS.
AMAZING. WITH THIS ...
YEAH, IT'S REALLY POWERFUL.

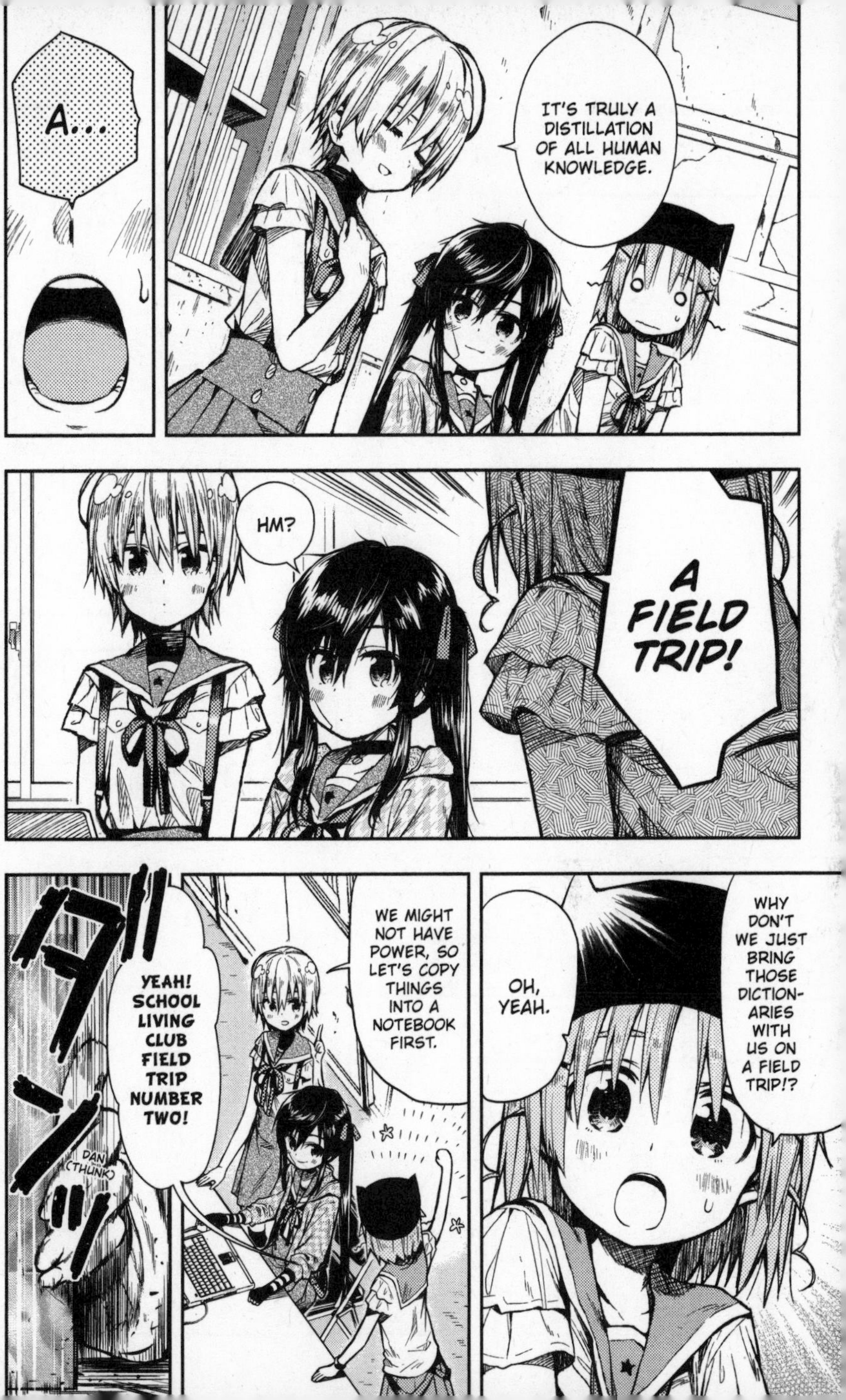
IT'S TRULY A DISTILLATION OF ALL HUMAN KNOWLEDGE.
A...
A FIELD TRIP!
HM?
WHY DON'T WE JUST BRING THOSE DICTIONARIES WITH US ON A FIELD TRIP!?
OH, YEAH.
WE MIGHT NOT HAVE POWER, SO LET'S COPY THINGS INTO A NOTEBOOK FIRST.
YEAH! SCHOOL LIVING CLUB FIELD TRIP NUMBER TWO!
DAN (THUNK)

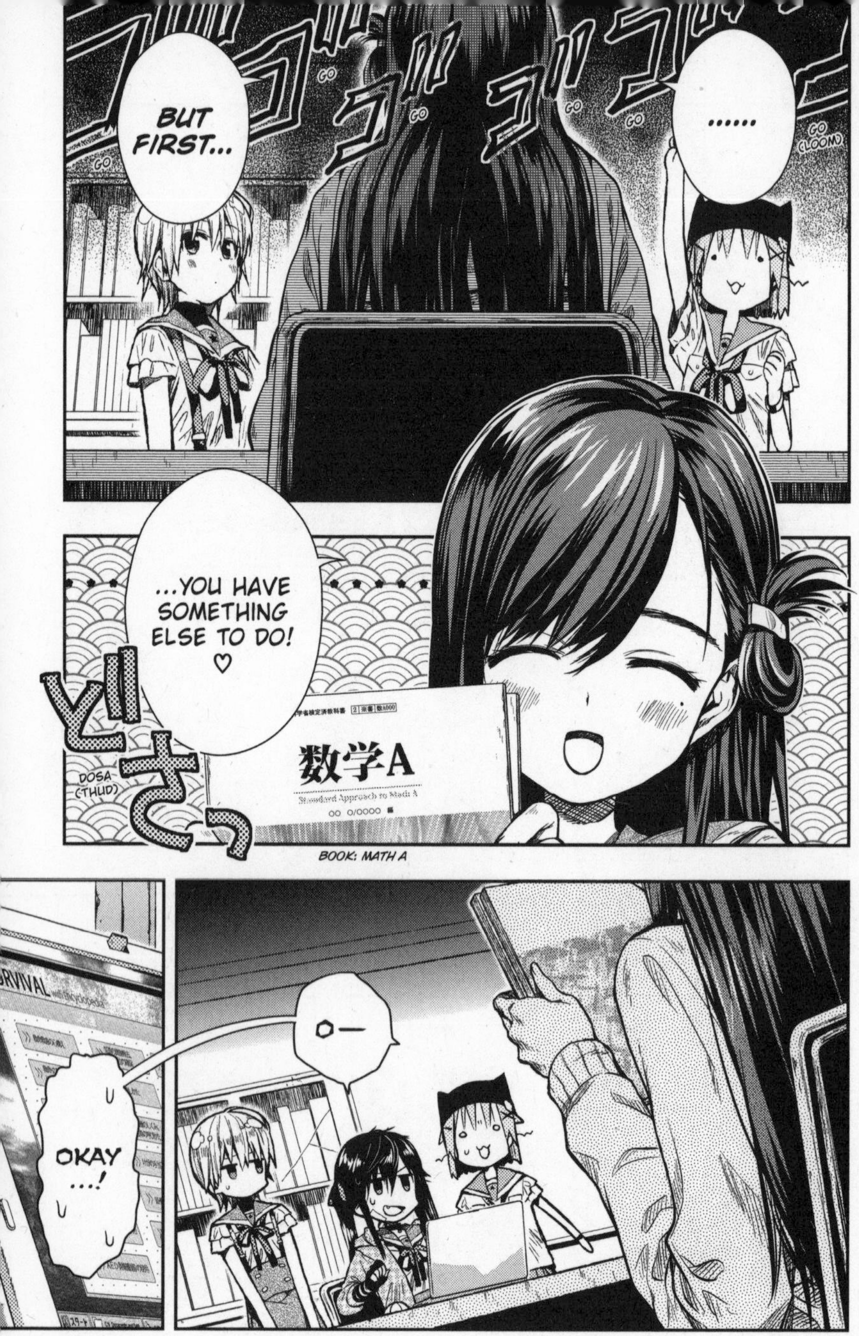
......
GO GO GO GO GO GO (LOOM)
BUT FIRST...
...YOU HAVE SOMETHING ELSE TO DO! ♡
数学A
Standard Approach to Math A
DOSA (THUD)
BOOK: MATH A
O—
OKAY...!

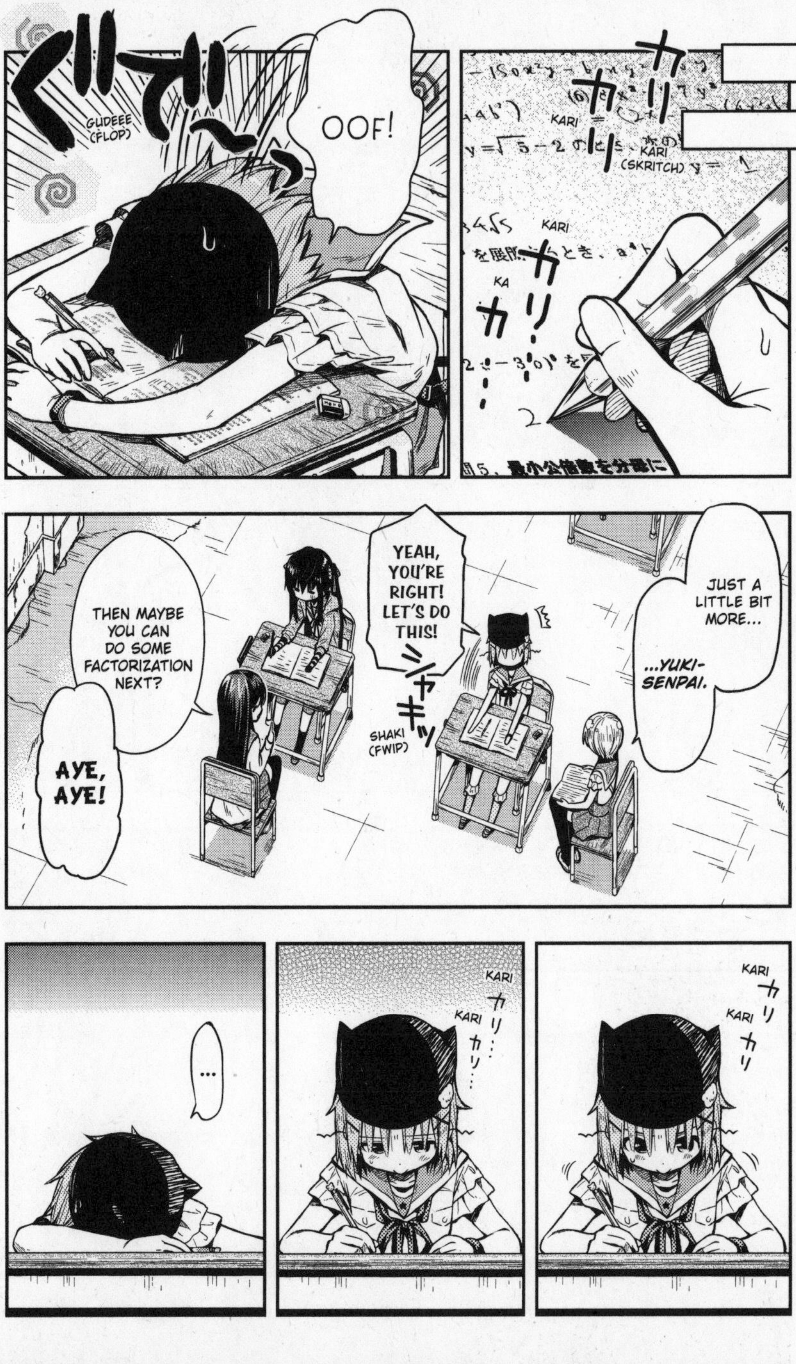
カリカリ
KARI
KARI
(SKRITCH)
KARI
カリ
KA
カ
ぐでーっ
GUDEEE
(FLOP)
OOF!
JUST A LITTLE BIT MORE...
...YUKI-SENPAI.
YEAH, YOU'RE RIGHT! LET'S DO THIS!
シャキッ
SHAKI
(FWIP)
THEN MAYBE YOU CAN DO SOME FACTORIZATION NEXT?
AYE, AYE!
KARI
カリ
KARI
カリ
KARI
カリ…
KARI
カリ…
...

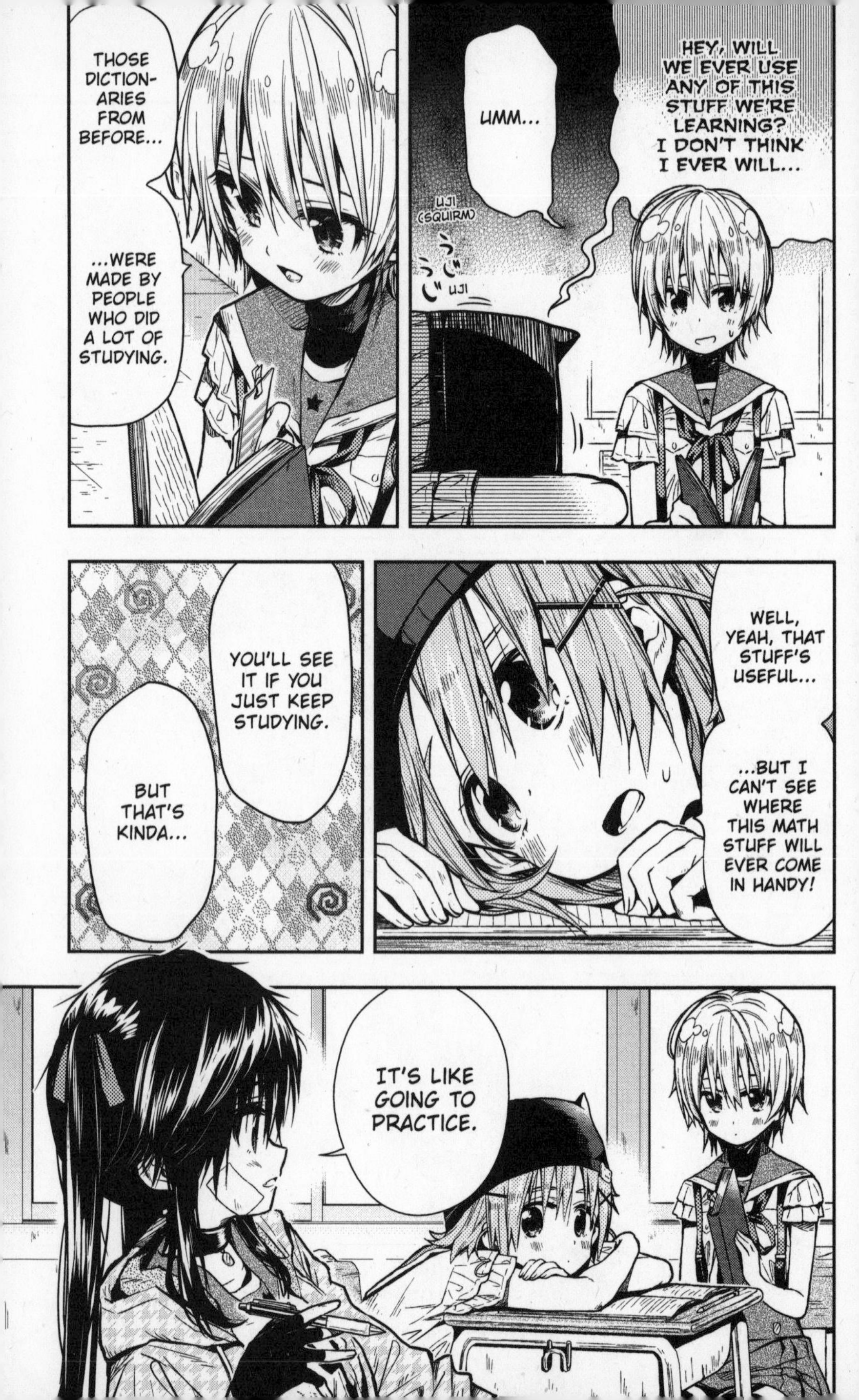
HEY, WILL WE EVER USE ANY OF THIS STUFF WE'RE LEARNING? I DON'T THINK I EVER WILL...
UMM...
UJI (SQUIRM)
UJI
THOSE DICTION-ARIES FROM BEFORE...
...WERE MADE BY PEOPLE WHO DID A LOT OF STUDYING.
WELL, YEAH, THAT STUFF'S USEFUL...
...BUT I CAN'T SEE WHERE THIS MATH STUFF WILL EVER COME IN HANDY!
YOU'LL SEE IT IF YOU JUST KEEP STUDYING.
BUT THAT'S KINDA...
IT'S LIKE GOING TO PRACTICE.

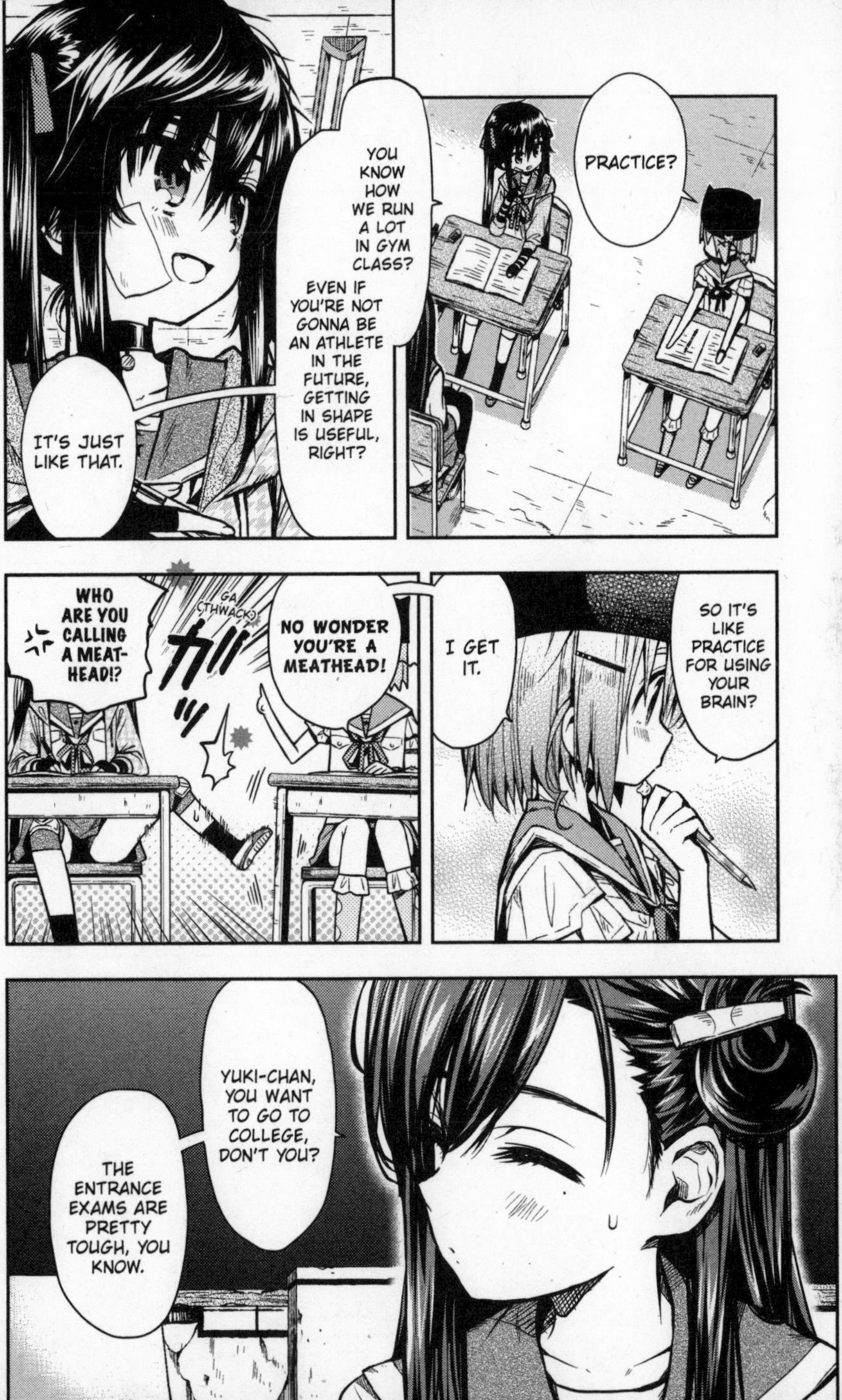
PRACTICE?
YOU KNOW HOW WE RUN A LOT IN GYM CLASS?
EVEN IF YOU'RE NOT GONNA BE AN ATHLETE IN THE FUTURE, GETTING IN SHAPE IS USEFUL, RIGHT?
IT'S JUST LIKE THAT.
SO IT'S LIKE PRACTICE FOR USING YOUR BRAIN?
I GET IT.
NO WONDER YOU'RE A MEATHEAD!
ガッ
GA (THWACK)
WHO ARE YOU CALLING A MEAT-HEAD!?
YUKI-CHAN, YOU WANT TO GO TO COLLEGE, DON'T YOU?
THE ENTRANCE EXAMS ARE PRETTY TOUGH, YOU KNOW.

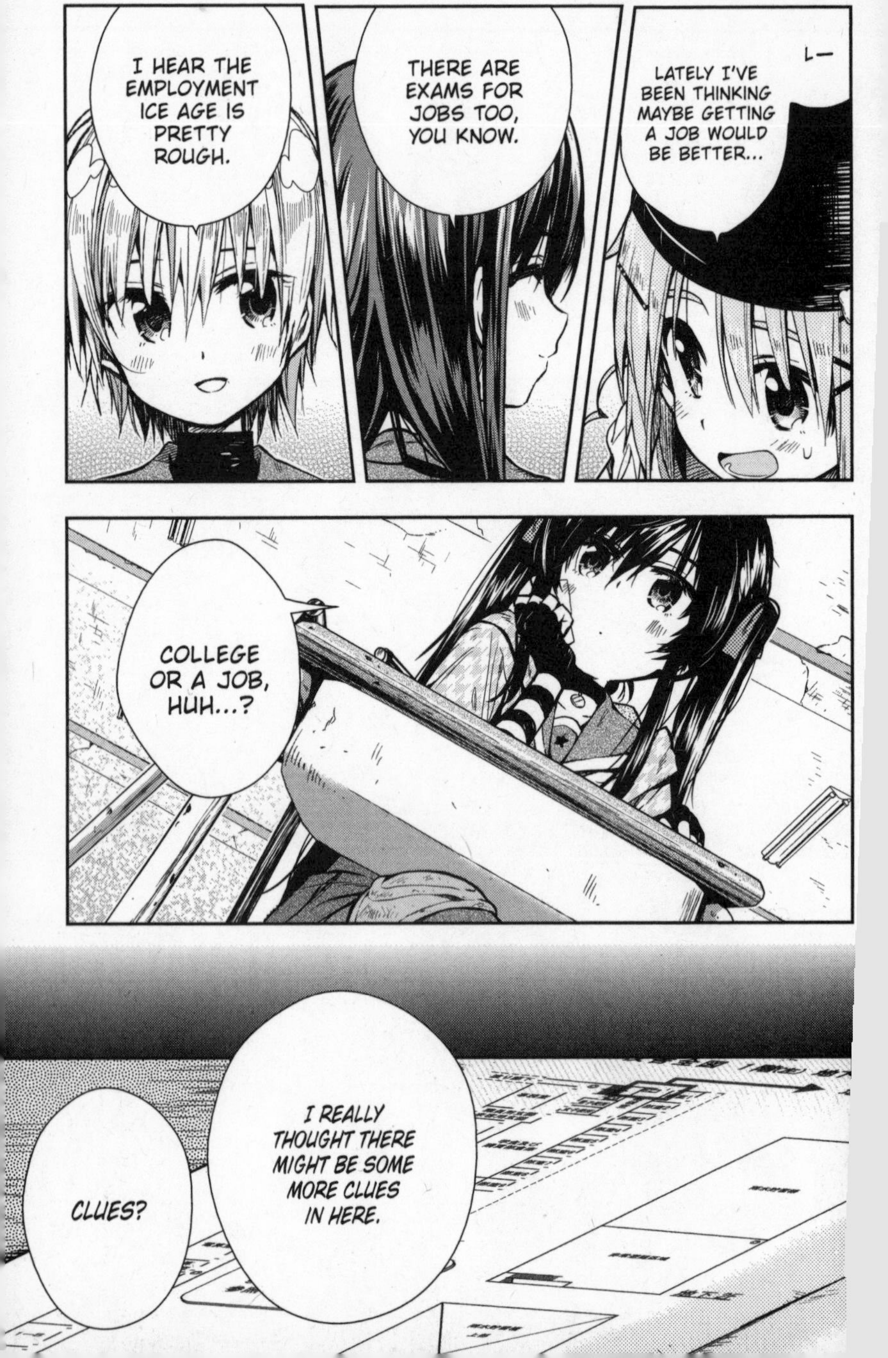
L—
LATELY I'VE BEEN THINKING MAYBE GETTING A JOB WOULD BE BETTER...
THERE ARE EXAMS FOR JOBS TOO, YOU KNOW.
I HEAR THE EMPLOYMENT ICE AGE IS PRETTY ROUGH.
COLLEGE OR A JOB, HUH...?
I REALLY THOUGHT THERE MIGHT BE SOME MORE CLUES IN HERE.
CLUES?

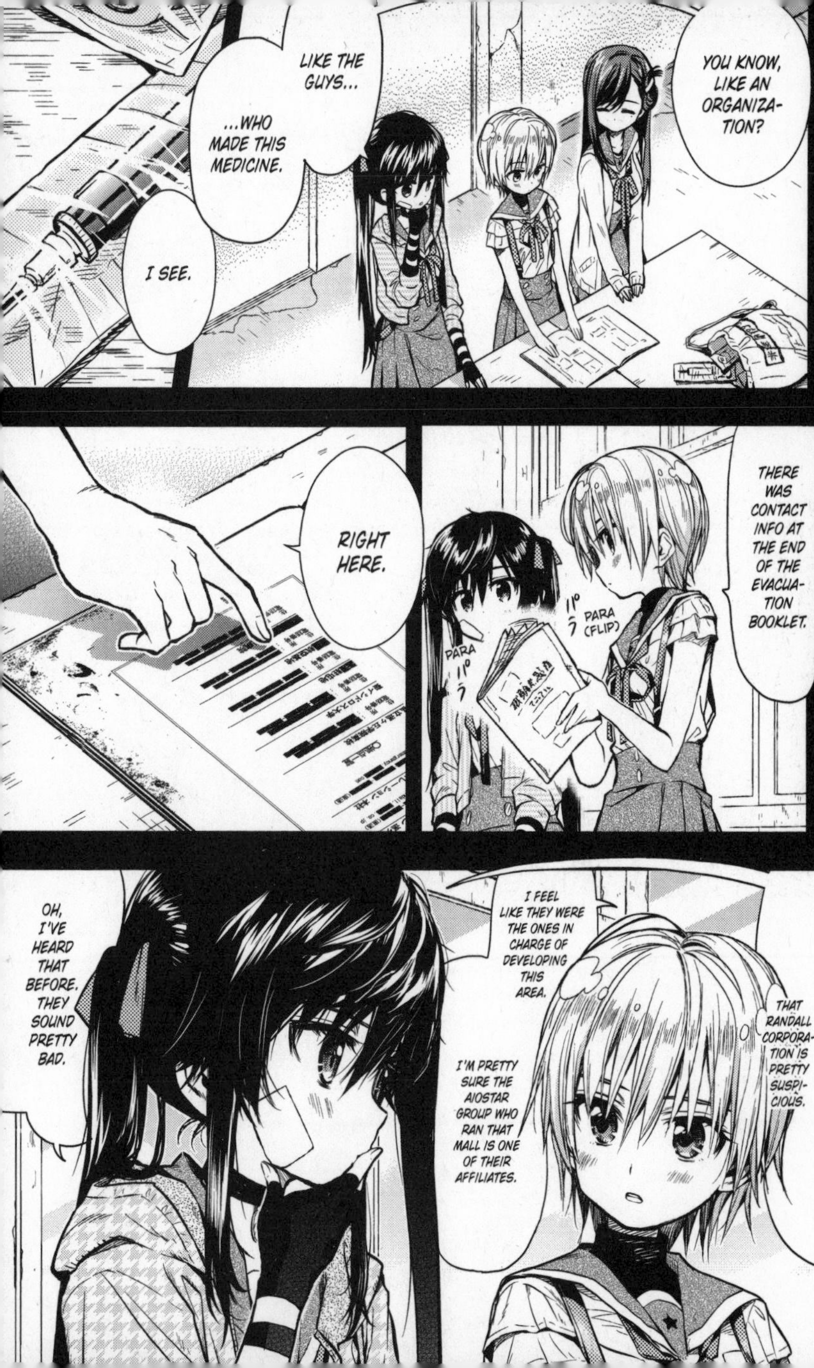
YOU KNOW, LIKE AN ORGANIZATION?
LIKE THE GUYS...
...WHO MADE THIS MEDICINE.
I SEE.
THERE WAS CONTACT INFO AT THE END OF THE EVACUATION BOOKLET.
パラ PARA (FLIP)
PARA パラ
RIGHT HERE.
THAT RANDALL CORPORATION IS PRETTY SUSPICIOUS.
I FEEL LIKE THEY WERE THE ONES IN CHARGE OF DEVELOPING THIS AREA.
I'M PRETTY SURE THE AIOSTAR GROUP WHO RAN THAT MALL IS ONE OF THEIR AFFILIATES.
OH, I'VE HEARD THAT BEFORE. THEY SOUND PRETTY BAD.

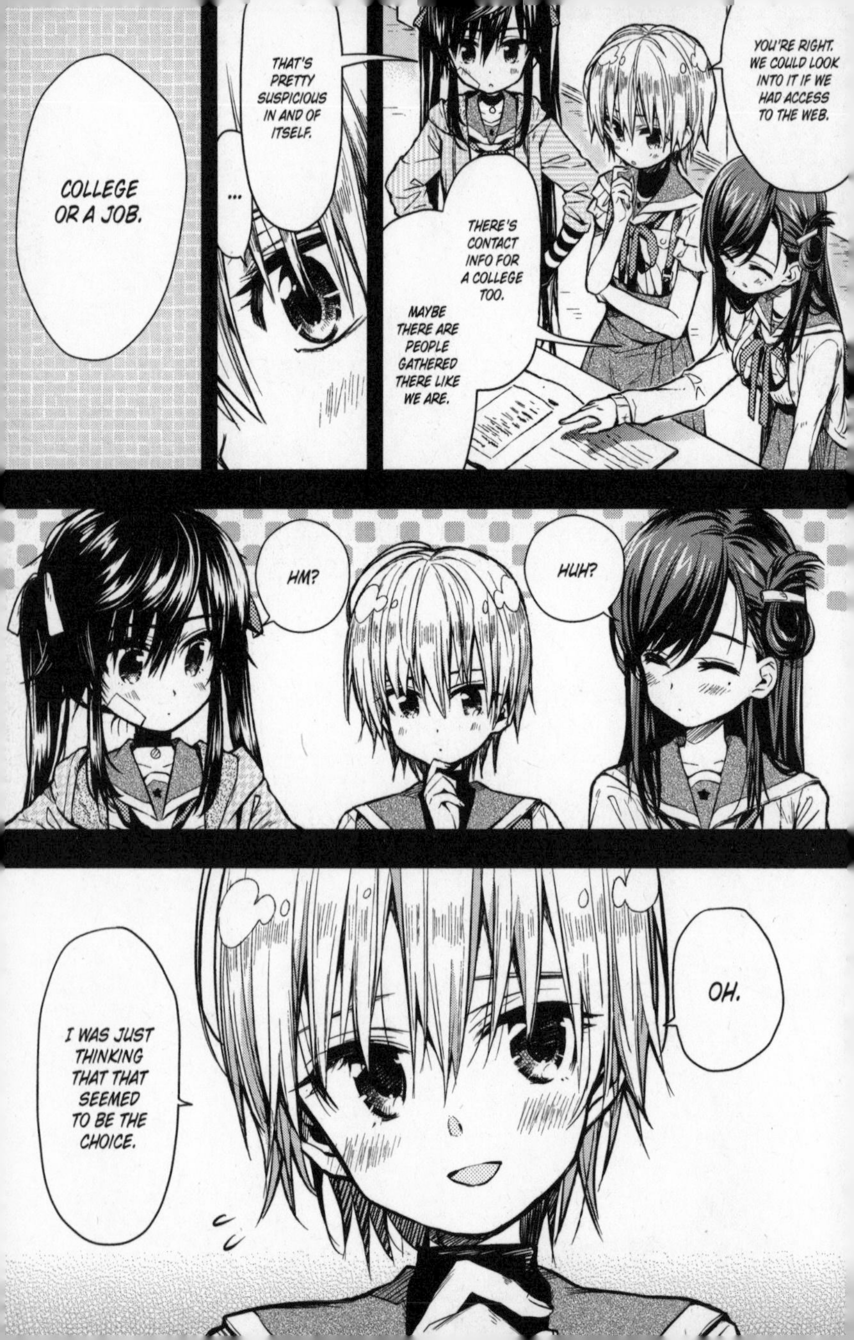

YOU'RE RIGHT. WE COULD LOOK INTO IT IF WE HAD ACCESS TO THE WEB.
THERE'S CONTACT INFO FOR A COLLEGE TOO.
MAYBE THERE ARE PEOPLE GATHERED THERE LIKE WE ARE.
THAT'S PRETTY SUSPICIOUS IN AND OF ITSELF.
...
COLLEGE OR A JOB.
HUH?
HM?
OH.
I WAS JUST THINKING THAT THAT SEEMED TO BE THE CHOICE.

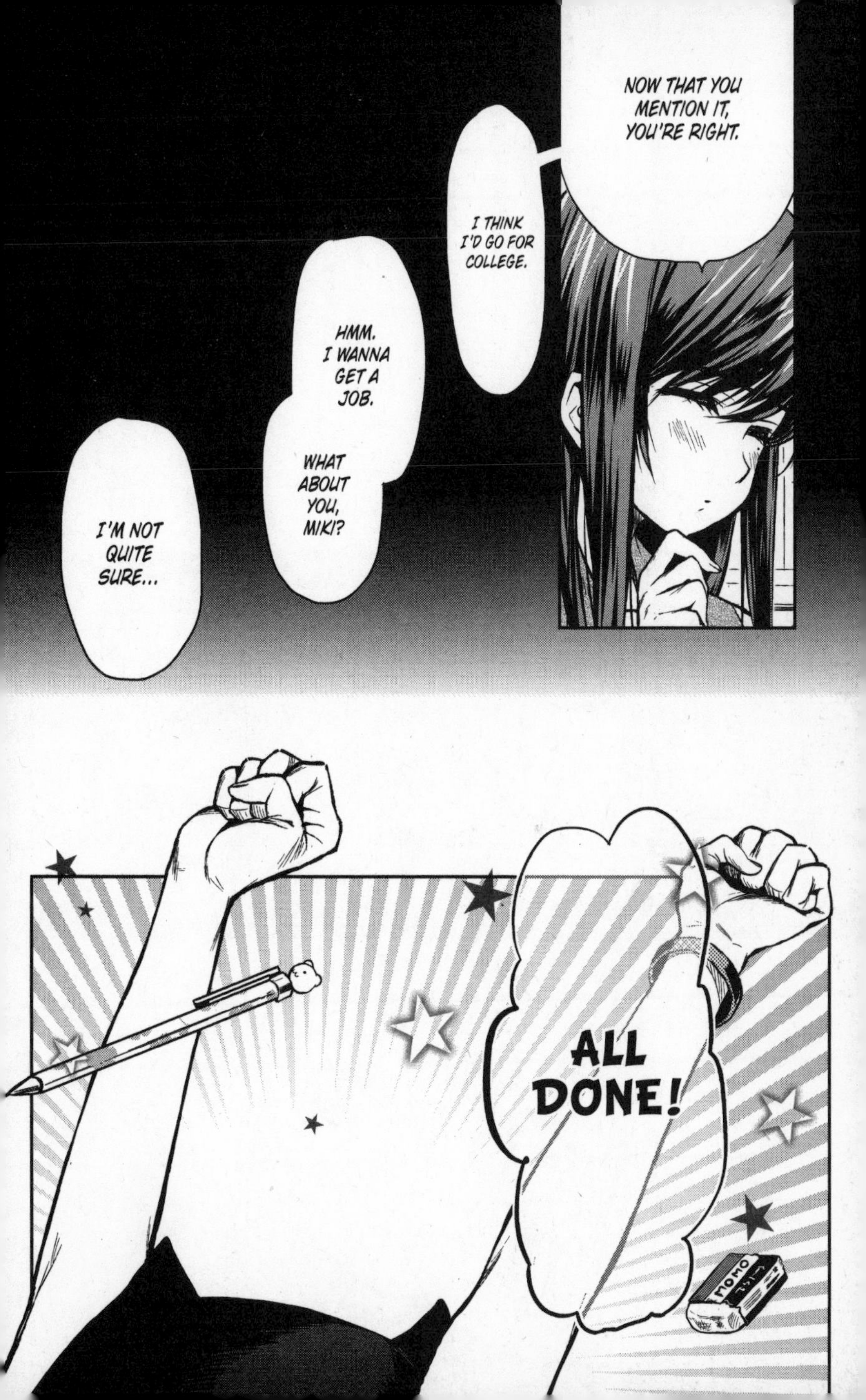
NOW THAT YOU MENTION IT, YOU'RE RIGHT.
I THINK I'D GO FOR COLLEGE.
HMM. I WANNA GET A JOB.
WHAT ABOUT YOU, MIKI?
I'M NOT QUITE SURE...
ALL DONE!
MOMO

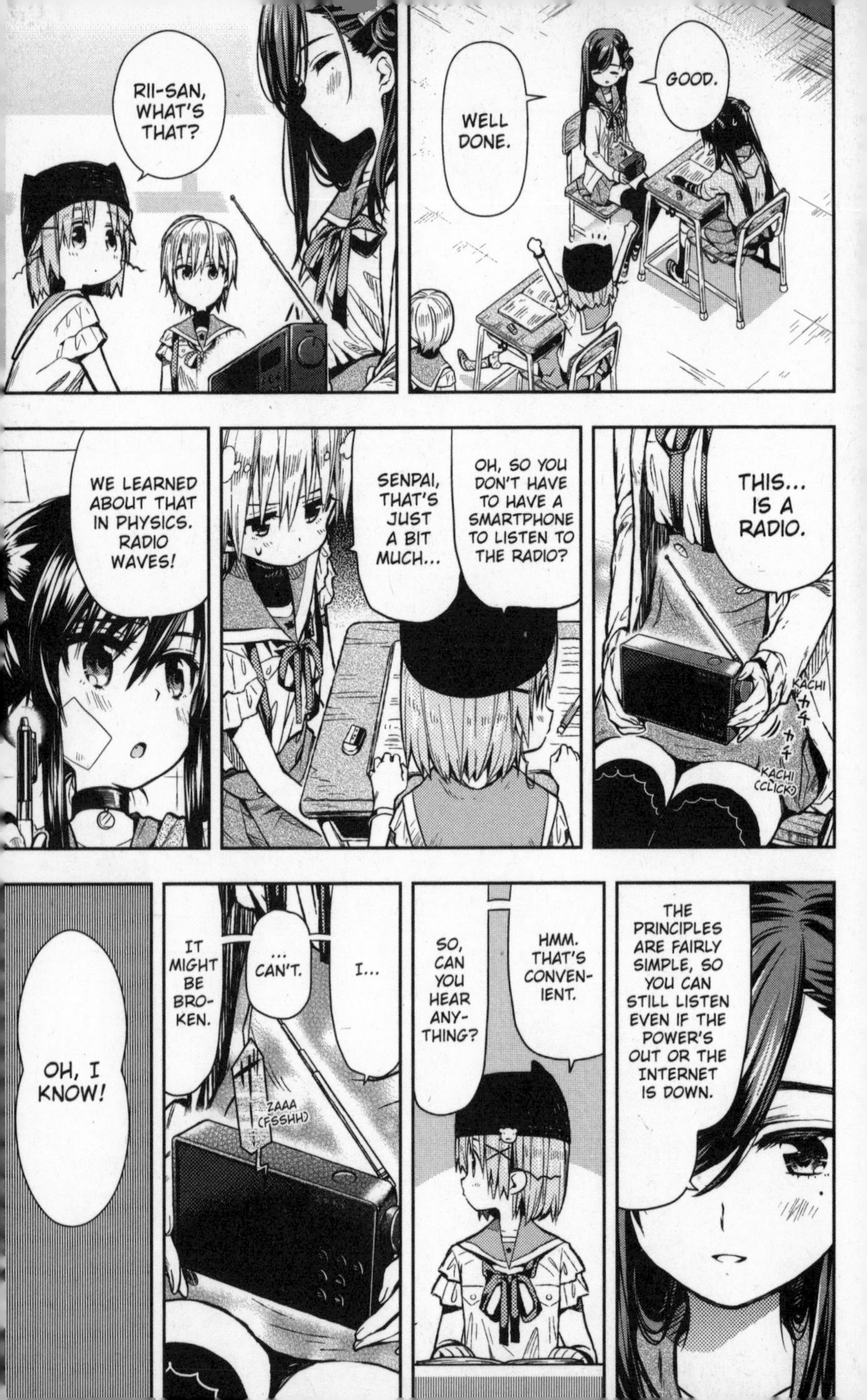

GOOD.
WELL DONE.
RII-SAN, WHAT'S THAT?
THIS... IS A RADIO.
KACHI
KACHI (CLICK)
OH, SO YOU DON'T HAVE TO HAVE A SMARTPHONE TO LISTEN TO THE RADIO?
SENPAI, THAT'S JUST A BIT MUCH...
WE LEARNED ABOUT THAT IN PHYSICS. RADIO WAVES!
THE PRINCIPLES ARE FAIRLY SIMPLE, SO YOU CAN STILL LISTEN EVEN IF THE POWER'S OUT OR THE INTERNET IS DOWN.
HMM. THAT'S CONVEN-IENT.
SO, CAN YOU HEAR ANY-THING?
I...
...CAN'T.
IT MIGHT BE BRO-KEN.
ZAAA (FSSHH)
OH, I KNOW!

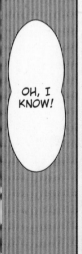

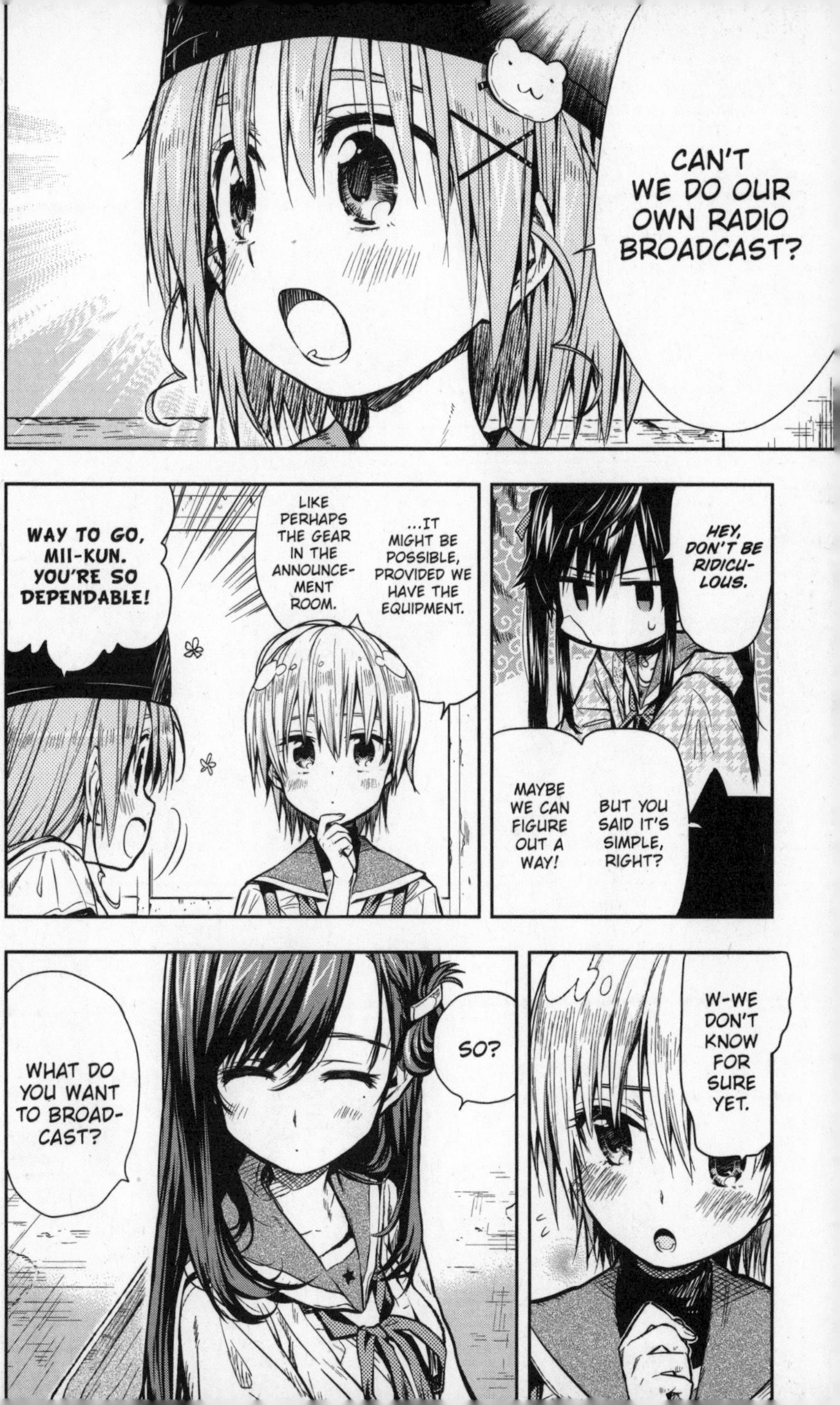
CAN'T WE DO OUR OWN RADIO BROADCAST?
HEY, DON'T BE RIDICULOUS.
BUT YOU SAID IT'S SIMPLE, RIGHT?
MAYBE WE CAN FIGURE OUT A WAY!
...IT MIGHT BE POSSIBLE, PROVIDED WE HAVE THE EQUIPMENT.
LIKE PERHAPS THE GEAR IN THE ANNOUNCEMENT ROOM.
WAY TO GO, MII-KUN. YOU'RE SO DEPENDABLE!
W-WE DON'T KNOW FOR SURE YET.
SO?
WHAT DO YOU WANT TO BROADCAST?

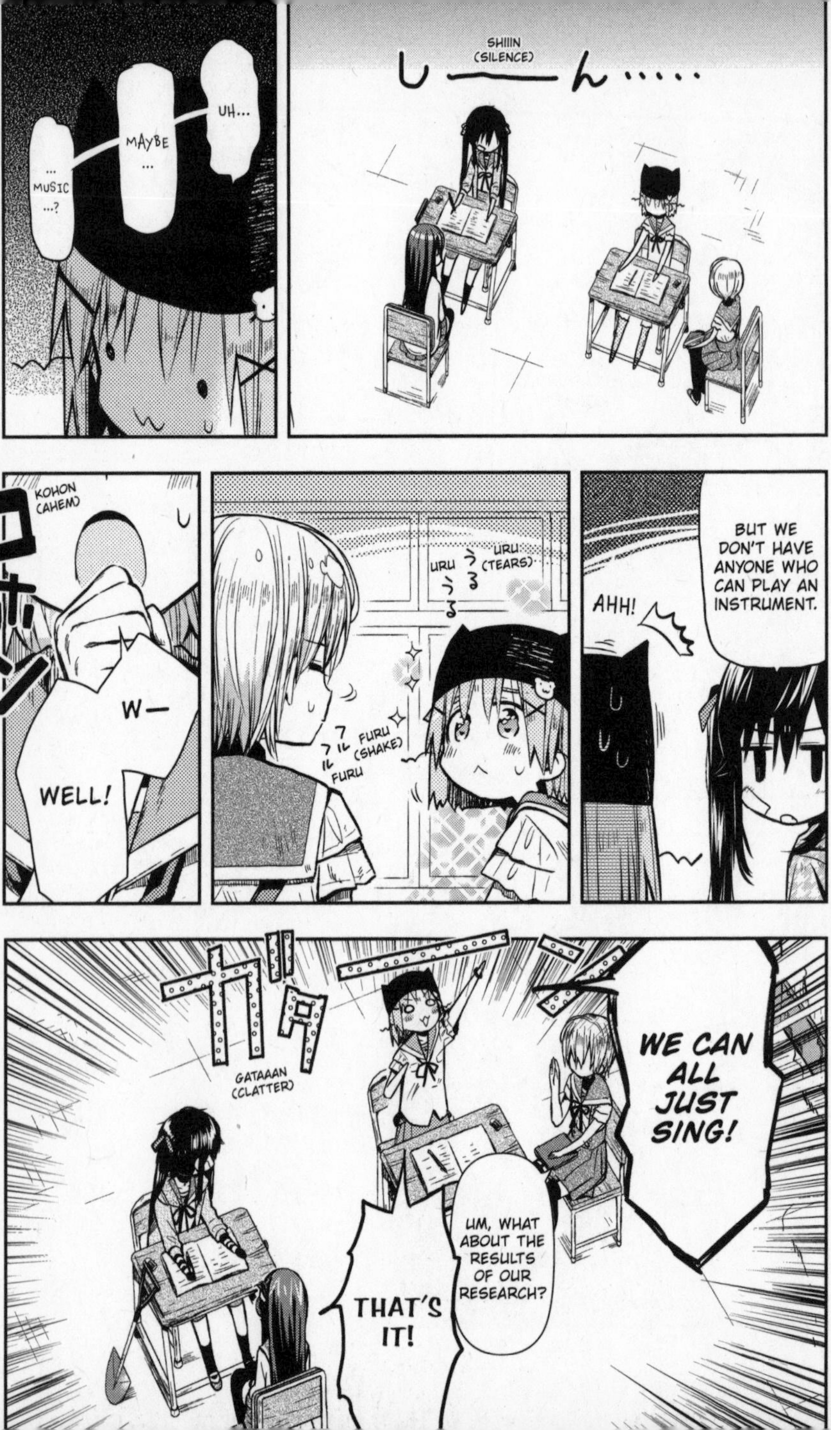

SHIIIN (SILENCE)
しーーん……
UH...
MAYBE ...
... MUSIC ...?
BUT WE DON'T HAVE ANYONE WHO CAN PLAY AN INSTRUMENT.
AHH!
URU URU (TEARS)
FURU FURU (SHAKE)
KOHON (AHEM)
W—
WELL!
WE CAN ALL JUST SING!
GATAAAN (CLATTER)
UM, WHAT ABOUT THE RESULTS OF OUR RESEARCH?
THAT'S IT!

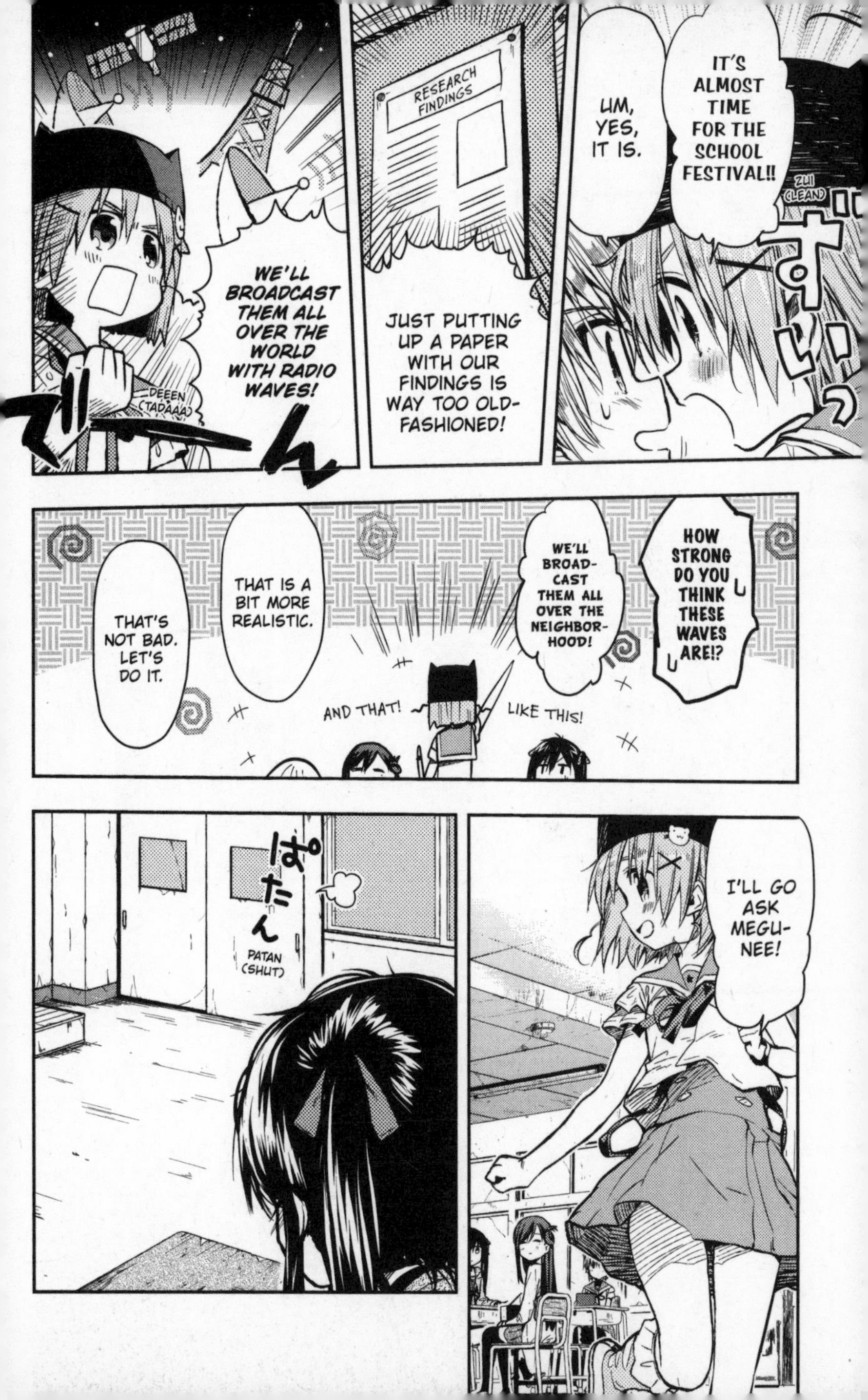
IT'S ALMOST TIME FOR THE SCHOOL FESTIVAL!!
UM, YES, IT IS.
ZUI (LEAN)
RESEARCH FINDINGS
JUST PUTTING UP A PAPER WITH OUR FINDINGS IS WAY TOO OLD-FASHIONED!
WE'LL BROADCAST THEM ALL OVER THE WORLD WITH RADIO WAVES!
DEEEN (TADAAA)
HOW STRONG DO YOU THINK THESE WAVES ARE!?
WE'LL BROAD-CAST THEM ALL OVER THE NEIGHBOR-HOOD!
LIKE THIS!
AND THAT!
THAT IS A BIT MORE REALISTIC.
THAT'S NOT BAD. LET'S DO IT.
I'LL GO ASK MEGU-NEE!
ぱたん
PATAN (SHUT)

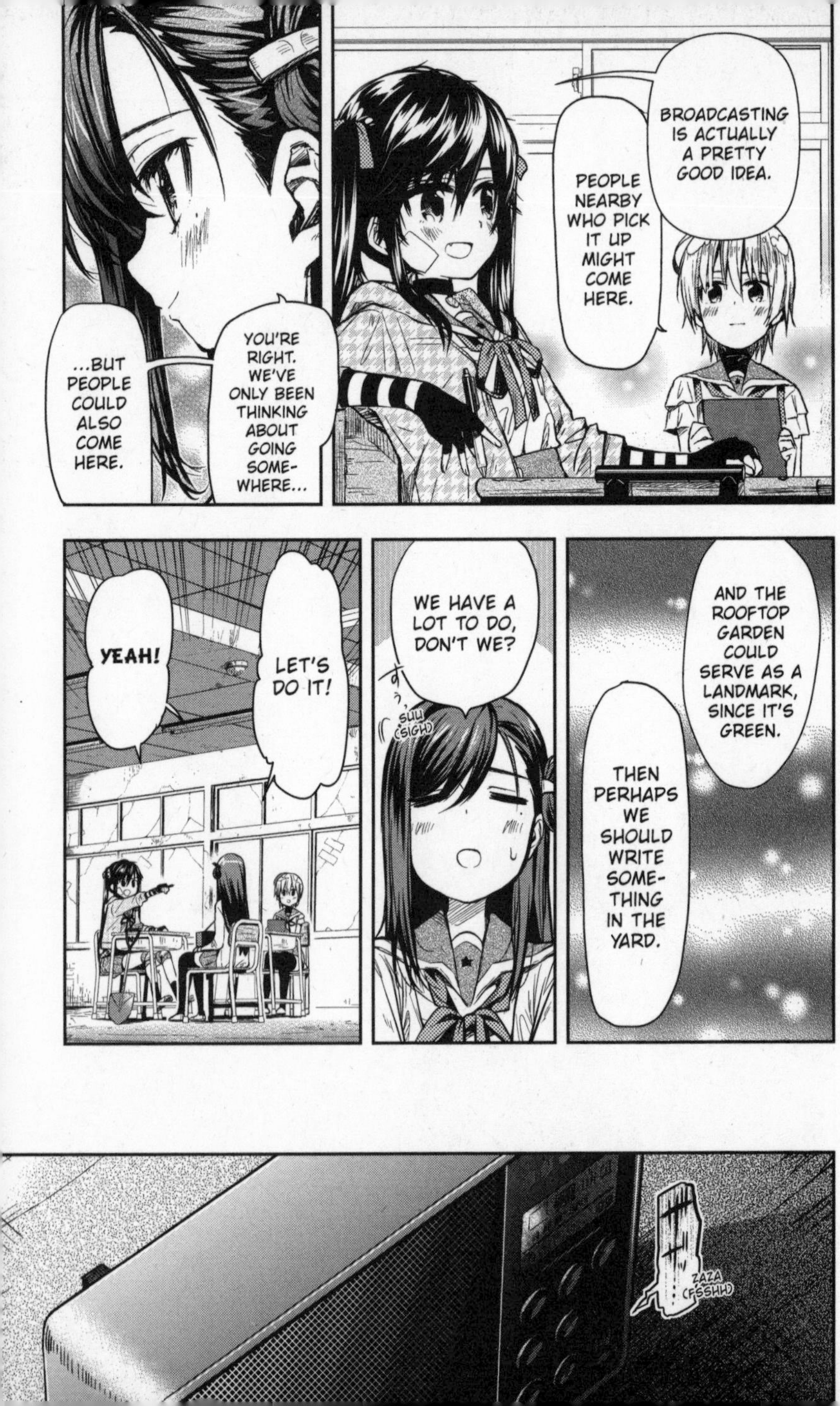
BROADCASTING IS ACTUALLY A PRETTY GOOD IDEA.
PEOPLE NEARBY WHO PICK IT UP MIGHT COME HERE.
YOU'RE RIGHT. WE'VE ONLY BEEN THINKING ABOUT GOING SOME-WHERE...
...BUT PEOPLE COULD ALSO COME HERE.
AND THE ROOFTOP GARDEN COULD SERVE AS A LANDMARK, SINCE IT'S GREEN.
THEN PERHAPS WE SHOULD WRITE SOME-THING IN THE YARD.
WE HAVE A LOT TO DO, DON'T WE?
SUU (SIGH)
LET'S DO IT!
YEAH!
ZAZA (FSSHH)

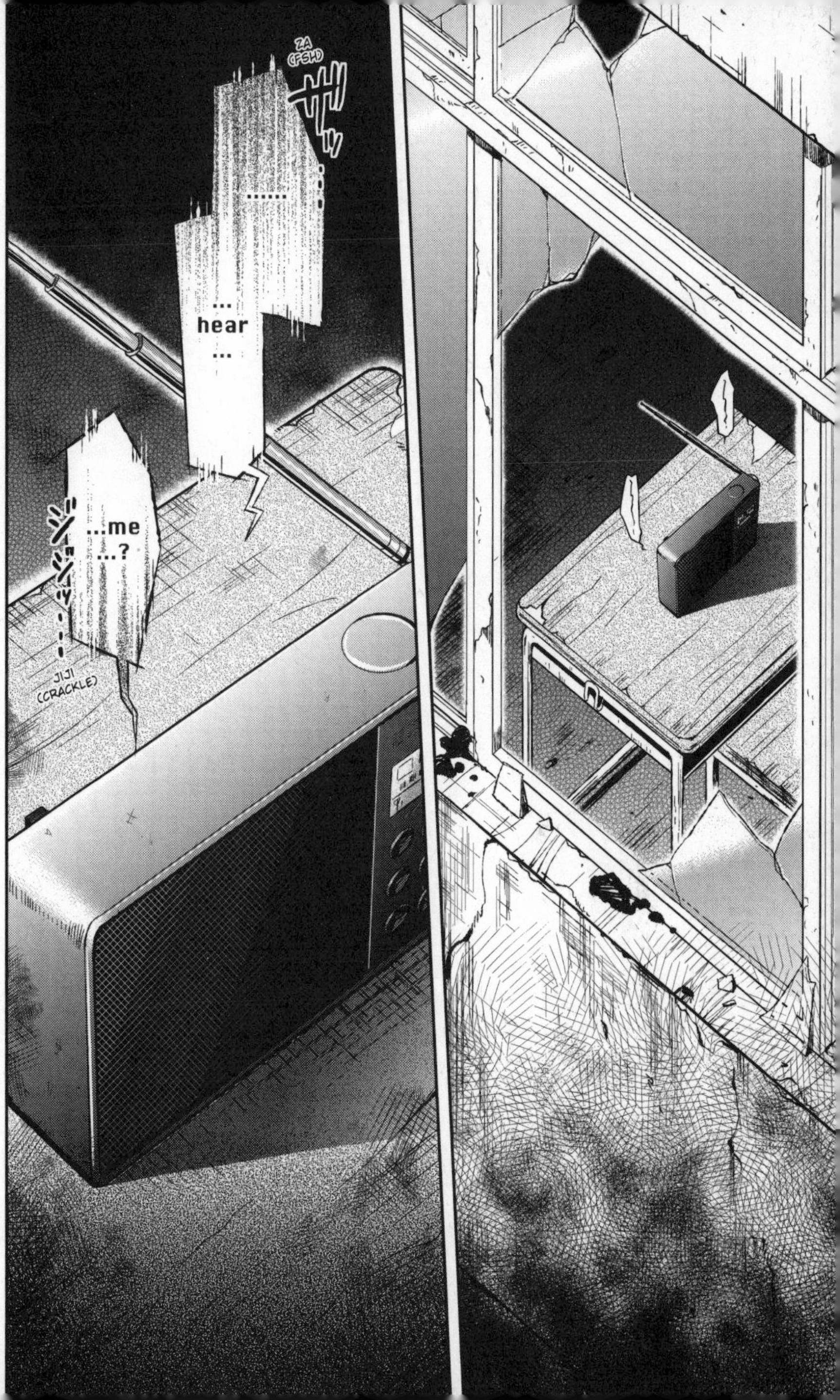
ZA (PFSH)
......
... hear ...
...me ...?
JIJI (CRACKLE)

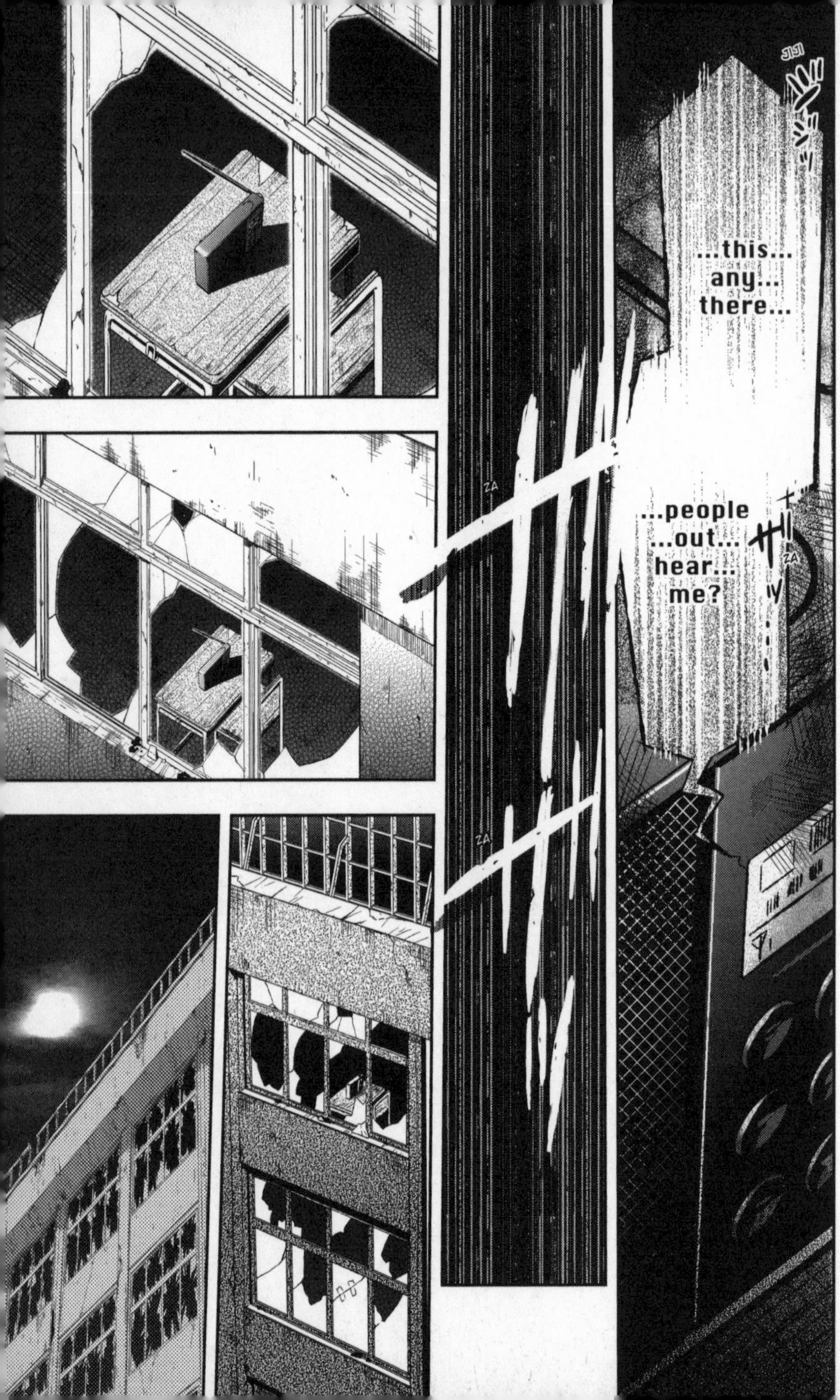
JIJI
...this...
any...
there...
...people
...out...
hear...
me?
ZA
ZA
ZA

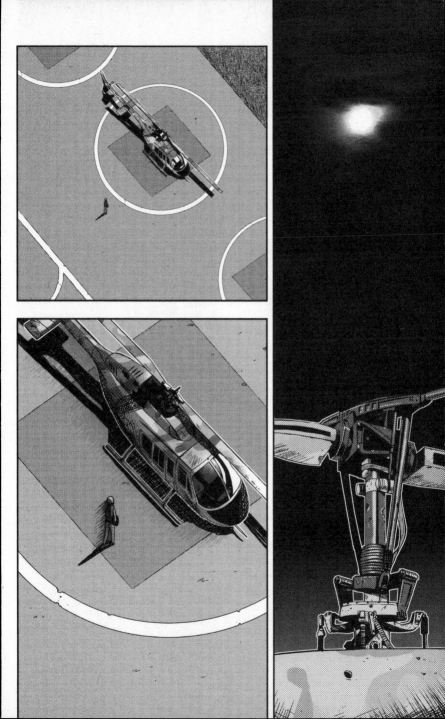

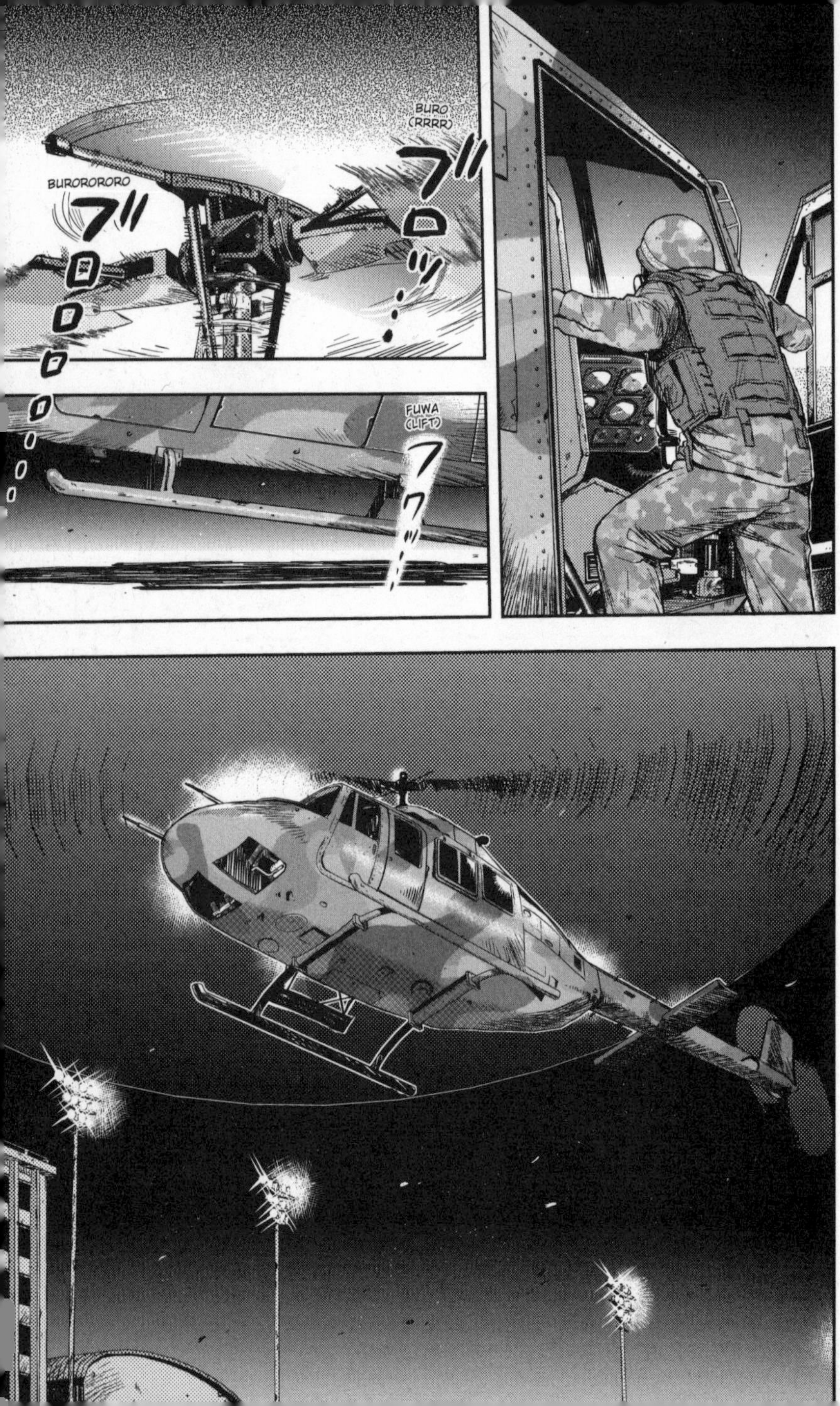
BURO (RRRR)
ブロッ…
BURORORORO
ブロロロロロ…
FUWA (LIFT)
フワッ…

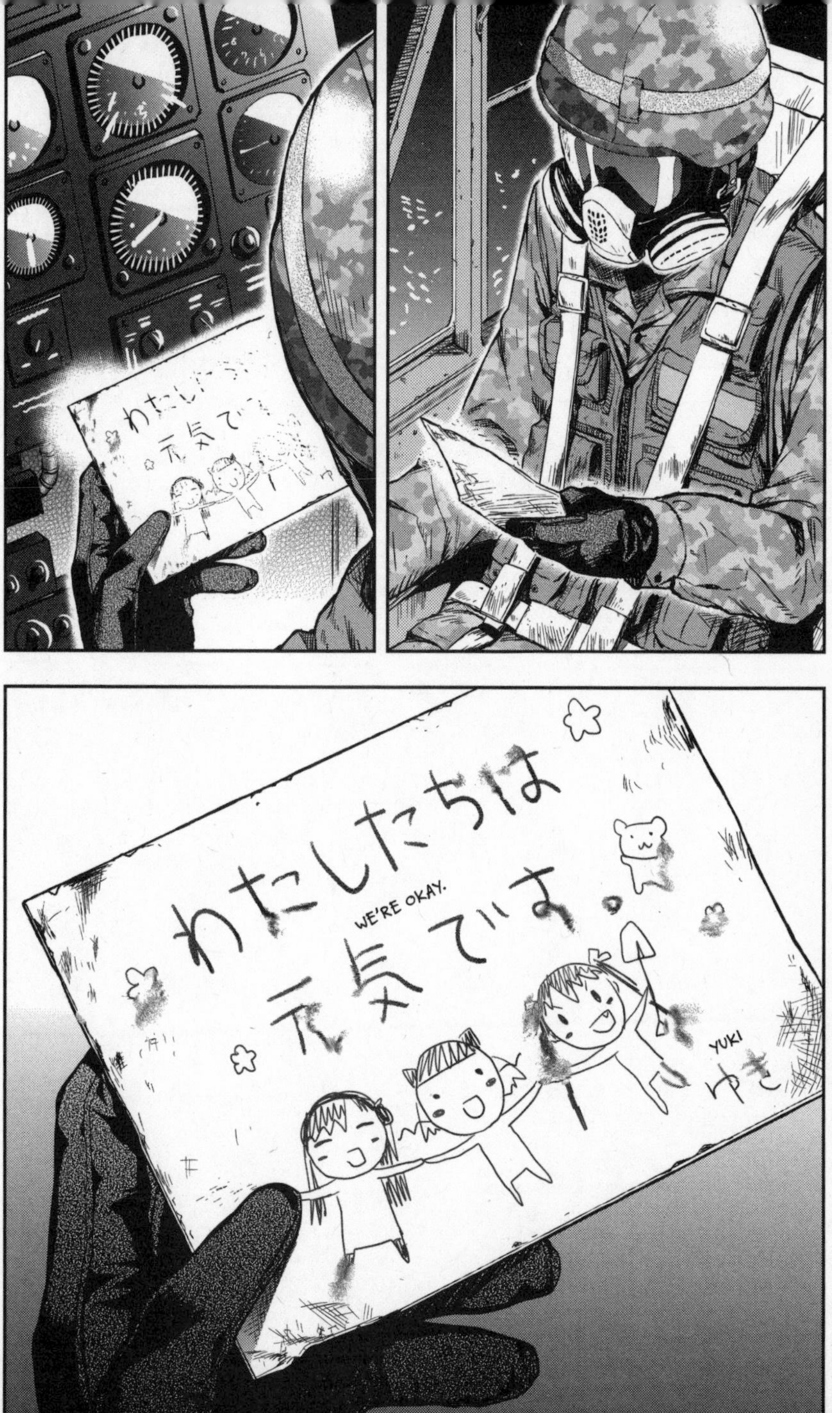
わたしたちは
元気です。
WE'RE OKAY.
YUKI
ゆき

サバイバル
Survival with Encyclopedia
百科事典
CD-ROM

AION SOFTWARE

SCHOOL-LIVE!

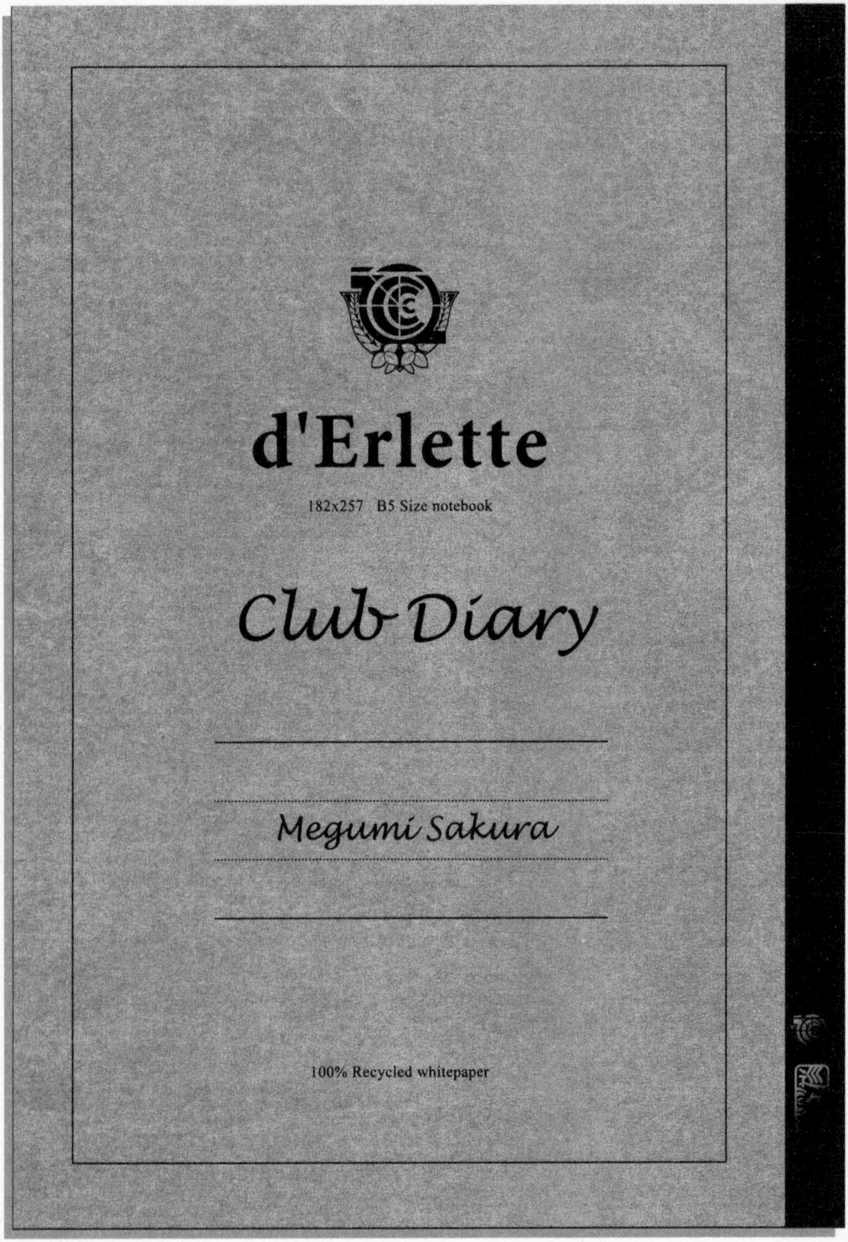
d'Erlette
182x257 B5 Size notebook
Club Diary
Megumi Sakura
100% Recycled whitepaper

It's calmed down a bit. We still can't say what will happen, but since we have a bit of breathing room now, I figured I'd put down some of my thoughts.

I'm still not quite sure what to write or where to start. I don't know what this notebook will become either. It could be my memoirs. Or maybe a letter. Or an accusation. Or perhaps my will.

I am Megumi Sakura. I ~~am was a Japanese teacher~~ am a Japanese teacher at Megurigaoka Academy Private High School. No, I'm still a teacher. I still have those girls.

I think I should write about that day. I think I should, but...

I feel sick when I think about it. I get chills. I can hear the screams deep in my ears. I've had some tea. I'll write about it bit by bit.

We have a vegetable garden for the Gardening Club on the roof of our school, so the students are allowed up there. Technically, only members of the Gardening Club are allowed there, and only during specific times, though that isn't enforced very strictly. It's not controlled very well, so we let it slide. That's how it is.

Yuki-san, Yuuri-san, and one other female student
were up on the roof when it happened. She must have
thought that I would be angry when she saw me
there.

She left the roof immediately. I regret that.
Yuki-san was the one who first realized what was
happening, and she pointed at the schoolyard.

We could tell there was some sort of riot, but
it didn't feel real. After that, Kurumi-san came
running up, out of breath, and then there were
countless students on the other side of the door.
And screams.

I just kept holding the door shut.

We're somehow managing to survive. I'm quite grateful that we have water and power, especially that the solar cells on the rooftop are all right. We even have hot water. It's like everything was set up for us to take shelter here. Actually, it's too perfect. I'll have to go to the staff room eventually and check on that.

We're making some headway on clearing out the classroom, so we have a bit of free time now. When I think, "Oh, I don't have anything to do," I choke and can't move. When I think about what we'll do from now on, my legs just stop. Yuki-san is doing particularly poorly. So am I, even though I'm a teacher. Even though I can't afford to weigh everyone down.

Yuuri Wakasa-san. She's very calm. She's a strong

person. She has the power to care for everyone.

That very same Yuuri-san asked me if I could hold

classes. Both to prepare for tomorrow and to make it

through today. I thought that was a very good idea.

It's a lie that teachers teach students. Teachers,

in fact, learn from their students. I thought I

understood that, but now that things are as they are,

I am reminded of that fact every day. So I can't say

it was a good thing, having class. Class is good, but I

feel like there are other things we should do as well.

We need to repair the rooftop gardens.

Yuki Takeya-san has cheered up quite a bit.

The School Living Club. It's not a bad name in my opinion. I'm the adviser, and the others are members.

We aren't trapped in here. We're living here. When we think of it as a school activity, we can start to see things we want to do and things we can do.

Even so, there are still times at night, in my sleeping bag, when I feel like I'm being crushed. I wonder what will happen to the girls, apart from their families like this.

For now, we'll just make it through the days, acting out our club activities. I'm sure there is some meaning to that.

Kurumi Ebisuzawa-san is a strong girl. She's an athletic girl from the track team, and she's always saving us.

We've been able to expand our sphere of existence because of her shovel. We probably never would have been able to do it by ourselves.

I do have some reservations about putting a student in danger. I would love to do it in her place if I could, but if I did that, there would just be more sacrifices.

What I can do is be there for her and protect her heart. That's what I believe.

Yuki Takeya-san ~~is~~. ~~She~~.

No, it may just be my imagination.

It may be my imagination, but I'll write about it

anyway.

She's always had a childish side, but lately she's

gotten even more childish. I don't understand it.

I just don't.

She's brightened up. She's gotten more cheerful.

Her smile truly does lend me strength.

But I'm not sure that it's for the best.

~~The stuff.com~~

He was a cute dog. He might have been someone's

pet. His coat was well groomed.

But —~~~~

It came back —~~~~

I think I know what this notebook will be.

This will probably be my will.

I have committed a sin.

I want whoever eventually reads this to understand

that.

About her.

It was my fault that Yuki Takeya's time stopped.

I was the one who wanted Yuki-san to smile. I was also the one who made the illusion that is the School Living Club. When she regressed, I thought that that was preferable. Even these circumstances were my fault. The other day, I finally went to the staff room. The evacuation manual. My responsibility. All adults' responsibility. There aren't any other adults left, so this is my responsibility.

You can't stop the flow of time. If one day those three can make it out of this school smiling...I don't care what happens to me to make that happen. Sending those girls off safely is my reason for living.

I am Megumi Sakura. I am a Japanese teacher at Megurigaoka Academy Private High School.

I wonder what the highlights of school life are.

In my case, it was putting everything I had into the school festival.

I'm sure there are some people for whom it was the field day. Or field trips. Or expeditions or tournaments as part of club activities.

Time just runs that slowly, and that time itself is the epitome of school life. That's the sort of stuff I was reminiscing about as I wrote the story for this volume.

There are laid-back days, and there are hard days. And that school life for Yuki and the others is happily getting an anime adaptation!

I personally can't wait for it.

I'd like to take this opportunity to give my sincere thanks to all the readers who have cheered us on so far and everyone who has supported this work.

Thank you very much, and please stick with us from now on too!

Thank you.

Norimitsu Kaihou

Next volume,
time for
good-byes...

~Special Thanks~
Itsuka Yamada (Parts design for the notes.)

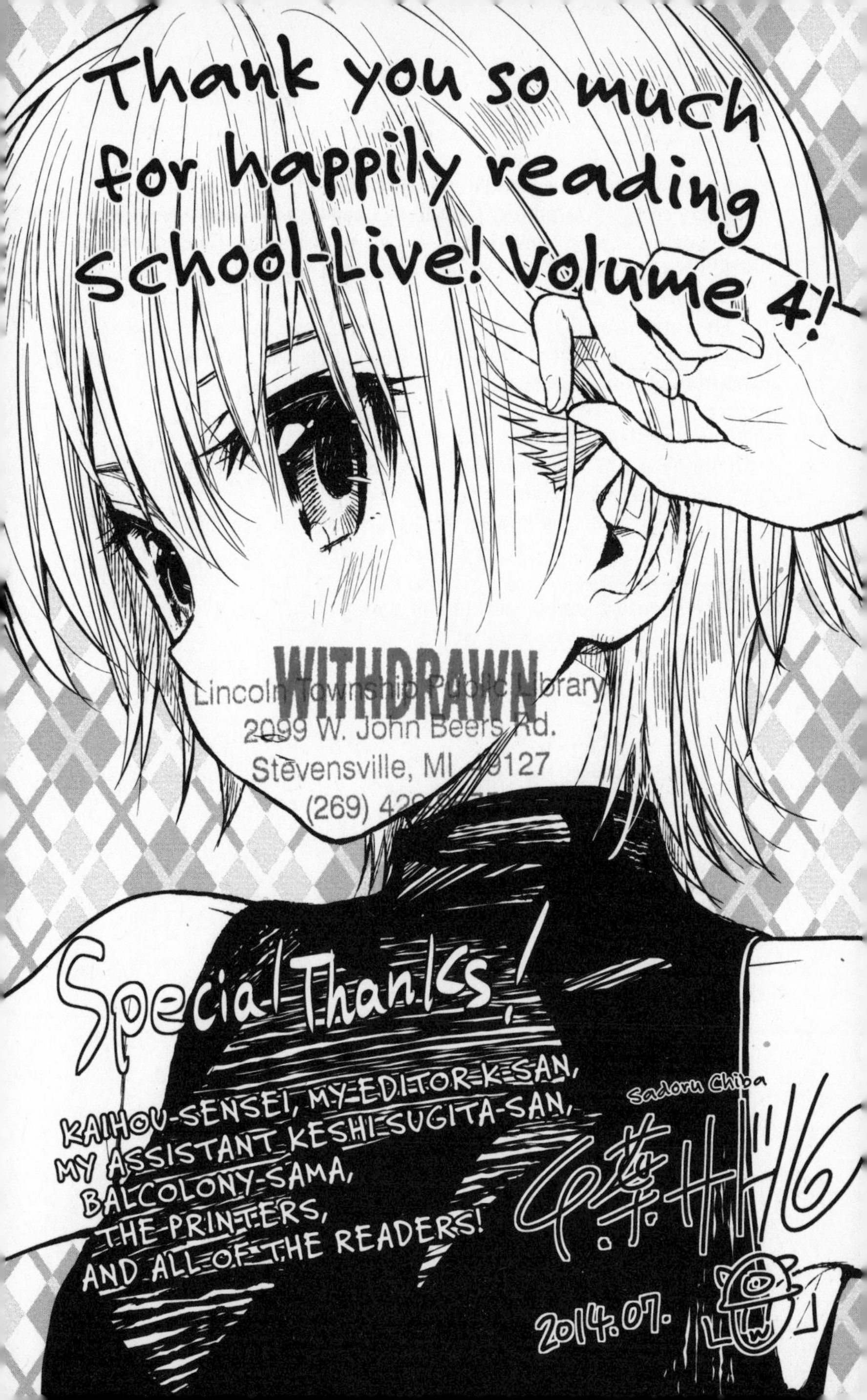
Thank you so much for happily reading School-Live! Volume 4!
Special Thanks!
KAIHOU-SENSEI, MY EDITOR K-SAN,
MY ASSISTANT KESHI SUGITA-SAN,
BALCOLONY-SAMA,
THE PRINTERS,
AND ALL OF THE READERS!
Sadoru Chiba
2014.07.

Translation Notes

Common Honorifics:

no honorific: Indicates familiarity or closeness; if used without permission or reason, addressing someone in this manner would constitute an insult.

-san: The Japanese equivalent of Mr./Mrs./Miss. If a situation calls for politeness, this is the fail-safe honorific.

-chan: An affectionate honorific indicating familiarity used mostly in reference to girls; also used in reference to cute persons or animals of either gender.

-senpai: A suffix used to address upperclassmen or more experienced coworkers.

-kouhai: A suffix used to address underclassmen or less experienced coworkers.

-sensei: A respectful term for teachers, artists, or high-level professionals.

-nee: Honorific derived from onee-san/-sama ("big sister"). When used alone after a name, *-nee* can mean closeness.

Page 147

Employment ice age: A phenomenon where young people aren't finding jobs when they graduate, and because many Japanese companies only hire new graduates, this locks many of these people out of full-time employment for a long time, if not the rest of their lives.

SCHOOL-LIVE! ④

SA
NORIMI

Translation: Leighann

GAKKOU GURASHI! Vol.
©Nitroplus / Norimitsu Kaihou, Sadoru Chiba, Houbunsha. All rights
reserved. First published in Japan in 2014 by HOUBUNSHA CO., LTD.,
Tokyo. English translation rights in United States, Canada, and United
Kingdom arranged with HOUBUNSHA CO., LTD through Tuttle-Mori
Agency, Inc., Tokyo.

English translation © 2016 by Yen Press, LLC

Yen Press
1290 Avenue of the Americas
New York, NY 10104

Visit us at yenpress.com
facebook.com/yenpress
twitter.com/yenpress
yenpress.tumblr.com

First Yen Press Edition: August 2016

Yen Press is an imprint of Yen Press, LLC.
The Yen Press name and logo are trademarks of Yen Press, LLC.

The publisher is not responsible for websites (or their content) that are not
owned by the publisher.

Library of Congress Control Number: 2015952613

ISBNs: 978-0-316-30995-0 (paperback)
           978-0-316-30999-8 (ebook)
           978-0-316-31000-0 (app)

10 9 8 7 6 5 4 3

WOR

Printed in the United States of America